How the Body Shapes Knowledge

How the Body Shapes Knowledge

Empirical Support for Embodied Cognition

REBECCA FINCHER-KIEFER

AMERICAN PSYCHOLOGICAL ASSOCIATION
Washington, DC

The opinions and statements published are the responsibility of the authors, and such opinions and statements do not necessarily represent the policies of the American Psychological Association.

Published by
American Psychological Association
750 First Street, NE
Washington, DC 20002
www.apa.org

APA Order Department
P.O. Box 92984
Washington, DC 20090-2984
Phone: (800) 374-2721; Direct: (202) 336-5510
Fax: (202) 336-5502; TDD/TTY: (202) 336-6123
Online: http://www.apa.org/pubs/books
E-mail: order@apa.org

In the U.K., Europe, Africa, and the Middle East, copies may be ordered from
Eurospan Group
c/o Turpin Distribution
Pegasus Drive
Stratton Business Park
Biggleswade, Bedfordshire
SG18 8TQ United Kingdom
Phone: +44 (0) 1767 604972
Fax: +44 (0) 1767 601640
Online: https://www.eurospanbookstore.com/apa
E-mail: eurospan@turpin-distribution.com

Typeset in Meridien by Circle Graphics, Inc., Reisterstown, MD

Printer: Sheridan Books, Chelsea, MI
Cover Designer: Anne C. Kerns, Anne Likes Red, Inc., Silver Spring, MD
Image: A.D. Waller, "Properties of human heart." Credit: Wellcome Collection. CC BY

Library of Congress Cataloging-in-Publication Data
Names: Fincher-Kiefer, Rebecca, author.
Title: How the body shapes knowledge : empirical support for embodied
  cognition / Rebecca Fincher-Kiefer.
Description: Washington, DC : American Psychological Association, 2019. |
  Includes bibliographical references and index.
Identifiers: LCCN 2018047601 (print) | LCCN 2019000437 (ebook) | ISBN
  9781433830846 (eBook) | ISBN 1433830841 (eBook) | ISBN 9781433829604
  (paperback) | ISBN 1433829606 (paperback)
Subjects: LCSH: Cognitive psychology. | BISAC: PSYCHOLOGY / Cognitive
  Psychology. | PSYCHOLOGY / Physiological Psychology.
Classification: LCC BF201 (ebook) | LCC BF201 .F56 2019 (print) | DDC
  153.4—dc23
LC record available at https://lccn.loc.gov/2018047601

British Library Cataloguing-in-Publication Data
A CIP record is available from the British Library.

Printed in the United States of America

http://dx.doi.org/10.1037/0000136-000

10 9 8 7 6 5 4 3 2 1

In memory of
Peggy Horne Smith
Kimberly Fincher Clabaugh
my embodiment of love

This book is dedicated to Will, Cody, Carter, Sam, and Karla—
each of you is bold and brave and you have inspired me,
in your own radiant way, to take on this challenge.
I have always wanted to do important things in your eyes;
I hope this is one of those things.

Contents

Preface

The theory of embodied cognition has been examined by philosophers, cognitive scientists, cognitive psychologists, and cognitive neuroscientists, and each group often has a different view of what *embodied cognition* means. The name of the theory suggests that these disciplines are curious about the influence of the body on the mind. I am an experimental cognitive psychologist, and I am interested in how knowledge is represented in the human brain. The view of embodied cognition that I adopt in this book is one that proposes that the body, or specifically sensory and physical experiences, is essential in determining how we understand the world and build conceptual knowledge. This view is shared by many experimental cognitive psychologists and cognitive neuroscientists and has been investigated for the last 15 to 20 years. In fact, it is a view that some psychologists have argued will unify the subdisciplines of psychology in terms of explaining cognition and behavior. It is my intent in this book to explore the empirical evidence that tests this theory of embodied cognition.

For readers unfamiliar with the different approaches to the theory of embodied cognition (or *embodiment*), let me provide a succinct but over-simplified description. Philosophers examine embodied cognition because they are interested in theories of consciousness, questioning, what is the *mind*? And, are our *bodies* involved in perception and thinking? Cognitive scientists, representing a field that emerged as computers were developed and artificial intelligence was advanced, are also interested in embodied cognition. They create computational models that simulate human cognition and raise the question of whether human brains need internal representations of thought. Perhaps the body itself, they argue, and actions related to goals of the body, are enough to explain cognition. Within cognitive science, robotics is a perfect test bed for this type of theoretical and experimental work.

However, philosophical debates about the need for internal representations in cognition are not part of the psychological literature. Psychologists assume that the activity of the brain, and its internal representations, affect behavior. Cognitive psychologists examine the theory of embodied cognition because we explore cognitive processes such as perception, attention, memory, emotions, and language, and we investigate how bodily experiences affect, or *constitute*, our internal representations of the world. Finally, cognitive neuroscientists examine embodied cognition and try to determine the specific brain activity related to the body's involvement in thought.

In this book, I will not do justice to the impressive philosophical and cognitive science versions of the theory of embodied cognition that have been detailed and debated in other books (Chemero, 2009; Gallagher, 2005; Shapiro, 2011, 2014; Varela, Thompson, & Rosch, 1991). Instead, I will put forth what appears to be the most straightforward and perhaps most agreed-on definition of embodied cognition within cognitive psychology. Embodied cognition means that the representation of conceptual knowledge is dependent on the body; it is multimodal (i.e., related to vision, audition, touch, etc.), not amodal, symbolic, or abstract. This theory suggests that our thoughts are grounded, or inextricably associated with, perception, action, and emotion, and that our brain and body work together to have cognition. I will use the terms *embodied* and *grounded* as essentially synonymous terms; grounded does not mean that the concepts are simply and loosely connected to sensory or motor information (as suggested by Mahon, 2015), but instead that the body plays a constitutive role in conceptual knowledge.

One aspect of the embodied approach to cognition that will be addressed in this book is that the function of human cognition comes from our evolutionary and developmental background. Cognition serves action for the purpose of survival and reproduction (Glenberg, 2015; Proffitt & Linkenauger, 2013). Thus, cognition arises from perceptual and motoric processes that are tailored to our specific individual morphology and physiology. This perspective suggests that the unique features and attributes of our own bodies and emotions determine the capacity to acquire and use sensory information, give it meaning—make it *knowledge*. From this view, the representation of knowledge must be multimodal; the body is no longer peripheral to cognition.

This book is far from being an exhaustive or complete review of the experimental psychology literature concerning embodiment. It has taken me over 3 years of teaching an advanced laboratory course on embodied cognition to realize what the central issues were and how to organize the topics to make a coherent package of empirical findings. Writing this book followed the same process I have used in teaching—picking and choosing those empirical "stories" that helped me understand a concept or a point of view, and these were the stories that I felt would be intriguing to my students.

Readers should understand that extensive experimental testing of the theory of embodied cognition has led some cognitive psychologists to claim that the theory may result in a paradigm shift for the whole discipline of psychology (e.g., Barsalou, 1999, 2008b; Glenberg, 2010, 2015; Glenberg, Witt, & Metcalfe, 2013). However, other theorists disagree and argue emphatically that the term *embodied* is vague and imprecise. They suggest the theory itself offers nothing new, or worse, cannot explain even basic cognitive processes (Goldinger, Papesh, Barnhart, Hansen, & Hout, 2016;

Mahon, 2015). However, even the opponents of the theory of embodied cognition recognize the wealth of existing empirical evidence that demands to be critically evaluated.

This book is intended to be of use to multiple audiences. Undergraduates who have the luxury in the later years of their psychology major to delve more deeply into this theory will find the book helpful. Psychology majors who take my advanced laboratory course in embodiment use the laboratory component of my course to design and conduct two studies that examine an interesting question within embodiment. The research described in this book could be the impetus for quality undergraduate research.

This book will also be useful to graduate students in any of psychology's subdisciplines who are trying to understand the theory of embodiment. The relevant chapters describe the research the way that I would in a class. This is not a book where an argument is made and research is simply cited—I discuss and interpret the studies that I have chosen to represent a particular topic. Hopefully, that will allow undergraduate or graduate students to learn how experimental psychologists have tested the theory of embodied cognition.

I have chosen those studies that I felt would make the empirical story from question to potential answer the clearest. In that way, this book is also for anyone who would like to teach a course on embodiment. One could use the research described in each chapter to structure a course and then supplement with the many studies that surely will have been conducted since this book was published.

Finally, I hope that this book is of interest to any curious person interested in the interplay between the body and the mind. One of my foremost goals in writing this book was its readability; I very much hope that I have come close enough to that goal for every reader to take away something intriguing about embodied cognition.

Acknowledgments

I would like to thank the many students who have already taken my advanced laboratory course in Thinking and Cognition at Gettysburg College and have been enthused enough about the lectures to make me consider writing a book that covers the topics we do in class. Without the excitement of young minds, I would never have thought about writing a book. The act of teaching helped me present embodiment through my experimental psychology lens, and students were integral in shaping and guiding what topics allowed this theory to come to life for all of us.

I am grateful for my colleagues and administration at Gettysburg College who have supported me through the year-long process of writing this book. Without a sabbatical at the beginning of this project, I would not have been able to dedicate all my energies to writing; a light teaching load for the second half of the year allowed me to bring the book to fruition.

I had the good luck of getting Chris Kelaher at the American Psychological Association (APA) at the other end of an e-mail when I naively asked about any interest APA might have in a book about embodiment, and I so appreciated working with him as my acquisitions editor. I am also extremely grateful to the one anonymous reviewer for reviewing my book proposal, as the encouragement and excellent suggestions sealed the deal for me. Finally, in the later stages of the book I had the pleasure of working with Tyler Aune, my development editor, who expertly summarized my three reviews and made the revision process tolerable and even exciting. I am thankful for two anonymous reviewers whose suggestions for revisions improved this book, and to my third, Art Glenberg, who was so kind to take on reviewing both the proposal and the entire book as well. He went above and beyond to provide me with wonderful suggestions for making the theory of embodied cognition accessible to all potential readers of this book.

I am grateful for so many friends (you know who you are!) who have kept me buoyant throughout this process. Carolyn Tuckey helped check all the references, a daunting task that required a lot of time and careful work.

I am grateful for her help on this task and for other formatting and editing changes that I just could not figure out without her assistance.

Dory Adams was my naïve-to-the-theory personal editor, happily and enthusiastically reading these chapters despite having little experience in experimental psychology. Her viewpoint was critical to me; it was a student's viewpoint, although she is surely the most engaged student one could ever hope for and her intellect definitely makes her the most intimidating. Her edits made this book better, and for her time and energy and focus, I will be forever grateful.

I would never have taken on this book without the encouragement and unwavering support of my mentor, fellow cognitive psychologist, brilliant professor and friend, Bob D'Agostino. He spent tremendous time and effort reading and helping to shape every chapter, culling what was tangential and improving what was critical, showing an uncanny ability to see through the trees to get to the heart of the forest. His constant mantra, "What is the story you are trying to tell?" comes from his extraordinary skill in the classroom, and it guided my writing at every stage. I owe him a debt of gratitude for so many aspects of my career, and this book is just one of those.

Finally, I thank my precious family and patient husband, Chris, for putting up with a very grumpy version of myself as I stepped outside my comfort zone to take on this challenge. I have always placed them before my work and my career, but there were times in this journey that I put this book ahead of some of my true joys. I can now return to the correct order of things.

How the Body Shapes Knowledge

An Introduction to the Theory of Embodied Cognition

Arthur Glenberg, the preeminent cognitive psychologist who has extensively tested and written about the theory of embodied cognition, starts his course on the topic with questions such as these: "Do left-handers perceive the world differently than right-handers, such that, for example, right-handers like objects on the right more than objects on the left, but lefties like the opposite?"; "When you say about a potential date, 'He leaves me cold,' do you literally feel cold?"; "Does getting a Botox injection to remove frown lines make it difficult to understand a sentence about sadness?"; and, "When you are leaning backwards, are you more likely to think about your past than your future?" These questions clearly implicate the body in thought, and the surprising answer to all is "yes." The empirical evidence that provides this answer supports the theory of embodied cognition.

Philosophical Roots of the Theory

Before describing how a philosophical version of the theory of embodied cognition evolved into a testable theory for cognitive psychologists, let me tell you how I start my course on this topic. My approach is a bit different from the above hook of Glenberg because it emphasizes the theory's approach to how we represent all the knowledge we have in our brain. The way I do this

http://dx.doi.org/10.1037/0000136-001
How the Body Shapes Knowledge: Empirical Support for Embodied Cognition, by R. Fincher-Kiefer

is to have my students play a few rounds of "20 Q"—an electronic version of the game "Twenty Questions"—with me on the first day of my advanced laboratory course in cognition. My goal is to give them firsthand knowledge of "symbolic knowledge representations," or *nonembodied knowledge*, and they come to understand this when playing this handheld game. Here's why: The electronic version begins just as the verbal version of the game does—you come up with your animal, vegetable, mineral, or "other" thought, and then the handheld device begins the electronic questioning by posing questions such as, "Is it bigger than a microwave?" You respond with the "yes," "no," or "sometimes" button press on the device. This continues for 20 questions, or fewer if the device decides it has an early guess.

My students are always amused when they see that this toy can in fact "read their mind" and, more often than not, guess their thought correctly. So I ask them, "Does this game have a *mind*?" (They can't be tricked into responding that it has a physical brain, but to ask if it has a mind is a different issue.) Most tentatively say no—the "mind" seems to be quintessential to being human, so it is hard to claim that an inanimate object has one. But of course some students answer, "Well, sort of . . ." I ask those pondering this, "Why do you think it has a mind?" They respond, "Because it's thinking and processing information and guessing." The mind is the game's intellect, and it clearly has one because it is able to guess what someone is thinking. "So *how* does it have this intellect?" I ask my students, and that makes them start thinking about how the computer chip inside this game stores knowledge, how it is structured and organized, and then I use the word *represented*.

Once it is acknowledged that the device has to have knowledge represented to play the game, then we can discuss what the nature of that representation is and what the processes are that eventually lead to it being able to guess what they are thinking (i.e., "20 Q" cognition). After playing the game, students intuit that once the first answer is processed (e.g., "Yes" it is an animal), that narrows the possibilities for what the correct guess is going to be and influences what questions should be asked (e.g., "Does it swim?"). Each new answer continues to constrain what the guess could be; by the time 20 questions are asked, the pruning of possibilities in the game's knowledge base has left very few, if not one, best guess. And students understand that the literal representation of that network of knowledge in "20 Q" is binary code, as in all computers.

What my students have described as they work through how "20 Q" makes its guess is that the game has a hierarchical semantic network of knowledge that uses the process of spreading activation to get to its response. This is exactly what cognitive psychologists theorized for human knowledge representation in the early days of the subdiscipline. In fact, the representation of knowledge was perhaps the central problem for cognitive psychologists when the subdiscipline first became recognized as a branch of experimental psychology in the late 1950s and early 1960s. Cognitive psychologists were questioning what philosophers had been debating for centuries—what is knowledge? Where does it come from? How do we derive meaning from our world? Some very early philosophy-of-mind theorists, starting with Descartes, argued for mind–body dualism, such that mental phenomena were completely separate from any body effects. However, in response to Cartesian dualism, Kant argued that knowledge results from the interaction of the mind and the external world and, as an early precursor to the theory of embodied cognition, suggested that the body is essential or central to human cognition.

More recently, some philosophers responsible for initially defining and developing the theory of embodied cognition have viewed cognition as serving the needs of the body as it meets the demands of real-world situations (hence the name). From this perspective, internal mental representations of the world are not essential, and there is little need to discuss the actions of "the brain" (see dynamical systems theory of Thelen & Smith, 1994, and Beer, 2003, as well as Brooks's 1991a, 1991b, work in robotics). This stance arose from a general philosophical belief that the concept of internal mental representations had been overused in explaining cognition, as well as a disillusionment with cognitive science's lack of interest in how perception and cognition were linked to action. This brought about the antirepresentational view of "radical embodied cognitive science" (Chemero, 2009; Gallagher, 2005; Thelen & Smith, 1994).

However, other philosophers flipped the relationship to suggest that the body serves the mind (cognition), such that the external world leads our body to respond in a way that will inform and guide the mental representations that constitute thought. For example, Clark's (1998; 1999; 2008) view is more moderate in terms of considering the role of internal representations in cognition and yet still suggests that the interaction of the body and the external world can explain much of what has typically been considered the work of the brain. Clark, as well as Varela, Thompson, and Rosch (1991), argued that the body is essential in the production of cognition; in fact, the body plays a constitutive role in cognitive processing. The position of these philosophers and cognitive scientists has been referred to as "embodied cognitive science," and the central issue that distinguishes it from radical embodied cognitive science is the presence of internal representations (Alsmith & de Vignemont, 2012).

There has been extensive discussion of how these philosophical approaches to the theory of embodied cognition emerged and how they differ (e.g., Shapiro, 2011, 2014; and M. Wilson, 2002), but it is important to remember that in the philosophical tradition, empirical work is often cited to support a view, but it is not essential in developing and testing the theory. Cognitive psychologists became interested in the theory of embodied cognition because we, too, were interested in the body–mind interplay. However, within the experimental psychological tradition, the theory's tenets required examination and testing. Cognitive psychologists adopted only one perspective of the theory of embodied cognition, and from a philosophical and cognitive science standpoint, it is considered a "narrow view" of the theory. This is because the perspective is "brain centered"—it assumes internal representations and, as such, shifts from the view that the mind operates to serve the body to a view that the body serves the mind. As M. Wilson (2002) stated,

> This takeover by the mind, and the concomitant ability to mentally represent what is distant in time or space, may have been one of the driving forces behind the runaway train of human intelligence that separated us from other hominids. (p. 635)

Psychological Roots of the Theory

Getting back to the historical roots of cognitive psychology, the issue of internal representations of knowledge was of central concern to the first cognitive psychologists. We were emerging from the ashes of behaviorism, and the interest in the mind was being driven by the emerging field of computer science. In 1956, John McCarthy, a professor of mathematics at Dartmouth College, organized a conference titled Summer Research Project on Artificial Intelligence, where the intent of the conference was to "proceed on the basis of the conjecture that every aspect of learning or any other feature of intelligence can in principle be so precisely described that a machine can be made to simulate it" (see McCarthy, Minsky, Rochester, & Shannon, 2006, p. 12). Mathematicians, computer scientists, linguists, and psychologists attended this conference, all united by this curiosity in understanding human thought and cognitive processes to the degree that a computer could mimic them.

Another important conference in the same year took place at the Massachusetts Institute of Technology, where the lingering interest in behavior was fading quickly and being replaced by an interest in the study of mental processes. At this conference, George Miller presented his idea that there are limits to human's ability to hold information in memory, that limit being somewhere around 7 "chunks" (G. A. Miller, 1956). Some psychologists were working on the "processing" aspect of cognition and were trying to understand perception, attention, memory, and reasoning. Others were working on the "structure" aspect of cognition—that is, how the knowledge we have is organized and coherent so that it can be retrieved and used by cognitive processes. Theories of knowledge were developed and tested, and they varied from feature comparison models (cf., Smith, Shoben, & Rips, 1974) to prototype models (cf., Rosch, 1973) to semantic network models (cf., Collins & Loftus, 1975; and J. R. Anderson, 1983). Figure 1.1 shows a semantic network from Collins and Loftus (1975), where the links between concept nodes are short or long depending on personal experiences with these thoughts: The shorter the link, the stronger the connection, and the faster the reaction time to respond to this connection in any object identification or categorization task (think "20 Q" responses and early guesses based on predictability in this network of knowledge). Semantic network theories were widely tested and modified to address results that could not be explained, but the newer versions became so general and flexible that they were criticized for being difficult to falsify, thus losing explanatory power.

In the 1980s, a new approach called *connectionism* gained favor, which was an approach to create computer models for representing knowledge that was based on what was known at that time about neural networks. These models were called parallel distributed processing (PDP) models of knowledge representation, and in some sense they were technological updates of more traditional semantic network models. These PDP models argued that neuron-like nodes are excited or inhibited by the action of other nodes, and thus knowledge was represented by patterns of excitation or inhibition rather than particular nodes. Spreading activation still flows through networks of linked concepts, but processes can occur in parallel, rather than the more

FIGURE 1.1

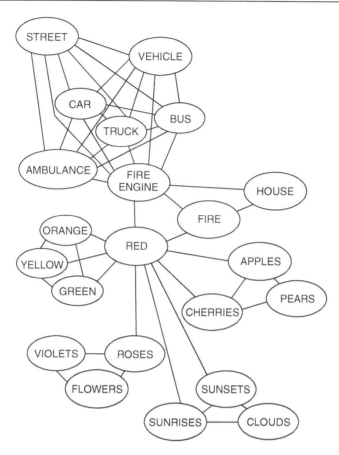

A schematic representation of concept relatedness in a stereotypical fragment of human memory (where a shorter line represents greater relatedness). From "A Spreading-Activation Theory of Semantic Processing," by A. M. Collins and E. F. Loftus, 1975, *Psychological Review*, *82*, p. 412. Copyright 1975 by the American Psychological Association.

hierarchical earlier models, and are distributed across brain sites (cf., McClelland & Rogers, 2003).

The zeitgeist of the subdiscipline of cognitive psychology for its first 40 or so years was to think about cognitive processes such as sensation, perception, attention, and memory as *modular*, that is, they existed in and of themselves with minimal interaction with each other (Fodor & Pylyshyn, 1988; Newell & Simon, 1972). The representation of knowledge was also functionally autonomous, and there was little discussion of how processes would affect or determine what was being represented. This could be likened to having a computer on one's shoulders with input and output modules that worked fairly independently from one another. This traditional view was that mental representations were symbolic in nature, quasilinguistic (propositional), and abstract. Any symbol (or word), for example, *chair*, was abstract in the sense that it referred to the general instance of the concept. Further, the symbol (word) was an arbitrary referent to the concept because the way in which it looked and sounded bore no relation to the physical or functional properties of the concept.

According to this view, these symbols that represented our knowledge of a concept were *amodal*; they were not tied to any specific modality or bodily action. Further, these symbols were organized propositionally, with their meaning emerging from relations to other symbols. Thus, this early theory holds that meaning is an internal process, and cognition is not shaped by perception or action. Newell and Simon's (1976) physical symbol system hypothesis (PSSH) was a theoretical instantiation of this view of knowledge: Abstract symbols can be found in both human thought (propositions) and computer representation (binary code), and thinking is the manipulation of these symbols, which does not involve perception or action.

As cognitive psychology grew as a discipline, there were many theoretical arguments and empirical results that undermined a PSSH system of knowledge representation. One of the most damning arguments against a wholly symbol system view of knowledge is the "symbol-grounding" problem (Harnad, 1990; Searle, 1980). This problem basically states that abstract symbols (words) that are arbitrary and have no connection to the external world can have no meaning. If thinking (or computation in a computer) is symbol manipulation that goes on internally, just within our heads or in the computer, and there are no external referents, then we have what Harnad (1990) referred to as the "symbol merry-go-round" problem. This is when symbols cannot be assigned meaning according to what they refer to (which would make them nonarbitrary); instead, their meaning is just in relation to other symbols. Glenberg (2015) likened this to trying to find the meaning of a word in a foreign language in a dictionary made up of only other foreign language words—the search would never be successful if none of the symbols have any meaning to the person searching. He described this problem in the following way:

> Imagine that you land at an airport, perhaps in China, where you don't speak the local language. You see what appears to be a sign consisting of logograms (or any other noniconic marks). Although you don't speak the language, you do have a dictionary written in that language. You look up the first logogram and find its definition, but of course the definition consists of more logograms whose meanings are obscure to you. Undaunted, you look up the definition of the first logogram in the definition, and you find that its definition consists of even more uninterpretable logograms. The point is that no matter how many of the logograms you look up, this closed system of abstract symbols will never produce any meaning for you. (p. 165)

What Glenberg (2015) pointed out about the standard cognitive models of knowledge representation is that in those models, understanding the meaning of a symbol could be likened to going round and round in an infinite circle. Looking for the meaning of one symbol involves trying to find the meaning of another arbitrary symbol, and the meaning of that symbol requires the same kind of internal search for another arbitrary symbol. If you look back at Figure 1.1, it seems as if the symbols (the ellipses that have the labels underneath) are meaningful—but that is because we are providing them with meaning. The shape is not related to the meaning, and the label (the word) is something we have provided. The words are there for the convenience of the reader; if we opened up someone's head and looked inside, we would not see labels on ellipses. Figure 1.2 more accurately represents the semantic network theory. Here the abstract symbols (ellipses) are not labeled, and thus they are authentically amodal, abstract symbols. This portrayal of the theory makes clear this symbol merry-go-round argument. One can start at any node and trace relations to any and all other nodes, but no matter how many relations are traced, no meaning will ever be available.

FIGURE 1.2

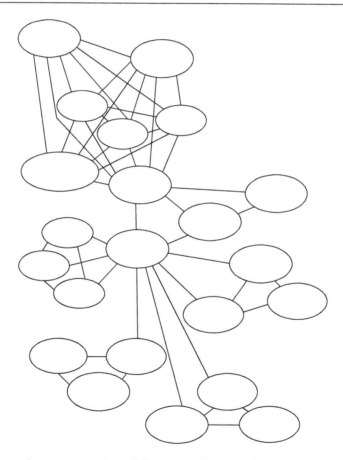

A schematic representation of the semantic network theory with amodal abstract symbols. Adapted from "A Spreading-Activation Theory of Semantic Processing," by A. M. Collins and E. F. Loftus, 1975, *Psychological Review, 82*, p. 412. Copyright 1975 by the American Psychological Association.

Never leaving "the head" (or the computer) to determine what a symbol is referring to in the external world would mean an infinite regress of search for meaning. We can only break from this symbol-grounding problem if the symbols refer to something in our external world, that is, have referents that *ground* those symbols in perception, action, and/or emotion. This grounding represents the meaning of the symbol. The embodied approach to cognition argues that all knowledge is grounded in sensory, perceptual, and motoric processes and that these processes are a function of one's own morphology (shape and size) and physiology (internal processes).

Evidence from cognitive neuroscience supports embodiment in revealing that thinking involves the reactivation and reuse of processes and representations involved in perception and action. For example, Hauk, Johnsrude, and Pulvermüller (2004) recorded neural activity while readers listened to action verbs such as *kick* and *pick*. They found that as readers read those action verbs, there was greater activation in the specific part of the motor cortex responsible for producing that action than other motor cortex areas. This suggests that understanding an action concept may be grounded in action-specific motor neurons.

The discovery of mirror neurons in the motor cortex of monkeys may help us understand a similar neural system in humans that would allow us to comprehend others' actions, goals, and intentions (e.g., Gallese, Keysers, & Rizzolatti, 2004; Iacoboni, 2009; Rizzolatti & Craighero, 2004). In monkeys, single-cell recordings from mirror neurons show that a neuron in this tract is similarly active when a monkey is performing a task as when the monkey is observing another monkey engage in the same task. Researchers have suggested that the purpose of having mirror neurons that are active both during action and during observation is that this provides the animal with the ability to infer goals and emotions to another. If an animal acts in a purposeful way, the neurons that fire during that action, and then are later "reused" while observing another's action, must reflect the meaning of that action. This is evidence for that neuron serving both action and cognition, supporting the view that the body plays a constitutive role in cognition.

This evidence seriously challenges the view that conceptual representations are abstract and amodal. Of course there are quite disparate views of the extent to which mental representations are modal or both amodal and modal. And even those that argue that meaning is found in modality-specific representations have quite different approaches to the theory of embodiment (see Gentsch, Weber, Synofzik, Vosgerau, & Schütz-Bosbach, 2016; A. D. Wilson & Golonka, 2013).

Tripartite Framework of the Theory

In this book, I will take a three-pronged approach to organizing and synthesizing the extensive experimental results concerning this theory. This is not entirely original, as others have noticed this tripartite distinction in the embodiment literature. Although the experimental work can be loosely organized within this tripartite framework, I will continue to remind the reader that these approaches are not contradictory but instead complementary.

These three approaches are represented by

■ Arthur Glenberg's (2010, 2015) view that *the body* is essential to knowledge (Chapters 2, 3, 4, and 5);

■ Lawrence Barsalou's (1999) perceptual symbol system hypothesis (PSS), which relies on representations that come about from perceptual experiences and *sensorimotor simulation* as the "core computational" process of thought (Chapters 6 and 7); and

■ Lakoff and Johnson's (1980) *Metaphors We Live By* proposal that *language* reflects our representation of knowledge (Chapter 8).

Although this book will allow the reader to compare and contrast these three approaches to embodiment, there is no attempt to choose one as the prominent or more persuasive perspective. Because it is at the core of my presentation of this topic, I will say it again: These approaches are not contradictory, but instead are complementary.

This book organizes results from different laboratories of experimental psychology examining multiple types of cognitive processes to give *weight* to the theory of embodiment. Why would I use such a metaphor concerning the weight of a topic? Very intentionally—it provides a way to illustrate what I am trying to do in this book. For instance, if I want you to understand the role of the body in this theory of embodiment, I would emphasize that when we hold something heavy, the perceived value of that which we are holding is increased compared with when it is light (Jostmann, Lakens, & Schubert, 2009). Further, our judgments concerning the importance of an object affect how heavy we believe that object to be (Schneider, Parzuchowski, Wojciszke, Schwarz, & Koole, 2015). These empirical examples suggest that our body is essential to our conceptualization of importance.

However, if I want you to understand that thinking involves Barsalou's (1999) PSS hypothesis of sensorimotor simulation, I would argue that it is the simulation of a prior experience of weight that underlies a judgment of value. In our life's physical experiences, more likely than not, heavier objects have been more important than lighter objects (e.g., full bottles of milk compared with empty ones), and these patterns of experience are reenacted in thinking about value (Barsalou, 2008b).

Or, if I wanted you to understand how we give meaning to something abstract, like importance, I would emphasize that we do this by linking abstract concepts to superficially dissimilar but understood concrete concepts. This is reflected in our language. For example, our metaphors concerning "weighty decisions" and "heavy topics" reflect that our mental representation of value or importance is linked to the concrete property of weight. Abstract concepts can be understood in terms of multiple linkages with concrete concepts, yielding expressions that could not be easily explained by embodied simulations (Landau, Meier, & Keefer, 2010).

In Chapters 2 through 5 of this book, I present material that supports the role of the body in different cognitive processes—perception of distance, perception of size—but also how our bodies affect our sense of control, power, even judgments about free will and include a discussion of how culture may mediate some of these judgments. Chapters 6 and 7 address how empirical results can demonstrate that sensorimotor simulation is the mechanism that provides meaning. Evidence will include such research as that demonstrating that emotional facial responses are simulations of others' emotional reactions even in the absence of motoric mimicry. Or how simulation, in the form of how we imagine our bodies moving in space, may determine our conceptual representation of time more so than the actual movement of our bodies.

Finally, in Chapter 8, I explore how language, specifically metaphor, reflects the grounding of meaning. In this chapter, I present results that demonstrate the bidirectionality of metaphor-consistent psychological effects. For example, in exploring the common metaphor that someone we care for is "warm," it has been shown that if we are physically warm (e.g., holding a hot cup of coffee), we feel closer to people in our lives (even strangers in our physical space) than when holding something cold, and when we are thinking about a time in which we were included in a social experience, we judge the temperature of a room to be physically warmer than when we remember a time of social exclusion. It appears that the conceptualization of affiliation may be grounded in the physical experience of temperature (Williams & Bargh, 2008).

I conclude with Chapter 9 that addresses the current status of embodiment and attempts to simplify the complex reactions to the theory. In the end, it will be left to experimental cognitive psychologists, cognitive neuroscientists, and cognitive scientists to continue with the empirical investigations and modeling of cognitive processes to determine if the theory of embodiment will in fact be the paradigm shift that unifies psychology as a discipline.

One final note about the book: At the end of each of these content Chapters 2–8, I have left a "takeaway" for the reader. This is simply a statement or two that represents the "big picture" of the chapter; the intent was to capture the essence of the empirical work discussed in that chapter. You will find some redundancy in these takeaways because they all are describing how embodiment theory explains cognition—and yet each explanation is within a specific area (e.g., perception, emotion, language) or specific to a concept (e.g., simulation). The takeaway pays homage to the primary theorists in each of the areas by simply stating their names, but of course the reader will understand that many others are cited in the chapter to support these views. I hope these takeaways serve as reminders of the overarching principles guiding the empirical investigations of the theory of embodied cognition.

The Body's Role in Perception

2

Questions:

- What is the role of the body in visual perception?
- How does the body provide meaning to our visual world?

In the study of human cognition, cognitive psychologists separate the investigation of sensation and perception because we believe in a hierarchy of cognitive processes. The environment presents physical information to our sensory organs, and then physiological processes immediately get to work to take the energy of light, sound, taste, and touch and transform it into neural code. Now sensation becomes internal information, and the question becomes: How do we get meaning from that code (called the *proximal stimulus* by cognitive psychologists)? That transformational process from proximal stimulus to semantics is *perception*.

The interplay of sensory and nonsensory information that results in a perceptual experience has long been debated by philosophers, cognitive psychologists, and neuroscientists. Visual perception is the focus of this chapter; more specifically, the role that nonvisual processes, or those bodily processes outside of the visual system, play in the perception of visual stimuli. Of interest in this exploration is what the empirical literature has to say about these nonvisual influences on a cognitive process that, in the tradition of the early schools of

http://dx.doi.org/10.1037/0000136-002
How the Body Shapes Knowledge: Empirical Support for Embodied Cognition, by R. Fincher-Kiefer

cognition, has been seen as a modular process where nonvisual influences were considered postperceptual (e.g., Fodor, 1983). Before beginning with this question of the body's role in visual perception, however, let's start with a broader view of embodiment that will get us to this specific question. Let's begin with a summary of Glenberg's view of embodiment, one that will be returned to many times throughout this book.

Glenberg's Perspective

Glenberg and his colleagues (Glenberg, 2010, 2015; Glenberg, Witt, & Metcalfe, 2013) have argued that thinking is not divorced from the body; their claim is that all psychological processes are influenced by the body's morphology, sensory systems, and motoric capacities. In his seminal article suggesting that embodiment theory could be a unifying framework for all of psychology, Glenberg (2010) emphasized how evolution, namely the pressures to survive and reproduce, has necessitated the role of the body in thought. His claim is that cognition evolved as our bodies evolved to thrive in our environment.

Glenberg's classic example is that of a mole being pursued by a predator—if the mole failed to represent its body's action capabilities accurately, for example by trying to fly instead of diving into a hole to escape, it would not have seen the dawn of another day. Cognition serves to control action, because without action, there is no survival. Given this is the case, then the primary goal of primitive but essential cognition is to determine the constraints and capabilities of one's body to act purposefully in our environment. This approach has its roots in the philosophical work of Varela, Thompson, and Rosch (1991). As detailed in their book *The Embodied Mind*, they write, "By using the term *action* [italics in original] we mean to emphasize once again that sensory and motor processes, perception and action, are fundamentally inseparable in lived cognition" (p. 173).

This view of cognition suggests that the evolution of thought starts with the body and becomes more advanced and sophisticated as the body develops. Of course this is an embodied view of cognition. There are some who have argued that cognition could still serve action without being embodied (e.g., Ernst & Banks, 2002; Firestone, 2013; Fodor, 1983), but the goal of this chapter is to focus on the empirical results suggesting that cognition, specifically perception, is embodied and evolved to serve action.

Glenberg et al. (2013) argued that evidence from both human and nonhuman research demonstrates that perceptual processes have evolved with the motor system. This general approach applied to the specific cognitive problem of visual perception is consistent with the earlier work of James Gibson (1977, 1979) and his theory of direct perception. Gibson argued that humans do not construct visual perceptions from sensory information; we do not simply perceive angles and lines that require further processing for a percept. Instead, the environment is perceived in terms of how it can be interacted with. Gibson's view has action, and therefore the body, central to perception. Meaning is established by what the environment affords the perceiver. Gibson's theory of affordances suggests that from visual stimulation, perceivers "pick up" information related to their ability to act on their world and its objects. A chair affords to be sat on, but that perception of the object as a chair is dependent on one's body shape—an adult would not perceive a dollhouse chair as an object to be sat on but instead as a toy to be picked up. Gibson also argued that affordances are inseparable from our bodies; for instance, the perceived edibility of an apple is dependent on the individual's shape of their mouth, their teeth, and even their digestive system.

Developmental Support for Action's Role in Perception

Gibson's (1977, 1979) view was supported by earlier animal research that examined how action plays a role in the development of perceptual skills. Held and Hein's (1963) classic research with kittens on a carousel illustrates how motor experience changes perception. A pair of kittens was harnessed to a small carousel, just like carousel horses across from one another, and exposed to a lit visual environment of vertical stripes on the curved walls of the carousel. It is important to understand that both kittens had been reared in darkness since birth, so both were receiving identical visual information for the first time. The difference between the kittens was that one kitten's harness allowed its feet to touch the ground, and it was able to move and rotate the carousel by itself. This was the active kitten condition. The other kitten was in a harness that kept its feet from touching the ground, so it was in a "gondola" that moved only when the other kitten was moving. Held and Hein called this the "yoked" gondola, or passive, condition. The point of this experiment was that although both kittens received the same sensory experience, or visual input, one could move actively while the other was deprived of self-controlled locomotion.

Results of this experimental situation demonstrated that kittens in both conditions had normal visual responses to light and moving objects, but the passive-condition kittens showed impaired blink responses (reflexive abnormalities) and impaired visually guided paw placement. These passive kittens also failed the visual cliff test. The visual cliff is an apparatus originally created by Gibson and Walk (1960) to investigate depth perception in humans and animals. This apparatus simulates the experience of walking to the edge of a cliff. It involves animals or humans (typically infants) walking or crawling across a sheet of see-through Plexiglass that has a high contrast checkerboard pattern on a cloth underneath. On one part of the Plexiglass, the checkerboard pattern is directly underneath, but on the other side, the cloth has been dropped about 4 feet below. This drop-off creates the perception of a visual cliff, or a change in depth below the Plexiglass.

When the passive condition kittens in Held and Hein's (1963) experiment were placed on the visual cliff, they walked over the "cliff"—or the place on the Plexiglass where the pattern below changed. This demonstrated that the kittens were unable to determine depth information from visual cues, which of course would yield serious environmental and survival challenges in the real world. The active kittens passed the visual cliff test; when placed on the deep side of the Plexiglass, they either froze or inched backward until they reached the shallow side of the cliff. The results of this study indicated that for the active kittens, moving through the environment had allowed the kittens to have a visual experience with meaning. However, for those kittens without self-produced action, they could not effectively interpret their visual world. (To respond to any worry concerning the later life experiences of the passive kittens, Held and Hein did find that once the passive kittens were given the opportunity to move around in a lit environment and experience the visual consequences of their action, their perceptual skills improved in a matter of days, and they passed all depth tests.)

An interesting aside here is an application of Held and Hein's (1963) research to the current pervasive use of satellite navigation systems (global positioning systems, or GPSs) and an impaired ability to self-navigate. Many of us have had the experience of not knowing how to travel somewhere when someone else has done the driving—similar to the yoked kittens' perceptual consequences. In addition, one could also question the cognitive ramifications of actually doing the driving but having an automated system doing the navigating. Research has suggested that continued use of GPS navigation systems may lead to an inability to create spatial maps as well as impoverished representations of the landscape that has been traveled (e.g., Ishikawa, Fujiwara, Imai, & Okabe, 2008; Leshed, Velden, Rieger, Kot, & Sengers, 2008; Weisberg & Newcombe, 2016).

Developmental research has also demonstrated interdependency between perception and action in infants that has clear consequences for perceptual development as well as for higher order cognitive development and emotional development (e.g., Campos, Bertenthal, & Kermoian, 1992; Dahl et al., 2013; Glenberg & Hayes, 2016; Lozada & Carro, 2016). As in Held and Hein's (1963) kitten research, work with infants has linked self-locomotion with the ability to have meaningful perceptual experiences (Campos et al., 2000). It has been shown that similar to the passive kittens, infants with little self-locomoting experience show less fear crossing the visual cliff than infants with experience in crawling, and this effect was independent of age (Campos, Bertenthal, & Kermoian, 1992). More recently, Dahl et al. (2013) gave pre-locomoting infants experience sitting in a wheeled device that they could move by kicking on the floor. Once infants gained experience moving with this device, they showed the appropriate fear to the visual cliff, measured by accelerated heart rate, compared with infants that did not get training with the mobility device.

Why is it that developmentally, locomotion is needed for a healthy (in terms of survival) fear of heights? The answer to this will help us determine whether the body is necessary for depth perception and thus this appropriate emotional response. Dahl et al. (2013) argued that the locomotor training in their research allowed for improved visual proprioception, which is the understanding of visual information that comes from one's own body movements responding to the environment. This visual proprioception comes from the development of a correlation between self-produced action and flow of visual information—most important, peripheral optic information (D. I. Anderson, Campos, & Barbu-Roth, 2003).

Infants receiving peripheral optic information show postural changes (body sway) that allow for stability. When there is a change in the peripheral optic flow (from locomoting near an edge), this leads to a decrease in postural compensation, which mediates fear of heights and the response to not cross over a deep visual cliff. Campos et al.

(2000) also argued that fear of heights could not simply result from developing depth perception. If that were the case, all 5-month-old infants would show visual cliff fear, and they do not. Instead, the converging evidence from multiple experiments suggests that it is *locomotor experience* that organizes the rudimentary perceptual skills existing in newborns and infants. This experience refines and dramatically tunes these skills, such as visual proprioception, to have meaningful perceptual experiences.

Piaget (1954) discussed the role of the body on the development of another perceptual skill, distance perception. He claimed that when infants begin to coordinate vision with reaching, they are then able to construct the perception of depth—but only within their reaching capabilities. Eventually, locomotor experience provides the information about space outside of reach, and only then can the infant estimate sizes and distances in vertical space. Piaget and others (Kaufman, 1974) have argued that the coupling of motoric and visual information allows the infant to "scale" optic information, essentially in motoric, effort-based units. This scaling process that was discussed by Piaget and Kaufman has been updated and detailed by Proffitt and colleagues (Proffitt, 2013; Proffitt & Linkenauger, 2013; Witt, 2011). Proffitt and his colleagues developed an "action-specific account" of perception that has been supported by a wealth of evidence from their laboratories, but their perspective and their data have also been challenged by other researchers (e.g., Durgin et al., 2009; Durgin, Klein, Spiegel, Strawser, & Williams, 2012; Firestone, 2013; Woods, Philbeck, & Danoff, 2009).

Proffitt's Perspective

Proffitt's embodied approach to visual perception began in the 1990s with a fairly bold statement that was reminiscent of Gibson's approach to perception: We perceive the world as a function of our ability to act within it. He claimed that perception does not involve thinking as much as it involves the body "reacting"—but within its unique action capabilities (Proffitt, 2006; Proffitt, Bhalla, Gossweiler, & Midgett, 1995; Proffitt, Stefanucci, Banton, & Epstein, 2003). This begins in infancy, when babies learn what they can and cannot do with their environment given their current behavioral status; in other words, they are learning environmental "affordances." These affordances change as an infant's body develops and action capabilities change. Throughout life we perceive the world as a function of the possibility for action needed to achieve our goals. To do this, we have to "scale" the world in terms of how our bodies can accomplish those goals (see Adolph & Hoch, in press, for a similar embodied perspective on the role of motoric development on psychological functions).

Perception of Slant

Proffitt and his colleagues initially found evidence of the role of the body on visual perception by exploring the perception of slant and distance. Proffitt, Bhalla, Gossweiler, and Midgett (1995) had participants who were regular runners come into their laboratory on the day that they were planning to do their most demanding run of the week. Before that run, Proffitt et al. had participants stand at the foot of a hill that had either a 5- or 31-degree slant (unknown to them) and make three estimates (in counterbalanced orders across participants) of that slant as they looked at the hill: a verbal estimate given numerically (after they were reminded that the horizontal ground plane was 0 degrees and a vertical surface was 90 degrees); a visual matching estimate, which involved looking at a handheld pie chart and adjusting the "piece of pie" until it matched the estimate of the hill's slant (see Figure 2.1, found in Proffitt, 2006); and a "haptic" (touch-based sensory experience) judgment of slant. This estimate involved standing at a small stand and adjusting a "palmboard" on top of that stand, without looking at their hands or the board, until the palmboard felt to be the same slant as the hill (see Figure 2.2, found in Proffitt, 2006).

Following this hill's slant estimation, the participants went on their hard run, and at the end they arrived at a second hill, which also, unbeknownst to the participants, had either a 5- or 31-degree slant (the starting and finishing hills' slants were different and their order was also counterbalanced across the two groups of participants). Participants were asked to make the same three slant judgments, and the results of

FIGURE 2.1

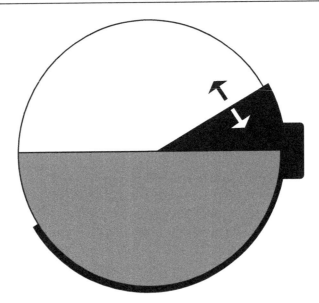

The visual matching device for slant estimation. Participants rotated the black semicircle so as to make the pie-shaped segment appear to have an angle equivalent to the cross section of the viewed hill. The disk was about 15 cm in diameter. From "Embodied Perception and the Economy of Action," by D. R. Proffitt, 2006, *Perspectives on Psychological Science, 1*, p. 111. Copyright 2006 by Sage. Reprinted with permission.

FIGURE 2.2

A participant using the haptic device (palmboard). Her task was to adjust the board to be parallel to the incline of the hill without looking at her hand. From "Embodied Perception and the Economy of Action," by D. R. Proffitt, 2006, *Perspectives on Psychological Science*, *1*, p. 112. Copyright 2006 by Sage. Reprinted with permission.

these estimations for before and after the run for both slants are found in Figure 2.3 (from Proffitt et al., 1995). As can be seen, the results for both slant conditions suggest that even before the run, the verbal and visual conditions were quite poor estimates of slant (sometimes incorrect by 20 degrees), but the haptic estimations were fairly accurate. Most important, the effects of fatigue on slant perception were significant in both slant conditions—participants estimated slant to be almost 10 degrees steeper after the run than before the run. Finally, the results cannot simply be attributed to just an inability to report angles in degrees. Proffitt et al. (1995) showed that participants, using the handheld disk used in the visual estimates, were accurate in knowing what angles, expressed in degrees, would look like on this disk when simply asked, for example, to "set the disk to 35 degrees."

Simply put, Proffitt et al. (1995) found a perceptual result that is so intuitively pleasing that it hardly seems surprising or even interesting—hills look steeper when we are tired. But why? And what does this say about how the body informs visual perception? Proffitt and colleagues proposed that perception is "mutable" or adaptive.

FIGURE 2.3

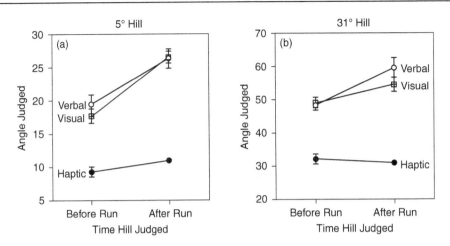

Mean slant judgments made by runners before and after their runs. Perceived slant was measured verbally, visually, and haptically for a 5° hill (left) and a 31° hill (right). Error bars indicate ±1 *SEM*. From "Perceiving Geographical Slant," by D. R. Proffitt, M. Bhalla, R. Gossweiler, and J. Midgett, 1995, *Psychonomic Bulletin & Review, 2,* p. 424. Copyright 1995 by Springer. Reprinted with permission.

We perceive the world not veridically but in terms of how our bodies will act within it. This is the essence of Proffitt's view of *embodied perception.* Visual perception takes the visual input from the environment and couples that, automatically and without conscious awareness, with a consideration of the energetic costs of body locomotion. We do this because of our internal, evolutionary-based drive to behave in an energy-efficient manner—we cannot expend more energy than we have available. Perceiving a hill to be steeper than it is in reality when we are tired is adaptive because it informs the action system to respond accordingly.

More evidence for the role of energetic costs, or bodily effort, on perception has been found in other work in Proffitt's laboratory. In another experiment where participants estimated slant using verbal, visual, and haptic judgments, Bhalla and Proffitt (1999) had participants wear either a light or a heavy backpack while standing at the bottom of a hill. They found that the heavy backpack condition yielded steeper slant judgments in the verbal and visual conditions, but not the haptic responses, as in the earlier studies. Bhalla and Proffitt also found that participants whose bodies were experiencing long-term energy deficits—those who were in poor physical condition and elderly participants—experienced the exaggerated overestimations in the conscious awareness of slant compared with their fit and youthful counterparts, yet their visually guided action of the palmboard was again unaffected by physiological potential.

Why are the haptic judgments, or measures of slant requiring visually guided action, not influenced by what Proffitt (2006) called "energetic considerations"? If the body influences some measures of visual perception but not this visually guided action, does that call into question the conclusion that the body affects visual perception? Proffitt et al. (1995) surmised that visually guided action is different from visual perception because they are informed by separate visual pathways.

It is now well recognized that beginning with a subdivision among retinal ganglion cells, there are two separate visual pathways in the human brain. One provides input to the inferotemporal cortex, identified as the *ventral system*, and another provides input to the posterior parietal cortex, identified as the *dorsal system* (Goodale & Milner, 1992; Milner & Goodale, 2008). The ventral system appears to be primarily responsible for "what" functions, or conscious visual awareness of object characteristics, whereas the dorsal system is nonconscious and carries out the "how" functions responsible for visually guided action.

The dissociation found in the different slant estimates from verbal and visual reports versus haptic judgments, especially that explicit judgments were affected by physiological states whereas action judgments were not, suggests that the basis for these different responses comes from different visual systems. Conscious perception appears to be influenced by the body, but nonconscious perception appears to be guided by purely visual information. The operation of both systems appears to be critically important to behavior. Despite our conscious perceptual system perceiving, for example, hills to be steeper than they are in reality to inform our actions, another visual system immune to nonvisual biases does allow us to act effectively. Thus, we do not inappropriately raise our feet 20 degrees for traversing a 5-degree slant or stumble when we take on a heavy backpack while walking along a terrain.

Schnall, Harber, Stefanucci, and Proffitt (2008) found another type of nonvisual influence on the perception of slant; this time, it was not a body effect, such as fatigue or age, but a psychosocial effect—the presence of social support. When participants either had a friend stand near them while estimating the slant of a hill or when participants imagined a friend beside them, they estimated the hill to be less steep than participants who stood alone or those who imagined a negative or neutral person beside them. As in previous studies, these effects occurred in the verbal and visual estimates of slant but had no effect on haptic judgments. Just as physical costs moderate the perception of the world, so do psychosocial resources similarly influence perceptual judgments. Interestingly, relationship quality mediated the effects of social support in this research; the longer the friendships and the stronger the feelings of closeness and warmth, the less steep the slant was perceived to be. These results from Schnall et al. suggest that conscious perception depends on energetic costs/resources, and psychosocial resources may offset those energetic costs or replenish them.

Perception of Distance

Proffitt, Stefanucci, Banton, and Epstein (2003) found that the same kind of energetic costs that affected slant perception also influence egocentric distance judgments, or perceived "extent," the distance from an observer to a target. This was demonstrated when participants who wore a heavy backpack and verbally judged distances to targets found the targets to be further away than participants who did not wear backpacks. Proffitt and colleagues argued that if egocentric distance is an environmental *affordance* (Gibson, 1979), then the perception of that distance must account for the costs of moving our body through that environment. In other words, perception of distance will not only be a function of visual input and variables that aid depth perception, such as optic flow and binocular disparity, but also be determined by the individual's ability to perform in that context. If distance perception is in part due to the nonvisual input of anticipated effort to traverse an extent, the next question to be asked is whether this anticipated effort is general or is it specifically applied to the behavior in question?

Witt, Proffitt, and Epstein's (2004) first experiment extended Proffitt et al.'s (2003) research by examining whether increased *throwing* effort also affected perceived distances (i.e., is this a general effort effect or specific to locomotion?). Participants in this study threw either a heavy ball or a light ball at targets placed in front of them and then judged the distance to the target. Witt et al. found that those who threw the heavy ball judged the targets to be further away than those who threw the light ball. This result suggested a general, or unconditional, effect of body effort on distance perception. Witt et al. further explored this coupling of energetic costs and visual input on distance perception to examine whether these effects influenced multiple measures of distance perception.

To that end, they used another measure of distance that had the potential to be less influenced by conscious perception, similar to the visually guided action measure of the palmboard in the slant perception studies. This was the distance measure of "blindwalking," where participants are blindfolded and asked to walk out a distance estimate instead of verbally providing that estimate. Blindwalking had been used before in a similar investigation with throwing effort (Rieser, Pick, Ashmead, & Garing, 1995) and had been shown to be insensitive to the nonvisual influence of effort. In fact, Witt et al. (2004) also found that when participants threw either a heavy ball or a light ball at targets at various distances and then were asked to blindwalk the distance estimates, unlike the verbal estimates, there was no effect of throwing effort on the blindwalk estimates. This of course calls into question whether these effort effects are truly occurring during perception or are strategic and only occur when participants are asked to make a verbal estimate of distance.

Witt et al. (2004) claimed that there is an interpretation of these results that is consistent with the proposal that online perception is a function of both visual input and anticipated effort required to move. In their first experiment in which participants were throwing balls in many trials with different distances, they knew they would be throwing in even more trials. Therefore, participants perceived their world as "throwers," and their distance estimates reflected effort in throwing. However, in Witt et al.'s later experiment in which participants were asked to "blind" walk after each trial of throwing, perhaps their intent was to be a "walker" and thus throwing effort was irrelevant.

To test the impact of intent, Witt et al. (2004) ran another experiment in which they manipulated intentions, or the action that the participants expected after each distance judgment. All participants threw a heavy ball three times at targets (different distances were used) and then estimated the distances to the target. However, half of the participants were told that after making each distance estimate, they would be asked to close their eyes and then throw to the target (blind throw distance estimate), and the other half were asked to put on a blindfold and then walk to the target (blindwalk distance estimate). Results demonstrated that when participants were intending to throw to the target, they overestimated distances compared with those who intended to walk to the target. This supports the contention that the effect of effort is specific to the task at hand; distances are perceived as further if one has been effortfully throwing and expects to throw again, but effortful throwing has little effect on perceiving distances that are expected to be walked. It is not just that bodily effort plays a general role in distance perception, but instead that the effect of effort specifically depends on the action that the perceiver intends to take. If one's perceptual world is that of a thrower, distance perception will be a function of the effort required for throwing. However, if one's intent is to be a walker, then distance perception will be affected by the effort specifically used in walking, and thus will be influenced by factors such as being encumbered.

Another factor that should influence distance perception if one's intent was to be a walker would be chronic pain that specifically affects walking. This would be another energetic "cost" that should automatically influence distance perception just as other nonvisual influences do. Witt et al. (2009) found participants who had chronic pain in their lower back and legs and had them make distance judgments to cones placed at various distances down a long hallway. They compared these distance estimates with those made by pain-free control participants. They found that participants who experienced chronic pain when walking perceived the distance to the targets as farther away than did the pain-free control participants.

Just as Schnall, Harber, et al. (2008) showed that psychosocial resources affected slant perception, other studies have found social/emotional factors that have influenced distance perception, and these factors may also work to alter the body's energetic resources. For example, Balcetis and Dunning (2010) found that desirable objects, such as money that could be won, were perceived as closer than less desirable objects. Their explanation for this result was that the bias in perception served an energizing function to approach items that fulfill needs. Similarly, Cole, Balcetis, and Dunning (2013) found that threatening stimuli, such as an aggressive male, was perceived as closer to their participants than stimuli that elicited disgust or no emotion. Cole et al. argued that this perceptual bias served to affect participants' action regulation, in this case, motivating the participant to move quickly away from the stimulus. Both of these emotional states, desire and fear, and perhaps other mood states (Riener, Stefanucci, Proffitt, & Clore, 2003), appear to affect the body's energetic resources in similar ways to being physically refreshed or encumbered.

Perception as a Phenotypic Expression

Proffitt and Linkenauger's (2013) conceptualization of embodied perception suggests an even stronger biological, body-based, foundation for perception. They argued that the transformation of visual angles, the computations involved in retinal disparities, and the ocular–motor adjustments that define visual information processing are all occurring through a scaling process that is specific to one's body.

Proffitt and Linkenauger's (2013) "perceptual-ruler" hypothesis suggests that during perception, we transform the visual angles that come in from the environment into units that are derived from our body. So, being quite tall, I will perceive the world differently than a shorter person, despite the same physical reality, because we are using different perceptual rulers. Eye height provides us with a perceptual yardstick that we use to judge and understand perceptual properties such as distance and object height (Sedgwick, 1986; Wraga, 1999). By using my body to scale the height of an object, the visual angles that the environment projects may hypothetically take up perhaps 40% of my perceptual yardstick, but to a shorter person, this same object could project angles that consume as much as 65% of their perceptual yardstick. This suggests that perception is a direct function of the body, and the meaning that comes from that perception is that a shorter person will see the world as bigger than a taller person. A child sees the world as bigger than an adult because the child's scaling process uses a ruler that is a dramatically different size than the adult's.

Proffitt and Linkenauger (2013) proposed that although our eye height scales distance and height, our hand size will be used to scale the size of graspable objects. Imagine how a child, having their hand serve as the scaling device, perceives the size of an apple compared with how an adult perceives that same apple. Similarly, one's arm is used for scaling the distance to reachable objects, and one's body's *ability*, in terms of physiological and behavioral potential, will be used to scale other aspects of the environment, such as slants and distances (see Figure 2.4, from Proffitt & Linkenauger, 2013). Proffitt and Linkenauger argued that the body does not just influence perception, it is necessary for perception.

Because our phenotype is how our genetic makeup (or genotype) is expressed as a function of our own personal environment, Proffitt and Linkenauger (2013) argued that perception is a "phenotypic expression" just as is any other biological process. There are three aspects of our phenotype that are important to perception:

- physiology—or the body's metabolic state;
- morphology—or the body's form and size; and
- behavior—or action, which is taken for different purposes and different goals.

Proffitt and Linkenauger (2013) also proposed that perception always occurs intentionally, or within the context of what we are asking our bodies to do. Perception is the intersection of purpose, body, and environment as shown in Figure 2.5 (reprinted from their 2013 chapter). Note that the lower half of this figure is a representation of how visual angles presented to the retina change as we move, necessitating the transformation from sensory information to a perception. This figure underscores the "grounding" problem mentioned in Chapter 1 because it shows that all visual information comes in in the form of visual angles. Therefore, as Proffitt and Linkenauger argued, what could possibly "ground" or scale these angles if not the body?

Perception requires what Proffitt and Linkenauger (2013) referred to as *phenotypic reorganization*, which means that the aspect of the body that determines perception

FIGURE 2.4

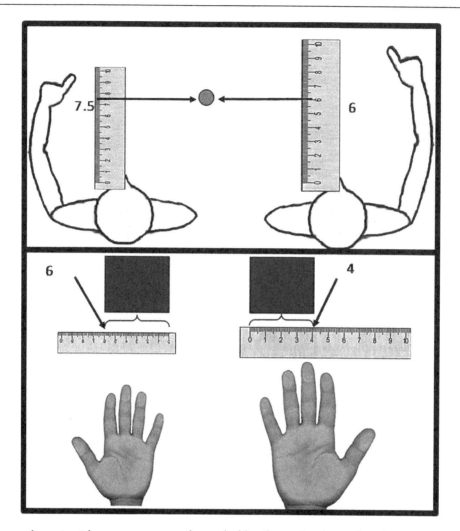

An extent in near space can be scaled by the action boundary for reaching (top panel) or grasping (bottom panel). From *Action Science: Foundations of an Emerging Discipline* (p. 183), by W. Prinz, M. Beisert, and A. Herwig (Eds.), 2013, Cambridge, MA: MIT Press. Copyright 2013 by MIT Press. Reprinted with permission.

depends on the action that you are engaged in. For example, relevant to the research described earlier, sometimes the body needs to perceive the world as a thrower, other times as a walker. Perception is then scaled to which aspect of the phenotype is relevant for that particular purpose. In the case of the thrower, perhaps the energetic costs to our physiology affect perception (i.e., if you have thrown a heavy ball and energy is depleted, perceived distances will be greater than if you have thrown a light

FIGURE 2.5

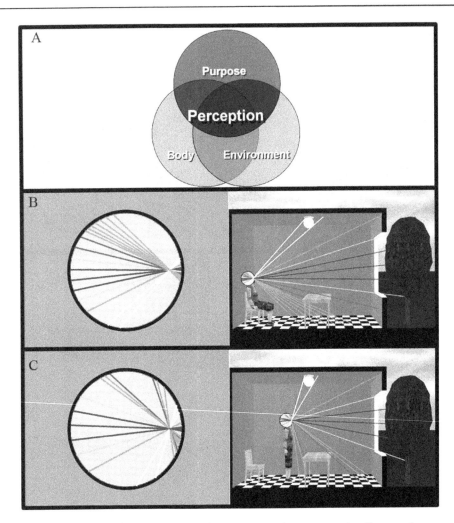

(A) Perception expresses the fit between environments, bodies, and purposes. (B & C) The visual angles projecting to the eye from an illuminated surrounding. From *Action Science: Foundations of an Emerging Discipline* (p. 173), by W. Prinz, M. Beisert, and A. Herwig (Eds.), 2013, Cambridge, MA: MIT Press. Copyright 2013 by MIT Press. Reprinted with permission.

ball). Other times, our body will be a "reacher," and that phenotypic reorganization requires perception to be guided by a different aspect of our phenotype—this time, our morphology, or the length of our arms. Finally, if performance goals are guiding perception (e.g., putting on a golf green), then past variability in our actions or behavior (are we an expert or a novice at this task/skill?) will be the most important aspect of our phenotype affecting perception.

PERCEPTION SCALED BY PHYSIOLOGY

There is growing empirical support for this view of perception as an expression of phenotypic organization. Let's start with perception that is a function of our body's physiology, or metabolic costs, given that the evidence that supports this contention comes from a corpus of studies that includes the studies presented earlier of Proffitt and colleagues (e.g., Bhalla & Proffitt, 1999; Proffitt, Bhalla, Gossweiler, & Midgett, 1995).

These studies demonstrated, for example, that participants who are encumbered or have more permanent energetic costs such as age or pain make perceptually biased slant or distance judgments. There have been criticisms levied at a number of these studies, suggesting that the results are due to the demand characteristics of the study instead of body effects on perception as Proffitt and colleagues suggested (Durgin et al., 2009). These concerns and others will be addressed in some detail in the last chapter of this book.

Proffitt and others have tested the influence of the body's physiology on perception while addressing the potential problem of possible participant awareness of experimental manipulations. For example, examining individual differences in bio-energetic potential, such as comparing elderly participants and young participants on slant estimations, is one way to eliminate the possibility of demand characteristics because there are no experimental manipulations. The finding that the elderly see the hills as steeper cannot easily be explained by postperceptual processes (Bhalla & Proffitt, 1999).

Proffitt's (2006) view is that perception of our environment must serve to "economize" our actions. Our bodies must be sensitive to the energy we have available and the energy required to act within the environment—perception will then be biased by those energetic considerations. Proffitt and colleagues have argued that when energy reserves are low, such as in the temporary state after a fatiguing run or in a more permanent state such as advanced age, perceptions are scaled by the amount of energy needed for an action relative to the amount of energy available. Hills will be perceived as steeper and distances as further away when resources are depleted and energetic costs to behavior are high.

In the early investigations of this account of perception, energy reserves were only assumed as they had never been directly manipulated or measured. Schnall, Zadra, and Proffitt (2010) conducted two experiments in which they manipulated metabolic energy to determine if it influenced spatial perception. In these experiments, Schnall et al. avoided demand characteristic concerns by making sure that their participants were completely unaware of the manipulation of their energetic state; that is, participants could not determine if they were in a high-energy condition or a low-energy condition. Schnall et al. had participants consume either a high-glucose drink or a no-calorie drink (they were identical in taste so participants would not have been able to guess whether they were consuming calories) and then estimate the slant of hills. Schnall et al. predicted that the availability of glucose from the drink allowed the participants to be in a state of high-energy reserves, and in fact they found that participants in the high-glucose drink condition judged the hill's slant to be less steep than the participants in the glucose-free drink condition. Further, independent of the glucose manipulation, individual differences in bioenergetics potential, such as amount of sleep, degree of personal fitness, nutrition, and stress, were used in a regression analysis to determine if those factors predicted variability in slant perception. Schnall et al. found that variables related to reduced bioenergetics resources were directly related to increased slant estimations.

Similar results have been found for cyclists (Zadra, Schnall, Weltman, & Proffitt, 2010) and walkers (Zadra, Weltman, & Proffitt, 2016) who were given either caloric supplements after exercise, leading to increased glucose levels, or noncaloric supplements, leading to reduced glucose levels, and then asked to make distance judgments. In both of these studies, many individual difference measures were also collected to assess physiological differences in participants and how those affected the variability in distance judgments.

For both the cyclists and the walkers, consuming caloric beverages increased glucose levels and decreased distance estimates (typically measured as a difference score between preconsumption to postconsumption). However, consuming noncaloric beverages after exercise did not affect the reduced glucose levels that had occurred because of the exercise (not surprisingly as they were absent of glucose), and pre- to postconsumption difference scores showed distances were perceived as greater in the posttest than the pretest. Both studies also found that distance perception was not just influenced by this temporary state of glucose fluctuations, but also by individual differences in energy output (the greater the output, the further the distance estimate) and fitness level (the more fit the participant, the smaller the distance estimate).

Zadra, Weltman, and Proffitt (2016) concluded that for actions in far space, morphological (body form and shape) action boundaries are not useful scales. Instead, the relative units for scaling that distance would be our physiology, and more specifically, bioenergetic considerations for how we might be able to travel that extent given our current metabolic state. These more recent studies provide direct evidence for the role of the body's physiological state on perception of slant and distant, and their results cannot be easily explained by artificial laboratory contaminants or by postperceptual influences.

PERCEPTION SCALED BY MORPHOLOGY

According to Proffitt and Linkenauger (2013), body morphology, or size and shape, can determine our perception if our action, purpose, and environment dictate that it should. Our morphology, which would include, for example, how far we can extend our arms to reach for something, constrains our action, yielding *action boundaries* (a term used by Fajen, 2005). To determine whether we can jump over a brook, or reach for a hanging apple, we must scale the visual information to our particular action boundary.

Reachability Affects Distance Perception

As a way of examining how our body's action boundaries for reaching affects distance perception, Witt, Proffitt, and Epstein (2005) manipulated reachability to a target. They projected a circle of light onto a table and had participants either point to where the target light had been with an outstretched arm (it was unreachable) or use a tool, a long baton, that allowed them to touch where the target light had been. They then had participants estimate the distance to the target. Witt et al. found that with both verbal distance estimates and with a visual matching task that assessed perceived distance, the targets appeared closer when the tool was used for reaching than when the arm pointed. They concluded that this result is due to an extension of the action boundary for the arm in the tool condition—because the tool could extend the participants' perceptual ruler and thus act on the target light (by touching it), the perceived distance was compressed. This result is similar to that found with macaque monkeys in Iriki, Tanaka, and Iwamura's (1996) research that examined tool use while recording neuronal activity in their brains' caudal postcentral gyrus, which is the area that receives converging somatosensory (body) and visual information. Iriki et al. found that monkeys using a tool to reach a distant object had modified visual receptive fields that included the length of the tool and the new accessible area. In line with Witt et al.'s conclusion, Iriki et al.'s data suggests that the use of a tool may neurally alter the representation of one's own "body schema" and that this will affect distance perception.

In a final experiment, Witt et al. (2005) demonstrated that simply holding a tool did not influence distance perception; the tool had to be pointed out and used to extend reach for it to compress the perception of distance. Witt et al. argued that this is evidence for action-based perceptual metrics—targets within reach are perceived as closer than targets beyond reach, but only when there is intention to reach (remember the overlapping circles in Figure 2.5 that couple action and environment with purpose).

In a follow-up study by Bloesch, Davoli, Roth, Brockmole, and Abrams (2012), participants merely observed another person reaching toward a target either with their arm or with a reach-extending tool. They found that observing action had the same perceptual consequences as acting; distances were more compressed when targets were reachable than when they were not. This finding suggests that the neural activity that allows distance perception to be modulated by action capabilities may be similar for action and for observation, suggesting that the same mirror neuron system found in monkeys and proposed for other cognitive processes may be involved (Buccino, Binkofski, & Riggio, 2004). Representing the action of others during observation would facilitate the comprehension of that action and could predict future action for ourselves (Iacoboni et al., 2005).

Finally, in an examination of what is now referred to as *tool embodiment* (Baccarini et al., 2014), L. E. Miller, Longo, and Saygin (2017) tested the boundary conditions of the recalibration, or perceptual scaling process with tool use. They found that when participants were looking in a mirror at their right arm so that it looked visually as if their left arm were doing the grasping of an object with a tool (but in fact it was completely stationary), their tactile perception of distance between points of contact on their left arm were perceived as larger (i.e., their arm as longer) than the tactile perception of distance between points on their forehead. In other words, the visual illusion of tool use with an arm was enough to get the same kind of recalibration, or scaling, found with the actual motoric use of the arm with a tool (Witt et al., 2005). This finding suggests that even just the visual experience of our body's activities shapes our perceptions of our body's dimensions and capabilities. L. E. Miller et al. argued that vision may bind other sensory feedback (e.g., coming from movement) into a multisensory representation of our body to be used when we scale the world we see.

More evidence for embodied perception and the scaling of our body comes from some fascinating data concerning handedness and perception. Linkenauger, Witt, Stefanucci, Bakdash, and Proffitt (2009) found that right-handed individuals' perceived length of their right arm was longer than the perceived length of their left arm (see Figure 2.4 as a reminder of the different perceptual rulers for right and left arms). For instance, it is not unusual for me, as a strong right-hand dominant individual, to behave as though I can reach further with my right arm than my left, often reaching across my body to grab something on my left that could easily be reached with my left arm. If I am going to stretch to get something just barely within my reach—for example, if something is hidden far beneath my couch, even if it is on the left of my body—I will automatically try to reach with my right arm.

Linkenauger et al. (2009) conducted a clever study in which they changed the orientation of a common object, a hammer, so that it was more or less easy to imagine grasping. Sometimes the handle was to the right of the participant and sometimes to the left, and both right-handed and left-handed individuals made judgments concerning how far away the hammer was to them. Across a number of experiments in which they manipulated graspability, Linkenauger et al. found that orienting the handle so that it was more difficult to grasp led to participants judging the hammer to be further away. Of course, the visual information specifying distance is not affected by the orientation of the hammer but ease of grasping is. Grasping ease affects perceived reachability, and reachability scales distance judgments.

In an interesting twist to this result, graspability only affected right-handed individuals in these studies; it did not affect the distance judgments of left-handed participants. Linkenauger et al. (2009) suggested that this is due to the fact that left-handed individuals are more ambidextrous, thus handle orientation does not dictate if the hammer is going to be difficult to grasp. If lefties can grasp objects with either hand with fairly equal ease, then graspability does not impact reachability; thus, distance perception will be similar across conditions of handle orientation.

Hand Size and Dominance Affects Perception of Object Size

Linkenauger, Witt, and Proffitt (2011) also found that perception of size of an object is scaled to the morphology of the body part that will be used for action. In their research, right-handed individuals judged objects to be smaller when in or relative to their right hand compared with their left hand. Linkenauger et al. suggested this was due to right-handed individuals perceiving their right hand to be larger and more effective in grasping than their left, and therefore the ability to grasp served as the "perceptual ruler" for the scaling process used for judging size. This conclusion was supported by the fact that this difference in object size estimates only occurred for graspable objects. If objects were too large to grasp, size estimates were similar whether the right or left hand was near.

Further evidence that hand size is used as a perceptual ruler for perceived object size has been provided by Linkenauger, Ramenzoni, and Proffitt (2010). They found that when participants wore magnifying goggles, causing their whole environment to be enlarged, both familiar and unfamiliar objects' sizes were unsurprisingly judged as larger than they were in reality. However, those same objects appeared to shrink in size when participants' hands were placed beside the object (despite the hands being magnified as well with the goggles), and interestingly, this effect was stronger when the right hand was visible than when the left hand was visible. This body-based rescaling effect, moderated by hand dominance, was predicted because only right-handed participants served in this study.

The results of this study (found in Figure 2.6) suggest that one effect of hand dominance is that the dominant hand is the better, or more efficient, perceptual ruler used in perception. In a second experiment, Linkenauger et al. (2010) showed the same result but in the opposite direction when participants wore "minifying" goggles. Despite the environment appearing smaller, objects were judged as larger

FIGURE 2.6

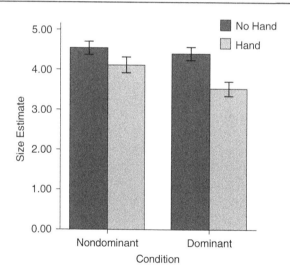

Mean size estimates, collapsed across all six objects, as a function of hand condition (dominant or nondominant hand) and hand pressure (i.e., whether the participant's hand was placed next to the object) in Experiment 1. Error bars represent 1 *SEM*, calculated within condition. From "Illusory Shrinkage and Growth: Body-Based Rescaling Affects the Perception of Size," by S. A. Linkenauger, V. Ramenzoni, and D. R. Proffitt, 2010, *Psychological Science, 21*, p. 1320. Copyright 2010 by Sage. Reprinted with permission.

when participants' hands were visible than when they were not visible. Yet another experiment in this article demonstrated that this "illusory" shrinkage and growth did not occur when it was another person's hand visible in the scene. Linkenauger et al.'s results provide strong evidence that perceptual rescaling is contingent on personal body metrics.

In yet another fascinating result concerning the body-scaling effect on perception of size that occurs with visible hands, there is a size–weight perceptual illusion that to date is not well explained but is well replicated and, as cited in Linkenauger, Mohler, and Proffitt (2011), it was apparently first noted by Charpentier (1891). It is the phenomenon that occurs when a number of differently sized objects of the exact same weight are presented to participants, and participants are asked to judge their weight. Despite their weight equality, participants will judge the larger objects to be lighter than the smaller objects, belying the intuition and typical reality that larger objects are heavier—thus the illusion. This illusion allowed Linkenauger, Mohler, and Proffitt (2011) to predict the following in their experiment: Given prior results that demonstrated that when participants' hands are visible, graspable objects appear smaller, the size–weight illusion should result in objects being judged as heavier when hands are visible compared with when hands are not visible. They found exactly this result for objects of various sizes. If a hand was visible, the participants, who were lifting objects on a pulley system to estimate weight, judged the objects to be heavier than in a condition in which a hand was not visible. The mechanism responsible for judging larger objects to be lighter is not yet clearly understood; however, the fact that visibility of a hand affects this illusion is yet another result supporting embodied perception.

PERCEPTION SCALED BY BEHAVIOR

The last aspect of our phenotype that plays a role in perception is when our bodies are used in ways in which we have a history of moving or acting, as in actions where we have developed a skill (Proffitt & Linkenauger, 2013). In this case, the appropriate scale for perception is the variability in our own behavior. For example, how would one explain the empirical result that golfers who have been putting well perceive the golf hole as larger than golfers who have not been putting well (Witt, Linkenauger, Bakdash, & Proffitt, 2008)? Or those softball players who have been hitting well see the softball as larger than those who have poorer batting averages (Witt & Proffitt, 2005)? Field goal kickers who are successful in kicking to their target perceive the distance between the goal posts as wider than those kickers who were not successful (Witt & Dorsch, 2009). Dart throwers who are better at hitting their target perceive the size of the target as larger than those who are less successful (Wesp, Cichello, Gracia, & Davis, 2004).

Proffitt and Linkenauger (2013) stated that as skill in any behavior develops, the consistency with which you perform that behavior increases. If that consistency is described as variability around one's typical performance (as in a probability distribution), then skilled performers implicitly understand that their actions cluster around that typical performance, whereas unskilled performers' actions vary sometimes dramatically around average performance. For example, skilled golfers tend to putt fairly close to the hole. Therefore, because perception is "scaled" by behavior, for skilled golfers the perception of the size of the hole is large compared with the smaller area surrounding their putts. However, unskilled golfers, whose putts are often quite far from the hole, perceive the hole as small compared with the surrounding area (representing the variability of their performance) that is large. This explanation would be supported by a result that showed that with any skill level in golf, if one had been putting near a hole and therefore having more success, the hole would be perceived larger than for the golfers who had been putting far from the hole.

Witt et al. (2008) found exactly this result with unskilled golfers who had been putting either near or far from the hole—perception of the hole's size was a function of their success in putting. This perceptual difference occurred even when the hole was in the golfers' sight, eliminating the argument that this effect is due to memory or some other postperceptual process. In the laboratory, Witt, Linkenauger, and Proffitt (2012) created an Ebbinghouse illusion (a circle closely surrounded by big circles appears smaller than the same size circle surrounded by little circles) on a putting green. They found that participants golfing toward the hole perceived the size of the hole bigger in the "little circle surround" condition compared with the "big circle surround" condition, falling prey to the illusion. It is important to note that participants putted more successfully to the perceptually bigger hole, demonstrating the link between perceived size and performance. Witt et al. and G. Wood, Vine, and Wilson (2013) suggested that the explanation for this effect may be that the illusion affected attentional control and motor planning, and perceiving the hole as bigger increased the confidence of participants putting to that hole. Clearly, our ability to act effectively in our environment influences perception, and the reverse is true as well—perception also influences our ability to act.

Conclusions

Glenberg's (2010, 2015) proposal that cognition serves action, and action is constrained and informed by the body, is consistent with Proffitt's conceptualization of embodied perception. Proffitt and colleagues argued that for a visual sensory experience to have meaning, those angular units of optical information must be transformed into linear units that allow us to perceive size and distance. Proffitt (2013) argued "the vehicle for this transformation is the human body. Perhaps this reflects my lack of imagination, but I cannot imagine how it could be otherwise" (p. 474). Proffitt goes on to state that the body provides the scaling devices, or perceptual rulers, for meaning to be derived from optical information. No one aspect of the body will serve as the appropriate perceptual ruler in all cases—which aspect is used will depend on the purpose of the action and the environment that the observer is in. For example, eye-height scaling is only appropriate for perceiving distances of objects that are on the ground, and hand-size scaling is only appropriate for the perception of size for graspable, but not ungraspable, objects. Metabolic costs may be used to scale the distances and slants that we are to traverse.

Is this account of embodied perception complete? Proffitt and Linkenauger (2013) claimed no; although their proposal that the body provides the ability to have meaningful percepts of our world is strongly supported by data, there are many spatial perceptions for which we have yet to determine the appropriate "perceptual ruler." There are also other critics of the findings presented in this chapter, and some of them are discussed in the last chapter of this book. However, to date, those opponents of embodied cognition, especially as it pertains to how action informs perception, have criticized methodologies and interpretations of empirical results but have been unable to suggest an alternative explanation for the many empirical findings that permeate the perceptual literature (see the arguments of Proffitt, 2013, and Witt, 2015).

Takeaway

- Sensory information must be transformed into meaningful perceptions. This sensory input is scaled by the body's morphology, physiology, and behavior, and this occurs within the context of the environment and the goals we have for acting on our world (Glenberg, Proffitt).

The Body's Role in Social and Emotional Judgments

3

Questions:

- What is the role of the body in the mental representation of affective decisions?
- How does the body inform our emotional responses?
- How do bodily experiences form a representation of *positive* versus *negative* or *good* versus *bad*?

A number of years ago, researchers investigated an intriguing hypothesis about the effects of the body on emotion. The hypothesis was simple: Does body position, specifically facial posture, directly influence one's emotions? It was a hypothesis that many of us heard from our mothers in our childhood: "If you smile, you'll feel better!" This facial feedback hypothesis was empirically tested by Strack, Martin, and Stepper (1988), who had participants hold a pen either in their teeth (with the tip pointing outward), such that their lips were forced upward into a smiling posture, or hold the pen between their lips, which inhibits those same smile muscles. Participants were told that they were adopting this facial posture because the experiment was investigating peoples' ability to perform various tasks with parts of their body that they would not normally use, such as when a physically impaired person has to learn to write with their mouth. Participants then performed several tasks, one of which was to rate the humor of some cartoons.

http://dx.doi.org/10.1037/0000136-003
How the Body Shapes Knowledge: Empirical Support for Embodied Cognition, by R. Fincher-Kiefer

The now-classic finding was supportive of the age-old adage about smiling—those participants who were in a facial posture that was smiling found the cartoons funnier than the participants experiencing the facial posture of a frown, despite the fact that participants were not consciously aware of the emotional value (valence) given to their own facial posture.

This general experimental approach of putting the body in a position that is associated with a particular valence has now been used quite often to test embodiment theory and to examine whether the body's position leads to compatibility effects in social and cognitive judgments. However, for these body position effects to be a true reflection of the body grounding conceptual knowledge, it must be clear that the body plays a direct, or causal, role in the resulting judgment. This can be achieved, as it was in the previously mentioned research, by ensuring that participants were unaware of the emotional valence of the body positions they were assuming (the researchers effectively masked the purpose of the study) or by investigating the physiological or neurological consequences of these body positions.

It is one thing for a theory that claims that bodily experiences shape the representations of thought to demonstrate how the body influences perceptual judgments such as distance or size, but it is quite another to be able to demonstrate that *abstract* concepts, those that we may never perceive or be able to act on, are also derived from the body. This chapter examines additional research that supports the argument that the body grounds valence (positivity vs. negativity) and motivation (approach vs. avoidance) in modality-specific systems just as it does concepts involving perception and action.

Bodily Action-to-Affect Effects

Years ago, Wells and Petty (1980) asked participants to nod their head vertically or shake their head horizontally to supposedly test whether the headphones they were wearing would slip off. Although participants were making these head movements, the headphones were surreptitiously presenting a simulated radio broadcast. Wells and Petty found that participants in the nodding head condition later agreed with the content of the broadcast more than the participants in the shaking head condition.

In another examination of how body movement might influence the acquisition of an attitude toward novel information, Cacioppo, Priester, and Berntson (1993) told participants they were in a study that was examining the effects of tension that came about from certain arm positions. Participants were asked to place the palm of their dominant hand on the bottom, or underneath, edge of the table and press upward firmly. This arm flexion position is classically described as an approach movement, given the muscle movements involved move the arm toward the body. Other participants were asked to press the palm of their dominant hand firmly down on the top edge of the table. This arm extension position has been described as an avoidance movement, given the muscles involved push the arm away from the body. Participants maintained these arm movements while they examined novel stimuli, Chinese ideographs on a computer screen, and decided whether they liked or disliked each figure.

Cacioppo et al. found an *action-to-affect* effect such that these ideographs were seen as more positive when participants were making the approach, or arm flexion, action, and they were seen as more negative when participants were making the avoidance, or arm extension, action. This effect occurred only when participants were making evaluative judgments about the ideographs (liking vs. disliking); it did not occur when making nonevaluative judgments, such as how complex the figures were. Cacioppo et al. suggested that a lifetime of experience with approach and avoidance movements and their positive and negative consequences establish automatic *evaluative* associations when judging novel information.

A number of other studies have demonstrated action-to-affect effects: When in body postures or when making motor movements that are associated with positive and negative affect (for example, slumping, which is associated with depression), attitudes toward that which is being processed become aligned with that affect (e.g., Duclos et al., 1989; Riskind & Gotay, 1982; Schubert, 2004). Because of these findings, it has been argued that attitudes appear to be determined, at least in part, by *embodied responses* (Niedenthal, Barsalou, Winkielman, Krauth-Gruber, & Ric, 2005).

A test of the hypothesis that body posture may embody a particular attitude, one that affects many social judgments, is Carney, Cuddy, and Yap's (2010) examination of "power" posing. Carney et al. described examples in humans as well as other species that are clear examples of bodily expressions of power—swans push themselves upward out of the water to expand their wings high and wide when in pursuit of a mate or guarding their young; gorillas bare their chest and put their elbows out wide to beat their chest when threatened; Wonder Woman stands with her feet planted wide and her hands on her hips as a symbol of strength. Are these expansive postures just typical body positions that have been modeled by others in positions of status and prestige, or do those postures *cause* a person to feel more effective and more powerful? In other words, is the abstract concept of power embodied in a particular stance in the same way that approach and avoidance may be embodied in patterns of arm movements?

Carney et al. (2010) conducted research on the effect of power posing and had participants pose in either high- or low-power positions that were based on two nonverbal dimensions universally linked to power: expansiveness and openness. To mask the true purpose of the poses, participants were told that the study concerned the accuracy of electrocardiography responses as a function of the placement of the electrodes (electrocardiogram [ECG] leads). The experimenter placed the sensors on the participants' calves and underside of their left arm and then manually configured the participants' bodies to place them into the positions seen in Figures 3.1a (high power) and 3.1b (low power). To further support the body position cover story, the participants were also told that the sensors needed to be certain distances from their heart, but of course no ECG data were actually recorded. Participants held each of the two positions for their power condition 1 minute while completing a filler task. After this, participants released their pose and had their risk-taking measured with a gambling task followed by their feelings of power measured in self-report scales. Saliva samples were taken before and after the poses (and also supported the cover

FIGURE 3.1

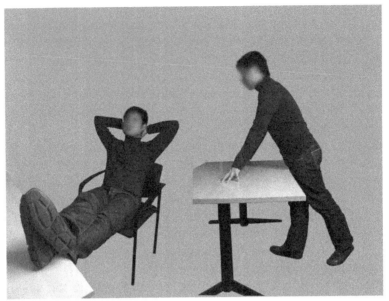

(a)

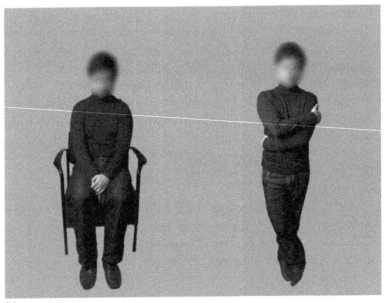

(b)

(a) The two high-power poses used in the study. Participants in the high-power pose condition were posed in expansive positions with open limbs. (b) The two low-power poses used in the study. Participants in the low-power pose condition were posed in contractive positions with closed limbs. From "Power Posing: Brief Nonverbal Displays Affect Neuroendocrine Levels and Risk Tolerance," by D. R. Carney, A. J. C. Cuddy, and A. J. Yap, 2010, *Psychological Science, 21*, p. 1365. Copyright 2010 by D. R. Carney, A. J. C. Cuddy, and A. J. Yap. Reprinted with permission.

story) to test the stress hormone, cortisol, which has been shown to be high in times of powerlessness and low when power has been achieved (e.g., Sapolsky, Alberts, & Altmann, 1997). These saliva samples also provided testosterone levels, which have been shown to be high in times of dominance and competition but low in times of defeat (e.g., Booth, Shelley, Mazur, Tharp, & Kittok, 1989).

Carney et al. (2010) found that high-power pose participants were more likely than low-power pose participants to take a risk in the gambling task by rolling a die to get a larger reward instead of choosing not to roll the die to keep a certain lesser reward. Further, high-power pose participants reported significantly higher feelings of both powerfulness and being in charge than low-power pose participants. Carney et al. concluded that a mere 1 minute of a powerful body posture has behavioral consequences of the activation of that knowledge. While Carney et al. also reported physiological changes due to power postures—higher testosterone levels and lower cortisol levels—these results have not been supported in replication studies (e.g., Ranehill et al., 2015). In response to a very public questioning of the veracity of their research, Carney, Cuddy, and Yap (2015) reviewed and summarized the extensive body of research that has explored expansive versus contractive body postures since their original studies. Although they reported that all 33 studies (at that time) either replicated or partially replicated their findings, others reported serious concerns with the methodology used and the statistical evidence from these replication studies (e.g., Simmons & Simonsohn, 2017). However, Cuddy, Schultz, and Fosse (2018) published another systematic review, based on 55 studies, that provides strong evidence for "postural feedback" (power-posing) effects on self-reported affective states, or feelings of power. In fact, beyond causing people to feel more powerful, the studies reviewed by Cuddy et al. also suggest that postural manipulations affected participants' emotions, mood recovery, and retrieval of positive and negative memories. One conclusion that now appears less controversial than others is that feelings of personal power and the emotions that follow appear to be a cognitive and behavioral consequence of body posture. It is worth examining several studies that provide converging evidence for this conclusion.

Huang, Galinsky, Gruenfeld, and Guillory (2011) explored the effects of body posture on the manifestations of power by comparing these bodily effects to effects that come about when the same power knowledge has been activated but cognitively—through what Huang et al. referred to as "role power." By independently manipulating the hierarchical role given to participants in a puzzle task (high-power manager or low-power subordinate) and body posture, they were able to explore which of these two was the "proximal correlate" (or more important determinant) of thought and behavior. Huang et al. conducted three experiments in which participants were given high- or low-power roles in an experimental task and placed in high- or low-power positions (expansive vs. constrictive). They found that on measures of action (a gambling task involving risk-taking), as well as measures of abstraction in thought (identifying fragmented pictures to determine the Gestalt), posture consistently produced stronger effects than role power. The role that participants were placed in did significantly affect self-reported ratings of power, but even on an implicit measure of knowledge activation (word-fragment completion), participants' posture had a stronger effect. Huang et al. concluded that their results indicated that to act and think like a powerful person, one merely needs to put their body in a position of power. Thus posture, not role power, is the more *proximate* correlate of thought and behavior.

Finally, Yap, Wazlawek, Lucas, Cuddy, and Carney (2013) explored a negative consequence of power postures—dishonest behavior. In a series of studies examining the effect of incidental postures of power in laboratory and field experiments, participants were put in situations where they could behave either honestly or dishonestly. Yap et al. found that whether consciously posed (and then given a cover story) or incidentally posed (in the field, due to the layout of the environment) participants in high-power, expansive postures committed more dishonest behavior, either failing to report too much money received or altering their responses to influence a monetary award in the task.

Interestingly, in another two studies, Yap et al. (2013) examined driving behavior when seated in an expansive car seat compared with a constrictive car seat. In one laboratory study, participants were seated in chairs similar to car seats and were asked to play a driving simulation game, and in a field experiment, participants were actually driving in different kinds of automobiles and parking behavior was observed. These experiments demonstrated that the more expansive the posture allowed by the seat, the more reckless the driving, measured by simulated accidents, and the more parking violations, measured by real-life double-parking. Yap et al. claimed that their results suggested that the relationship between expansive posture and dishonesty, and between expansive posture and risky driving, is mediated by the sense of power embodied in the body posture. Their use of different participant populations and real-world data in their field experiments indicates that this posture effect is ecologically valid.

One final study needs to be presented that indicates the effects of action on affect because it further supports the ecological validity and the universality of the body posture effect. Ijzerman and Cohen (2011) examined body "comportment," a term they prefer to posture because it is more general and includes a sense of demeanor or how one carries oneself. Because of the universal nature of certain human postures and the similarities of those postures to ones in nonhuman species, Ijzerman and Cohen argued that the connection between posture and affect seems to have an evolutionary, or "prewired," base. For example, they suggested an evolutionary link between a person's upright, chin-high posture and their experience of pride, dominance, maybe even happiness. Similarly, a downward gaze, chin-down posture may be prewired or linked to the experience of shame, submission, perhaps sadness. Ijzerman and Cohen pointed out that this prewired nature does not necessarily mean "determined" because culture and gender provide a context in which these connections are either triggered or not. They also proposed that the relationship between body and culture is bidirectional—with the body causing certain cultural values to become salient, and when those values are salient, they cause specific bodily effects.

In a series of three experiments, Ijzerman and Cohen (2011) tested men and women from "honor cultures" (Latino Americans and Arab and Turkish participants from the Netherlands), which are cultures that value family loyalty, high social esteem, and chastity of women. They also tested both sexes from "dignity cultures" (Anglo Americans and Dutch participants), cultures that value the individual worth of each person and thus believe that individuals show character strength when they are independent from others. They had their participants stand in either a position in which their head was high and chin up or in a position with head and chin down, ostensibly holding this position for the purpose of exploring differences in oxygen intake on a visual acuity test.

As can be seen in Figure 3.2, in one of several experiments, Ijzerman and Cohen (2011) found that for Latino Americans, where honor is a particularly salient cultural value, men in the head-high body posture showed greater sensitivity to honor-related words than men in the head-down body posture. However, this posture effect was not found with Latino American women. Latinas in honor cultures do not embody honor with this same body posture; in fact, women in these cultures believe that deference and modesty is honorable, and thus the head-down position would be associated with their cultural values (Cohen, 2003). In fact, as seen in Figure 3.2, Latinas in Ijzerman and Cohen's experiment showed greater sensitivity to honor words in the head-down than in the head-high position. Anglo American men and women participants, whose dignity culture does not make pride a particularly salient value, showed no posture differences in their honor-word sensitivity measures.

Ijzerman and Cohen's (2011) final experiment reversed the causal direction of body posture and cultural values. In a field experiment, body postures were observed

FIGURE 3.2

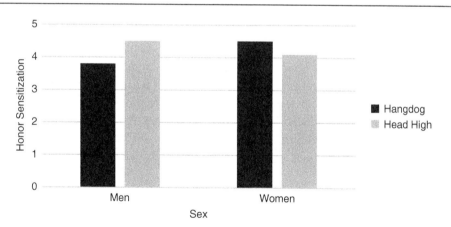

Number of letters of H-O-N-O-R read by Latino Americans on the "vision test" as a function of body comportment and participants' gender. From "Grounding Cultural Syndromes: Body Comportment and Values in Honor and Dignity Cultures," by H. Ijzerman and D. Cohen, 2011, *European Journal of Social Psychology*, *41*, p. 463. Copyright 2011 by Wiley. Reprinted with permission.

and rated for "swelling" or "shrinking" when participants from both honor and dignity cultures filled out a questionnaire that made salient an honor norm (protecting a family member even if there was potential for violence). Only men served as participants, and results showed that those from honor cultures became more expansive (swelled) when endorsing honor-related violence and tended to become smaller (shrink) after not endorsing such violence. However, men from a dignity culture, who tend to believe in each person's worth and feel stronger when they do not answer insults with violence, became more expansive when *rejecting* honor-related violence and tended to shrink when they did not reject it.

These experiments refine our understanding of the embodiment of culture. Ijzerman and Cohen (2011) found that body posture may not by itself necessarily represent a particular abstract concept, such as honor. Despite the fact that we may be "prewired" to represent abstract affective responses in our bodily expressions, that determination will be dependent on cultural context, gender, and an individual's personal adherence to their cultural norms.

Embodiment of Valence

Ijzerman and Cohen's (2011) suggestion that abstract concepts, such as honor, are grounded in one's body in unique, variable representations is a view that is consistent with Casasanto and Lupyan's (2015) proposal that all concepts, categories, and word meanings are represented in patterns of neurocognitive activity that are different from one thought to the next and from one person to the next. Casasanto and Lupyan argued that even for shared knowledge of concrete concepts (e.g., "dog"), our neurocognitive representations are idiosyncratic because they are dependent on our own social and physical experiences and are constrained by the context at both construction and retrieval. Casasanto (2009) had previously argued that our bodies are always part of the context in which we construct knowledge and, thus, if our bodies influence the representations that we form, then people with different bodies should think differently. This is Casasanto's body-specificity hypothesis, and it is consistent not just with Ijzerman and Cohen's data demonstrating that cultural context shapes how our bodies ground our abstract concepts, but also with what has been discussed in an earlier chapter, that our unique bodies constrain our perceptions and actions (Proffitt, 2013).

According to Casasanto's (2009) body-specificity hypothesis, an individualized bodily basis for our mental representations of concrete actions and objects seems fairly intuitive. For example, if thinking about a concrete object would involve mentally simulating its color, color-blind versus noncolor-blind individuals should show different patterns of activation in their neurocognitive representations. Similarly, thinking or reading about an action, like throwing, would involve a mental simulation that would be specific to how one's own body performed that action. Right-handed individuals would differ from left-handed individuals; in fact, we would expect contralateral hemispheric activation of the motor cortex as a function of body dominance during thinking about an action like throwing. This is exactly the result that has been found when participants of different handedness were reading about or imagining bodily actions (e.g., Willems, Hagoort, & Casasanto, 2010; Willems, Toni, Hagoort, & Casasanto, 2009).

A convenient test bed for Casasanto's (2009) body-specificity hypothesis was handedness, because what better way to examine whether people with different bodies might actually represent thought differently? Imagining how the mental representations of abstract concepts, such as good versus bad, would differ for differently bodied individuals is not as straightforward though. If the representations of valence are variant, or body specific, then right- and left-handers should show opposite patterns of thinking about good and bad, in line with their own personal body dominance. Alternatively, representations of these concepts may be universal and invariant, which would be consistent with pervasive patterns in language and culture that suggest a spatial-valence mapping of right is *good* (e.g., "right-hand man") and left is *bad* (e.g., "two left feet"). Casasanto conducted five experiments to explore the embodiment of valence.

In Casasanto's (2009) Experiment 1, both left- and right-handed participants performed a pencil-and-paper diagram task (often referred to as the "Bob task") where they first listened to a brief story about a person, Bob, going to a zoo. The story described that Bob would get to see zebras, an animal he liked very much, and pandas, an animal that he hated (this affective connection to the type of animal was counterbalanced across participants). In front of the participants was a simple diagram of a cartoon of Bob's head. The diagram also included two boxes, one on the right and one on the left side of the head, which was the horizontal condition, or the two boxes were above and below the head, which was the vertical condition (see Figure 3.3a and 3.3b for these conditions). Participants were randomly assigned to these two conditions and were told to draw a zebra in the box that best represented good things and a panda in the box that best represented bad things (this order was also counterbalanced across participants).

Casasanto (2009) predicted that if the spatial representation of good and bad is dependent on universal linguistic and cultural tendencies, then in the horizontal condition, the good animal should always be placed in the right box, independent of handedness. However, if right- and left-handed participants ground positivity and negativity (valence) in their bodies, they may do so differently given their body dominance differences. This would then be seen in their different placement of the good and bad animals in the left or right boxes. The vertical condition was an important control because of the lack of correspondence between handedness and the up/down dimension, resulting in the prediction that all participants should use the linguistic and cultural convention that *up* is *good* (e.g., "I'm feeling really up today!") and *down* is *bad* (e.g., "down in the dumps"). That led to Casasanto's prediction for the vertical condition that both right- and left-handers would place the good animal in the box above the cartoon head and the bad animal in the box below.

Figure 3.3c and 3.3d provide the results from Casasanto's (2009) Experiment 1, and clearly demonstrate that in the horizontal position (3.3c), left- and right-handers

FIGURE 3.3

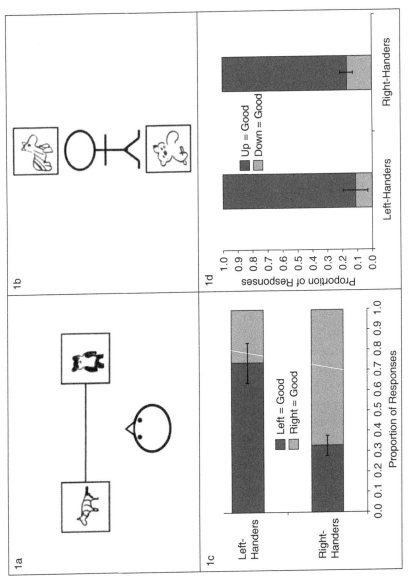

Top: Examples of stimuli and responses from Casasanto's (2009) Experiment 1. (a) Horizontal condition. (b) Vertical condition. Bottom: Results of Experiment 1. (c) Proportion of left- and right-handers who drew the good animal in the left box (dark bars) and the right box (light bars). (d) Proportion of left- and right-handers who drew the good animal in the top box (dark bars) and the bottom box (light bars). Error bars indicate standard error of the mean. From "Embodiment of Abstract Concept: Good and Bad in Right- and Left-Handers," by D. Casasanto, 2009, *Journal of Experimental Psychology: General, 138,* p. 354. Copyright 2009 by the American Psychological Association.

show the opposite pattern of preference for putting the good animal in which box. The fact that right-handers put the good animal in the right box but left-handers put it in the left provides support for the hypothesis that the representation of valence is body specific. The results of the vertical condition (3.3d) show the universal influence of a space-valence mapping that comes from something other than specific body influences (because there were no handedness differences), presumably the linguistic and cultural convention of up being good and down being bad.

Linguistic conventions cannot explain the horizontal condition's results, as de la Fuente, Santiago, Román, Dumitrache, and Casasanto (2014) also found that cultural conventions in language do not modify this association between valence and left–right space. Their study examined this mapping by using the Bob task with participants from an Arab culture and participants from a Spanish culture (all participants were right-handed; these researchers could not find left-handers in the Arab culture that they sampled from, presumably because the taboo against the left is so prevalent). They predicted that if the association between space and valence is affected by culture, it should be greater in an Arab culture, which holds very strong values that favor the right and actually disparage the left (e.g., Muslims can never touch food or drink with their left hand because it represents dirty and bad). They replicated Casasanto's (2009) effect for right-handers in the Bob task but found no difference between participants from these different cultures. These results suggest that the implicit association between good and right and left and bad for right-handers is not moderated by the strength of cultural norms.

To examine how this body-specific, space-valence mapping might affect decisions in the real world, Casasanto (2009) put right- and left-handed participants in a job-hiring scenario where they had to choose which of two people should be hired for several positions (programmer, security guard, etc.). The job titles were in the middle of the page and the brief job qualifications of people supposedly applying were on the left and right columns of the page. These qualifications were written to be equal in valence; both of the fictional candidates sounded comparable but were distinctive, and participants simply had to circle which candidate they would hire. In a second part of this task, participants had to perform a similar shopping task, in which they were supposedly shopping for several products (mattress, carpet, etc.), and they were to decide on which product of a pair they should buy based on their descriptors on the left and right side of the product's name. Casasanto found that for both the job and the shopping tasks, preferences depended on handedness, corroborating the results of the other experiments; left-handers believed candidates and products were better if they were on the left of the page, but right-handers believed the good was on the right.

An outside-of-the-laboratory finding that provides converging evidence for associating "good" with one's dominant side was found by Casasanto and Jasmin (2010) in examining gestures of left- and right-handers during the final debates of the 2004 and 2008 presidential election. By analyzing the speech and gestures of the two right-handed candidates (Kerry and Bush) and those of the left-handers (Obama and McCain), Casasanto and Jasmin found that positive speech was associated with right-hand gestures and negative with left-hand gestures in the right-handers, but the opposite association was found with the left-handed candidates. It appears that when people communicate about positive and negative ideas, there is visible evidence of the body-specific grounding of valence.

Casasanto (2011) argued that his results across a series of experiments demonstrate that at least some abstract concepts, namely those with positive and negative valence, have an embodied origin. This origin comes from a developmental process of interacting with the environment. Those people who have a more dominant body side are more comfortable (fluent) interacting with objects on that side than the other. Right-handers have comfortable interactions and are more "coordinated" when writing, kicking, and handling objects on their right, whereas left-handers' fluency is just the opposite. Because of this, Casasanto proposed that these motor fluencies result in implicit associations of "good" with whatever side is more fluent and "bad" with the less fluent side. These fluencies are the basis of the mental representation of valence. This is supported in part by data that shows that for ambidextrous individuals, spatial preferences for good and bad are not consistent.

The fluency-based explanation of these spatial-valence mappings was also explored by Casasanto and Chrysikou (2011), who examined the effects of long- and short-term disability of the dominant hand and its effect on how people think about "good" and "bad." They found that for right-handers who had suffered a unilateral stroke, if the stroke had preserved their natural right-handedness, they showed the same "right is good" preferences on the Bob task used by Casasanto (2009). However, for participants whose stroke had disabled their right hand and their handedness poststroke had effectively been reversed, they showed the opposite "left is good" spatial-valence mapping. In a second experiment in which Casasanto and Chrysikou handicapped participants' dominant hand for only a few minutes with a bulky ski glove while performing the cartoon diagram task, they found again that even short-term changes in motor fluency can reverse the association between valence and right–left space. Although this reversal is presumably temporary, these data support the conclusion that motor experience causes this space–valence association.

Casasanto and colleagues suggested that it is motor fluency, or bodily action, that provides the grounding for the affective states of good and bad. Neuroscientific evidence that other emotional states are linked to action comes from Brookshire and Casasanto's (2012) examination of handedness differences in approach and avoidance motivational states. Prior research had shown that for right-handers, the left frontal lobe (controlling the dominant hand) was active for approach motivational states; however, the right frontal lobe (controlling the nondominant hand) was active during avoidance motivational states (Davidson, 1992). Casasanto's (2009) body-specificity hypothesis would argue that if right-handers' right hands are used for approach actions and their left hands are used for avoidance actions, this pattern should reverse for left-handers. Casasanto claimed that the evolutionary or developmental process would establish the dominant hand to be used for approach (as in a sword fighter approaching his enemy with his dominant hand), but the nondominant hand would be raised to avoid an attack (the shield being held by the nondominant hand). Brookshire and Casasanto (2012) tested handedness differences in what they called the *sword and shield hypothesis* and found that although electroencephalogram (EEG) activity replicated prior results for approach and avoidance lateralization in right-handers, the EEG activity for left-handers was the opposite. Approach activity was found with this group in the right hemisphere (corresponding with their dominant hand), but avoidance activity was in the left hemisphere. This suggests that emotional motivation, like affective states, is differentially embodied as a function of handedness. This evidence provides strong support for Casasanto's contention that when our bodies are different, we think differently, and even abstract thoughts may depend on how our bodies interact with our physical environment.

The Body Language of Victory

What do we do when we have won a race and are breaking through that ribbon? We immediately throw up our arms, push out our chest, throw back our head and open our mouths in elation. Some of the most compelling data to suggest that a body posture can embody an abstract, emotional concept, like victory, is this automatic, nonconscious, rapid bodily response of an athlete who has just been victorious in his or her sport. It is a universally human response to a triumphant moment, and interestingly, you see a very similar pose in animals when they are victorious in battle for territory or mate. And even more fascinating, blind athletes make these very same poses and facial gestures when they have triumphed—even though they have never seen them modeled before. The body language of victory, known as the "triumph" or "dominance threat display" (Hwang & Matsumoto, 2014; Matsumoto & Hwang, 2013), is a nonverbal display of emotion that is so universal that it provides compelling evidence for the embodiment of the abstract concept of victory. However, as Ijzerman and Cohen's (2011) study also showed with the embodiment of the abstract concept of honor, this embodied response is constrained by one's culture.

Tracy and Matsumoto (2008) examined nonverbal displays of pride and shame in sighted, blind, and congenitally blind individuals from over 30 different countries when competing in judo for the 2004 Olympic and Paralympic Games. They found that the prototypical components of the pride, or victory, expression—head back, arms raised, open mouth, fists clenched—were found in response to winning in all individuals from every culture. The fact that the congenitally blind athletes produced the same body posture to winning that occurred with sighted athletes suggests that it is not a modeled, or learned, response. That it also occurred cross-culturally suggests that this is an innate behavioral response that embodies the abstract construct of success.

Interestingly, the components of the body posture for shame—shoulders slumped, chest narrowed—were found in athletes that lost their matches, but culture did play a role in their expression. Sighted athletes from individualistic and status-oriented cultures (Western countries such as the United States) were less likely to display these bodily postures when they lost than individuals from cultures that were more collectivistic (Asian countries). Tracy and Matsumoto (2008) suggested that this was because the collectivistic cultures view shame as an appropriate response to social failure, whereas individualistic cultures typically suppress their expression of failure as it is a fairly stigmatized emotion.

The evidence for cross-cultural differences does not undermine the proposal that body posture embodies the emotion of shame; instead, it appears that certain higher arching goals, such as social communication, may play a role in whether an individual's body posture reflects that underlying representation of thought. Further evidence supporting this contention is that the strongest expression of shame was found in the congenitally blind athletes from all cultures, shown even to a greater extent than athletes who had lost their sight later in life. Individuals who have never seen others show or suppress emotions are less sensitive to culture-specific norms for regulating emotions; thus, their bodies should most clearly represent the evolved, innate behavioral marker for that emotion.

Conclusions

The evidence for the role of the body in emotion can be found in research examining the influence of facial musculature, the effect of actions that represent approach and avoidance (rudimentary emotional responses), the consequences of body postures to behavioral measures of an emotional response (such as power), and the differences between emotional responses as a function of one's individual body dominance. Each of these areas of research provides converging evidence to suggest that the body plays a direct, causal role in emotion.

This may occur through an evolutionary process that has yielded a universal, innate expression of an emotion (such as pride), perhaps to serve the purpose of social communication. In other emotional expressions, the role of the body may occur through a developmental process that yields evidence that demonstrates the constraints of age, culture, and unique body skills and limitations. However, the evidence suggesting that the body influences affective decisions and emotional responses is undeniable. Embodiment theory can account for these results; further research will determine if another theoretical framework might have the same explanatory power.

Takeaway

■ The body determines, through facial action, postural feedback, and body dominance, what emotional response is given in a particular situation (Cuddy, Casasanto). Embodiment theory suggests that this reflects the grounding of emotional knowledge in brain areas that are responsible for bodily movement.

The Body's Role in Higher Order Cognition

4

Questions:

- How does the body inform higher-order cognitive judgments?
- What evidence exists to suggest that the body is involved in the acquisition of cognitive skills and the representation of knowledge about complex abstract concepts that do not involve perceiving or emoting?

The above questions are challenging and seriously test the central tenets of embodiment theory. If embodiment is to be considered a fundamentally unique theory of knowledge representation, it must provide evidence that the body's role in cognition is more than just a byproduct, or a downstream consequence, of activated symbolic knowledge.

If we have an abstract concept, such as *time*, we need to determine whether the body plays an essential role in our representation of that concept. Embodiment requires that conceptual knowledge is not symbolic and amodal but a multimodal representation that involves the body directly and automatically—perhaps in muscle movements or in action, or evidenced in neural networks associated with motor activity. Evidence from the developmental literature suggests that cognition develops because of bodily action, and there is also evidence of the body's involvement in the representation of several different abstract concepts that have been used as tests of this theory—free will, time, and numerosity.

http://dx.doi.org/10.1037/0000136-004
How the Body Shapes Knowledge: Empirical Support for Embodied Cognition, by R. Fincher-Kiefer

Developmental Evidence for the Role of Action in the Acquisition of Cognitive Skills

Piaget (1952) was one of the first developmental psychologists to argue that the coordination of sensory processing and self-produced locomotion (like crawling) laid the ground work for cognitive development. His main thesis was that development was determined by biological maturation and interaction with the environment, which placed action central to the acquisition of cognitive skills. Piaget and Inhelder (1966/1969) later argued that infants' action capabilities served as the foundation for objective thought; mental activity was based on bodily activity. However, only recently have the psychological consequences of independent locomotion been subjected to empirical study (see Campos et al., 2000, for a review).

Overwhelming evidence now suggests that locomotion is not just a maturational milestone that precedes psychological change in an infant, but instead, self-produced locomotion is a causal agent producing significant cognitive development. D. I. Anderson et al. (2013) claimed that the significance of independent locomotion is that it not only facilitates a number of psychological changes, but it is also available across the lifespan, so it may play a role in tuning and maintaining these same psychological skills.

Developmental psychologists have examined the ontogeny of two cognitive skills that are often considered precursors of significant cognitive growth: wariness of heights and search for hidden objects (D. I. Anderson et al., 2013). Campos, Bertenthal, and Kermoian's (1992) research on the wariness of heights, discussed in Chapter 2, suggests that this important cognitive skill (which is biologically adaptive) is due to visual proprioception, the optically induced sense of self-movement that is derived from optic flow. Campos et al. found that infants without locomotor experience lack fully developed visual proprioception, and independent locomotion plays a causal role in establishing this perceptual skill. Once an infant acquires visual proprioception, he or she can maintain postural stability when navigating the environment. It is the loss of postural stability linked to visual proprioception that produces fear of heights; thus, without independent locomotion, there is no fear of heights.

Another cognitive skill that is not perceptual in nature is understanding *object permanence*, which is demonstrated in the search for a hidden object. When an infant searches for an object hidden from his or her view, it is an important milestone in cognitive development because it marks the awareness of an object's permanence despite the lack of visual evidence (Piaget, 1952, 1954). Piaget (1954) found that infants between the ages of 8 and 9 months can successfully retrieve an object hidden (typically under a small cloth) in their direct view from one location, but they fail to search for the same object when it is hidden in a new adjacent location also in their direct view. When they continue to make the error of searching in the old location for the hidden object even when they have seen the object hidden in a new location, this is referred to as the *A-not-B error*. Infants' performance in this search becomes even poorer as the delay increases between when the object was hidden in a new location (again, in their direct view) and when they are permitted to search for it.

An infant's successful search in this task has been considered evidence for his or her understanding of spatial relations, which appears to underlie not only object permanence but also a variety of other cognitive advances, such as concept formation, linguistic-cognitive spatial skills, even the development of attachment and other emotions (Haith & Campos, 1977; Oudgenoeg-Paz & Rivière, 2014). Interestingly, although Piaget (1954) argued that this search behavior would be a function of motoric experience and exploration of the infants' environment, others have explained this advance primarily as a function of cortical maturation, specifically dorsolateral prefrontal cortex (Diamond, 1990).

Evidence to support Piaget's view has been found by Kermoian and Campos (1988), who grouped 8.5-month-old infants into prelocomotor infants, prelocomotor infants who were given walker experience, and locomotor infants who had experience crawling on hands and knees. All infants were given a series of tasks to search for a partially hidden object, and these tasks varied in difficulty from simply retrieving the hidden toy under one cloth to the A-not-B task with delays between when the object was hidden and when they could search. Results demonstrated that the locomoting infants—those who had been crawling and the infants given walker experience—performed significantly better on the search tasks than the prelocomotor infants. Examining the locomoting experience more carefully, those infants who had been crawling longer showed a linear trend in success on these tasks. Kermoian and Campos also found that there were no real differences between the crawling and walker groups, but both performed better on the search tasks than prelocomoting infants and another control group of infants who were "belly crawling," which is more effortful and does not move the infant ahead as the hands-and-knees crawling does.

These results offer strong support for the contention that the onset of locomotion leads to the development of spatial search skills. These findings have been replicated and extended using cross-sectional and longitudinal designs, and have also been found in another culture. Chinese infants, whose mobility is typically delayed due to cultural norms to avoid crawling (because of an aversion to infants getting dirty), performed poorly on the A-not-B test until they began to locomote. Their performance improved dramatically as a function of locomotor experience, regardless of the age at which they began to have independent locomotion (see Campos et al., 2000).

Of course these data beg the question: For children with impaired motor abilities, does their impairment lead to delayed development of spatial-cognitive skills? There is evidence to support an affirmative answer to this question from a longitudinal study of infants with spina bifida, a neural tube disorder associated with delays in locomotor development (Campos et al., 2009). Infants were tested on a hidden search task as well as another spatial-cognitive task assessing the infants' ability to follow the experimenter's point and gaze both before and after the onset of their independent crawling. The ability to crawl was delayed for the infants with spina bifida (typically about 1 year); however, dramatic improvements on both tasks followed the onset of their crawling. Campos, Anderson, and Telzrow (2009) reported that these infants searched for the hidden objects on only 14% of the trials prelocomotion, but they successfully found the hidden objects 64% of the time postlocomotion.

Converging evidence from both typically developing as well as delayed developing infants supports the link between locomotor experience and spatial-cognitive skills; however, how locomotor experience specifically leads to success in spatial skills remains unclear. D. I. Anderson et al. (2013) proposed mechanisms such as improved attentional strategies, ability to delay goal attainment, and refined understanding of others' intentions, but more experimental work needs to be conducted to test these possible causal factors.

Questions are also now being addressed that concern how the brain changes as a function of locomotor experience (D. I. Anderson et al., 2013). The hippocampus, known to play a critical role in learning and memory, has been identified as a brain center that has shown dramatic structural change as a function of aerobic activity (Thomas, Dennis, Bandettini, & Johansen-Berg, 2012). If self-produced locomotion facilitates the development of the hippocampus, it then becomes possible that locomotion plays a role in another higher order cognitive skill—the development of memories.

Glenberg and Hayes (2016) developed a hypothesis that involves the maturation of the hippocampus and the ability for infants to form episodic memories, or memories for personal experiences that are linked to a time and place. Infantile amnesia (IA), or the inability to remember much at all from the first few years of life, is a well-known and well-researched phenomenon. Because other species whose young are also incapable of moving around on their own after being born (altricial species such as dogs, cats, and rodents) show signs of IA, Glenberg and Hayes argued that an explanation of IA cannot involve human attributes, such as underdeveloped language skills or an inability to have a self-concept. Instead, Glenberg and Hayes suggested that something that these species share with humans, self-locomotion, may be responsible for this memory problem.

They argued that because self-locomotion produces consistent correlations between optic flow, head direction, and proprioception, this leads to specific hippocampal cells, notably place cells (coding location information) and grid cells (coding spatial relations among the locations), becoming "tuned" to the environment. These correlations cannot occur when an infant is carried around for two reasons: first, an infant's head is free to move around while the adult is moving, so the optic flow does not necessarily match the direction of movement. Second, because the adult is producing the movement and not the infant, the correlation between the infant's proprioception (very little) and optic flow (produced by the adult) is broken. Thus, just like a passenger not learning the route that the driver takes on a journey, the carried infant does not have the opportunity to tune hippocampal place and grid cells to the environment. Without the correlations that underlie the tuning of the hippocampal cells, prelocomoting infants will not have the ability to form stable episodic memories that link an event to a time and place.

Glenberg and Hayes' (2016) explanation for IA is one that falls squarely within embodiment theory because it details the role of the body in this memory phenomenon. Their claim is that self-locomotion will eventually tune place and grid cells in the hippocampus to the environment, allowing for the opportunity to develop an episodic memory. However, even then these memories will be fleeting, which accounts for another memory phenomenon in childhood called *continued rapid forget-ting*, or *childhood amnesia* (CA).

As the infant transitions from crawling to walking, new correlations develop between head direction (which has changed from looking down in crawling to look-ing forward in walking), optic flow, and proprioception, disrupting the old correla-tions. Memories encoded during that earlier phase of crawling are forgotten at a rate faster than that of an adult (resulting in CA). Glenberg and Hayes proposed that when walking and exploration of the child's environment has finally advanced to the degree that spatial relations in the environment are understood, the hippocampal system will then code the location of an event with the specific time and place to form an adult-like episodic memory.

Glenberg and Hayes' (2016) hypothesis will need to be empirically tested, but there are some studies that already provide support. For example, Winter, Mehlman, Clark, and Taube (2015) found that in active rats exploring their environment, hippo-campal grid cell firing increased with returns to specific locations, but this relation-ship was disrupted and disorganized in passive rats that were pulled in a cart around their environment. This supports the contention that at least in rats, self-locomotion tunes the grid cells in the hippocampus to location, providing the opportunity for the development of memories that are tied to place. Additionally, Riggins, Blankenship, Mulligan, Rice, and Redcay (2015) found a positive correlation between episodic memory skill and hippocampal volume for 6-year-olds, but not for 4-year-olds. Although there may be multiple explanations for this correlation, it does suggest that hippocampal development may be related to memory advances.

As stated by Glenberg and Hayes (2016), their hypothesis concerning the acqui-sition of episodic memories is also consistent with the data concerning the loss of episodic memories with aging. Given the decrease in active movement and novel exploration in the aged population, Glenberg and Hayes suggested that with age, the hippocampal place and grid cell firing may become disorganized and less associated with place, disrupting the formation of episodic memories. Interestingly, the hippo-campus does show dramatic decreases in volume with diseases such as Alzheimer's and depression (Thomas et al., 2012), both conditions associated with a sharp decline in mobility.

Recent research lays a strong foundation for the idea that the maturation of certain brain structures that are involved in locomotion, or bodily action, are critical for the development of higher order cognitive processes, supporting embodiment theory. One more relevant study to consider tests an embodied perspective on the development of executive function. Executive functions are cognitive processes used to choose actions, sustain attention, and inhibit distractions. They are typically con-sidered working memory processes, developed for the primary purpose of controlling action (Gottwald, Achermann, Marciszko, Lindskog, & Gredebäck, 2016). Gottwald et al. (2016) hypothesized that although executive function is eventually used to con-trol mental action, it must develop in conjunction with the ability to control motor action (i.e., executive function is grounded in motor control).

Gottwald et al. (2016) predicted that if executive function emerges from develop-ing motor control, then as soon as executive function can be measured, we should see evidence of this relationship. In their study, 18-month-old infants performed several executive function tasks, including a simple inhibition task where the infants had to inhibit their reaching for an attractive toy because the experimenter discouraged touching it, and a working memory task that was a version of a hide-and-seek task where a toy was hidden in the infant's view in a chest of drawers, and after a 5-second delay, the infant could search for the toy. The infants were also given a task that assessed motor control in the smallest observable units of action, the speed with which infants moved, called "peak velocities" of first movements. Gottwald et al. found that infants with higher peak velocities of their first movements, indicating more developed motor control abilities, also showed superior performance in the simple inhibition task and in the working memory task. They claim that the ability to plan reaching actions, as measured in these movement units, is related to higher order executive control. These data are consistent with the earlier data presented that suggest that cognitive skills emerge from motoric skills (i.e., cognitive skills are grounded in the body).

To summarize what has been covered so far, embodiment theory would suggest that if higher order cognitive skills are grounded in the body, we should find evidence for the ontogeny of these skills in bodily action. This is indeed supported by

1. The development of fear of heights, particularly important for survival, as a function of self-produced locomotion.
2. The finding that self-produced locomotion plays an essential role in an infant's ability to search for a hidden object, which is the hallmark of several cognitive advances such as object permanence, understanding spatial relations, and action planning.
3. Glenberg and Hayes' (2016) proposal that the developing hippocampus in young children is responsible for the formation of episodic memories. This can be tied to locomotion because cells in the hippocampus become tuned to place and location with the onset of locomotion; over time, this allows a link to occur with an event in a child's life, resulting in a memory.
4. Finally, there is evidence that executive function, an essential cognitive skill, is related to our ability to act. It appears that executive function, the ability to control and manipulate cognitive processes, depends, at least initially, on our ability to control action.

There are many other cognitive abilities that will need to be examined to determine if they are based on bodily action.

The Role of the Body in the Representation of Abstract Concepts

There is growing evidence for the role of the body in the *acquisition* of higher order cognitive skills. If we leave the developmental research, another direction for embodiment theory to take would be to find evidence for the body's role in the conceptualization of abstract thought. This evidence is important because it demonstrates that our understanding of abstract concepts is linked to our body's state or stance or action. And this evidence is particularly striking when it involves abstract concepts that have nothing to do with the body or with emotions, for example, *time*.

FREE WILL

Let's start with the abstract concept of free will. Research has shown that most people believe in free will, loosely defined as one's ability to control their own actions, make their own decisions, and be free of external constraints when following their dreams (Monroe & Malle, 2010). How do we mentally represent this abstract concept of free will? Ent and Baumeister (2014) examined the embodiment of free will by exploring how an individual's bodily state may determine their belief in this concept. If this concept is grounded in one's bodily ability to control their actions, then those individuals who have medical disorders that limit that control should report less belief in free will compared with individuals who do not have any such limitations.

In their first study, Ent and Baumeister (2014) gave a survey about the belief in free will to three groups of individuals: individuals with epilepsy, a disorder characterized by unpredictable seizure activity; individuals with panic disorder, a disorder also characterized by a sense of lack of control and unpredictability; and individuals who had neither disorder. They found that individuals with epilepsy and panic disorder believed less in free will in general than the control individuals (responding to questions such as, "Free will is a basic part of human nature"). These disorders did not affect people's beliefs in their own free will (responding to questions such as, "I am in charge of the decisions I make"), which was not significantly different than the control individuals' beliefs. Although correlational in nature, this result provided preliminary evidence that one's bodily state can affect the general representation of a concept that captures how you think about how controllable the world is while not necessarily altering one's belief in their own free will.

Study 2 surveyed individuals in temporary bodily states of physical need. Ent and Baumeister (2014) predicted that an immediate state of need would nonconsciously remind the individuals that they lacked complete control over their body, perhaps affecting their beliefs about their own personal free will (general belief in free will was not measured in this study). Participants self-reported their hunger, thirst, need to urinate, desire for sex, and physical fatigue. Ent and Baumeister found that with the exception of the scale for hunger, the higher the scores on the scales indicating physical needs, the lower the scores on the personal free-will scales.

Coupled with Study 1, these data provide further evidence that bodily states seem to determine belief in free will. Study 3 provided a fascinating test for a potential explanation for Study 2's result that the state of hunger did not affect the belief in free-will measure. Ent and Baumeister hypothesized that for those individuals who responded to Study 2's survey, there were certainly both dieters and nondieters, and they reasoned that dieters may have a very different view of one's ability to control their body than nondieters. Because dieting involves resisting the urge to eat, those who are successful must be constantly reminding themselves that they have control over that physical need—reinforcing their belief in free will. However, nondieters experience hunger just as any other physical need, and this results in lower belief in free-will scale values. The two groups' belief in free-will scores when combined (as in Study 2) counter each other, making it appear as if hunger does not affect this measure.

In Study 3, dieters and nondieters were identified and then given the physical need (hunger) survey and the personal free-will survey. Figure 4.1 shows the interaction found between level of hunger and dieting status in the belief in free-will measure. As Ent and Baumeister (2014) predicted, nondieting individuals experience physical need (hunger), and this reduces their belief in their ability to control their body (just as other physical needs did in Study 2) compared with when they are not hungry. However, when dieters are hungry, their belief in free will shows the exact opposite trend. As dieters resist this physical need, it strengthens their belief in the ability to control their actions and life, evidenced by higher belief in free-will scores for dieters when hungry than when not hungry. Although much of embodiment research has focused on experimental manipulations of the body to determine their effects on cognition, this survey research suggests that our chronic bodily states may be linked to our cognition, changing our representations of abstract philosophical constructs such as free will.

FIGURE 4.1

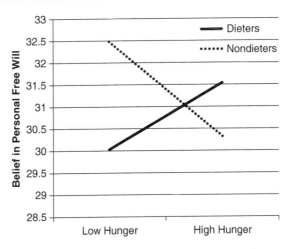

Dieting status interacted with hunger to predict belief in personal free will. From "Embodied Free Will Beliefs: Some Effects of Physical States on Metaphysical Opinions," by M. R. Ent and R. F. Baumeister, 2014, *Consciousness and Cognition*, *27*, p. 152. Copyright 2014 by Elsevier. Reprinted with permission.

TIME

How do we construct our mental representation of time? Prominent metaphors found across cultures use a spatial dimension to represent time (e.g., length—a *short* exam or a *long* lecture) or explicitly link time with a spatial dimension (e.g., a front/ back axis—her future is *ahead* of her or his past is *behind* him). Because of this, it has been assumed that we use the domain of space to structure our understanding of time (Boroditsky, 2000, 2011; Casasanto & Boroditsky, 2008). (The idea that metaphors reflect how we mentally represent abstract concepts is the substance of Chapter 8.)

Our bodies are inherently structured to link time and space through perceptuo-motor interactions with the world: The fronts of our bodies allow us to see ahead of us and move toward objects that have not been experienced (i.e., the future), and as we move, those things that have already been experienced are behind us (i.e., the past). The body's sensorimotor systems that regulate movement may ground our conceptual understanding of time, such that forward movement provides the conceptual underpinnings of the abstract concept of future, whereas backward movement provides the underpinnings of the concept of past. This embodiment of time is metaphorically revealed in language (e.g., "going back in time" and "jumping ahead") but may also be revealed in motor movements.

Miles, Nind, and Macrae (2010) tested the hypothesis that our body's forward movement is linked to thoughts about the future whereas backward movement is linked to thoughts about the past by measuring spontaneous postural sway when participants were engaged in mental time travel. Participants were fitted with a move-ment sensor on the left side of their leg, being told this was for preparation for a later part of the study. They were blindfolded (for the purpose of encouraging vivid mental imagery) and told to stand comfortably in one spot and follow specific imagery instruc-tions. They were told to either recall what their everyday life was like 4 years ago and to image the events of a typical day, or they were told to imagine what their everyday life would be like 4 years in the future and to image the events of a typical day. Miles et al. found that mental time travel had an observable behavioral consequence: Those that were asked to remember the past showed postural sway in the backward direction (from neutral), but those that were asked to imagine the future showed postural sway in the forward direction. None of the participants were consciously aware of any body movement that they had made. These researchers argued that thinking about time is grounded in the perception–action systems used for actually moving through space.

This evidence of postural sway may support the body's role in representing time, but it is also consistent with prevalent metaphors for past/ahead and future/behind. This makes it difficult to determine if the body movement was from metaphors being activated, and thus time is represented in language, or if the movement reflected the concept being grounded in the motoric system. Evidence that the abstract concept of time is internally represented in the physical dimension of space, which is always relative to our body, is particularly interesting when that evidence does not involve linguistic conventions. We do not have linguistic conventions that link the past to the left side of space and the future to the right side of space (e.g., Tuesday is the day *before* Wednesday; Tuesday is not to the *left* of Wednesday), and yet the evidence that the mental representation of time is grounded in a mental time line running from left to right space is now quite strong.

Response time studies have provided strong evidence for a left–right mental time line. For example, Santiago, Lupáñez, Pérez, and Funes (2007) had participants respond to words presented on a computer screen with one hand if the word referred to the future or with the other hand if the word referred to the past. Response times were faster when the left hand responded to past words and the right hand responded to future words than the opposite (this effect was independent of handedness).

Weger and Pratt (2008) also found a time–space congruency effect with non-linguistic stimuli. They had participants decide whether an actor was popular before or after the participants were born. Pictures of these actors (e.g., James Dean vs. Brad Pitt) were responded to with participants' left (if earlier time: before born) or right (if later time: after born) hand. Despite the fact that the names themselves did not convey temporal information as did the words in the Santiago et al. (2007) study, participants were still faster when the picture was compatible with the left–right representation of time.

Recently, this time–space congruency effect has been replicated by Ding, Feng, Cheng, Liu, and Fan (2015), but they found asymmetry in the strength of this effect based on how distant the past and future events were. Specifically, Ding et al. found that when judgments were made with participants' right and left hands about events in their near past or near future (e.g., yesterday or tomorrow), the typical congruency effects were found. However, when judgments were made about more distant past or future events (e.g., last year or next year), the congruency effects were found for the distant past but not the distant future events. Ding et al. suggested that past and future may be represented asymmetrically in the mental time line, with the spatial representation of the past being stronger than that for the future. They suggest the reason for this is that the construction of the representation of the past is based on real events, whereas the representation of the future is only imagined. These data provide interesting further support for the mental time line; the representation of certain memories may indeed be linked to a spatial representation, but one that is based on the reality of the experiences within a time context (i.e., episodic memories are coded on a mental time line).

This left–right mapping of past to future suggests that our understanding of time is directly linked to this physical domain, and it appears to be independent of linguistic conventions. Although languages around the world use spatial metaphors to describe time, these metaphors do not explicitly use the left–right mapping. This suggests that the mapping of time to space is not at the linguistic level of representation but instead at a deeper, conceptual representation. However, it also appears that the reading/writing (or linguistic) experience of one's culture may determine the direction of the mental time line. Fuhrman and Boroditsky (2010), using nonlinguistic stimuli, examined whether participants used culturally determined spatial representations when reasoning about time.

In one experiment, Fuhrman and Boroditsky (2010) asked English and Hebrew speakers to arrange pictures of natural events in any order that they wished, and in another experiment, these participants had to make rapid temporal order judgments about pairs of pictures presented one after the other using one hand for an "earlier" response and the other hand for a "later" response. Fuhrman and Boroditsky found that English and Hebrew speakers arranged temporal sequences in the direction of their reading (English: left to right and Hebrew: right to left). Further, English speakers made faster "earlier" judgments with their left hand and "later" judgments with their right hand, but Hebrew speakers showed the reverse pattern. These data suggest that writing/reading experience shapes or "spatializes" peoples' representation of time, and this culturally specific spatial representation is automatically accessed when making temporal judgments on nonlinguistic tasks just as it is on linguistic tasks.

De la Fuente, Santiago, Román, Dumitrache, and Casasanto (2014) extended this argument by suggesting that individuals' space–time mappings are not only determined by their writing/reading experience, but also by their cultural attitudes toward time (e.g., Arabic speakers think of the future as behind and past as in front, despite front/future—back/past metaphors in Arabic that are similar to those in English). De la Fuente et al. examined this question with participants from Morocco (an Arabic culture) and Spain, and these participants were categorized as younger (mean age was 26 years) or older participants (mean age was 76 years). Using a variation of Casasanto's (2009) "Bob task" described in the previous chapter, De la Fuente et al. found that when asked to put certain objects from a participant's past and other objects from the participant's future in a box either in front of or behind the drawing of the fictional "Bob," both young and older individuals from an Arabic culture (Moroccans) and only older Spanish individuals put objects from the past ahead (or in front of) Bob and items from the future behind Bob. The representation of the past in front of Bob reflects the attention that Arab cultures give to the past, and older Spaniards doing the same reflects the tendency for older individuals to be more past focused than future focused. However, younger Spaniards put the objects from the past behind Bob and the objects from the future in front of Bob, which is consistent with linguistic conventions. These data strengthen the argument that these space–time linkages that provide us with a representation of time are often independent of entrenched linguistic influences.

Although there is strong evidence from these multiple paradigms to suggest that thinking about time is affected by spatial information, the question could still be asked: How connected are our representations of time and space? Is it possible that time and space share the same representational system, such that one cannot think about time without thinking about space (Boroditsky, 2000)?

Eikmeier, Schröter, Maienborn, Alex-Ruf, and Ulrich (2013) used a novel paradigm to examine the representational overlap between time and space. In their first experiment, participants were presented sentences on a screen that referred to either the past or the present, for example, "Yesterday, Hannah repaired the bike," or "The boss will sign the application tomorrow morning." Participants were asked to vocally respond as quickly as possible with the words "in front" or "behind" in the experimental condition, and in the control condition, participants' vocal responses were "past" or "future." Eikmeier et al.'s hypothesis was that if the dimension of time is strongly connected to the dimension of space, the difference in response times for the experimental and control conditions should be small. However, if there is little overlap between time and space, then the control group should be faster in making the correct responses than the experimental group.

The response times and error rates for congruent conditions (in which the participants were told to respond to the sentences with correct responses; i.e., "in front" or "future" to future-related sentences and "behind" or "past" for past-related sentences), and for incongruent conditions (in which the experimenters could examine interference because participants were asked to make the opposite responses to past and future-related sentences) can be found in Figure 4.2. As can be seen in this figure, the difference between the congruent and incongruent conditions was the same for the experimental and control conditions, indicating a strong degree of overlap between the representations of time and space.

FIGURE 4.2

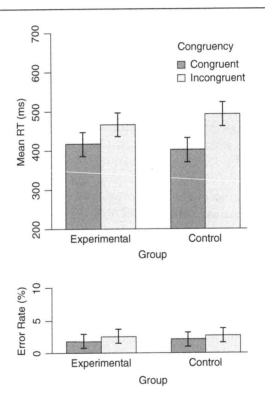

Experiment 2: Mean reaction times (RTs, upper panel) and error rates (lower panel) as a function of group and congruency. Confidence intervals were computed as recommended by Masson and Loftus (2003). From "Dimensional Overlap Between Time and Space," by V. Eikmeier, H. Schröter, C. Maienborn, S. Alex-Ruf, and R. Ulrich, 2013, *Psychonomic Bulletin & Review, 20*, p. 1123. Copyright 2013 by the Psychonomic Society. Reprinted with permission.

The second experiment examined whether this overlap also occurred with non-linguistic stimuli, and instead of sentences, tones were placed either in front of or behind participants. In this experiment, participants in the experimental condition were to respond "past" or "future" after hearing the tone coming from one of those locations, and participants in the control condition were to respond "in front" or "behind" after hearing the tone. As in Experiment 1, there were also congruent groups (who were responding with the correct mapping of time and space) and incongruent groups (who were responding with the opposite mapping). Results replicated those in Experiment 1; the difference between congruent and incongruent conditions was again the same for both the experimental and control conditions, indicating that time and space are strongly connected (and in this case, past and future are mapped onto a front/back axis).

Eikmeier et al. (2013) argued that the results of these two studies are consistent with either the position that the representations of time and space essentially overlap or, if not overlapping in the sense of intersecting, the representation of time may be embedded in our representation of space. This view is consistent with data that suggests that time and space share neural networks (Basso, Nichelli, Frassinetti, & di Pellegrino, 1996). Bueti and Walsh (2009) claimed that the neural pathways for time and space are found in the parietal cortex, which is responsible for guiding action. Thus, the representation of time may be coded in the same neural pathways that provide us with spatial information, and these pathways also prepare the body for action.

In a fascinating study that provides further support for the representation of space and time sharing neural underpinnings, Saj, Fuhrman, Vuilleumier, and Boroditsky (2014) examined the mental time line in individuals who have an inability to spatially represent information on the left side of their bodies. Left-side spatial neglect is a cognitive impairment that results from brain damage to the right hemisphere of the brain, specifically the inferior or posterior areas of the parietal lobe. This is a syndrome where, on the contralateral (opposite) side of the lesion, the patient's ability to perceive, identify, and even move toward objects in that physical space is impaired (even in the absence of any motor deficits). Patients with left-side spatial neglect show such a strong right side of space bias that they may not eat food on the left side of their plate, shave and groom only the right side of their face, and miss words while reading that are on the left side of the page (Azouvi et al., 2002). Left-spatial neglect is also often associated with representational difficulties, that is, an inability to generate or remember information that has been presented from right space. Thus, patients with right-hemispheric damage will have difficulty drawing the left side of objects from memory or retrieving landmarks from the left side of a familiar space (Bisiach & Luzzatti, 1978). Right-side spatial neglect from left-hemispheric damage is apparently rare because the left hemisphere, unlike the right, has few neural pathways critical for spatial processing; thus, as long as the right hemisphere is intact, spatial deficits are unlikely (Beis et al., 2004).

Saj et al. (2014) hypothesized that if spatial representations are needed for the representation of events along a mental time line, then patients with an inability to represent the left side of space due to spatial neglect should have difficulty representing the "left side" of time. Saj et al. compared performance on a memory task for French right-hemisphere stroke patients, some with left-side spatial neglect and others that showed no spatial neglect, with performance for healthy control patients. Participants were given an encoding phase where they learned a list of things that a fictional character liked 10 years ago and other things that the character will like 10 years from now. The items on the list were line drawings of objects (e.g., in the food list: eggs, a hamburger, etc.), and each item had a cue above it (a white cap or a black top hat) to indicate whether this was something from the character's past or would be liked in the future. Four lists were given, but after each list, the participants had a recall phase, followed by a recognition phase in which the old items and four new items were presented on the screen and the patient verbally responded whether they remembered the item and if it was from the character's past or future.

The results of the recall and the recognition phases showed the same pattern: Patients with left hemispatial neglect showed a significant impairment in recalling (and recognizing) those items across the lists that were presented as items from the character's past (on the left side of their mental time line). When remembering items from the future, patients with neglect did not show any memory deficits from the other right-hemisphere stroke patients or the controls, but they were more likely to misattribute items from the past as items from the future. These findings demonstrate that an inability to represent space (from hemispatial neglect) results in an inability to represent events along a mental time line. These data provide more supportive evidence for the contention that some neural pathways in the posterior parietal cortex, where these patients' lesions were located, are shared for the representation of space and the representation of time.

NUMEROSITY

Like the abstract concept of time, the abstract concept of numerosity, or number magnitude, appears to be represented in the spatial dimension of left to right. Because this dimension is body specific, an embodied perspective of number magnitude follows along a mental number line: What is to the left of our body may be representing smaller numerosity than what is to the right of our body (Restle, 1970). This argues against an abstract, amodal representation for the representation of magnitude. We can find evidence of this representation of number magnitude in bodily effects. Eerland, Guadalupe, and Zwaan (2011) hypothesized that if we mentally represent numbers along a mental number line, then making people lean slightly to the left or slightly to the right, surreptitiously, would affect their number estimations.

Participants in Eerland et al.'s (2011) study answered estimation questions (about diverse dimensions such as the height of a building or the percentage of alcohol in a beverage) in two experiments while standing on a Wii balance board. They were asked to maintain an upright neutral position, and to help them in doing so, their "center of pressure" readings were supposedly shown on a computer screen positioned in front of them. They had to keep their center of pressure within the cross hairs of a circle shown on the screen and could rebalance their bodies any time they needed to accomplish that. Unbeknownst to the participants, the experimenters manipulated their body posture (the magnitude of displacement on either side of center was only 2%) so that sometimes the participants were leaning slightly to the left and sometimes they were leaning slightly to the right.

The numerical estimation questions appeared on the screen above the display that indicated they were centered (when actually they were not), and the experimenters recorded their responses. Figure 4.3 presents the standardized average estimations across the questions answered during the times when the participants were leaning left, right, or were upright. The results of both experiments indicate that when leaning left, participants gave number estimations that were smaller than when they were leaning right (however, number estimations in the upright position were not statistically different from those in the leaning right position). These postural influences on number estimation suggest that numerosity is represented on a mental number line grounded in a spatial dimension of left to right.

Body posture influencing quantitative estimations is certainly consistent with the embodied view of number cognition, but converging evidence is needed. The mental representation of magnitude and parity (the odd vs. even nature of numbers) was examined by Dehaene, Bossini, and Giraux (1993). In a series of experiments that had participants sometimes making parity judgments and sometimes making magnitude judgments, participants' responses were made with their left and right hands. Across task types and independent of handedness, Dehaene et al. found that left-hand responses were faster than right-hand responses for small numbers, and the converse was true for large numbers.

They referred to this association of large numbers with right space and small numbers with left space as the Spatial-Numerical Association of Response Codes (SNARC) effect. They found the SNARC effect even on parity judgment tasks, where participants were responding with their right or left hand to the odd versus even

FIGURE 4.3

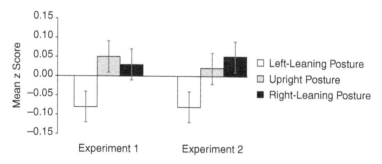

Mean *z* scores (±1 *SE*) for participants' estimates in the three posture conditions in Experiment 1 (*N* = 33) and Experiment 2 (*N* = 58). From "Leaning to the Left Makes the Eiffel Tower Seem Smaller: Posture-Modulated Estimation," by A. Eerland, T. M. Guadalupe, and R. A. Zwaan, 2011, *Psychological Science, 22*, p. 1512. Copyright 2011 by Sage. Reprinted with permission.

number task. This task did not have participants explicitly responding to magnitude information, and yet relatively small numbers were responded to faster with their left hand and relatively large numbers were responded to faster with their right hand. This suggested to Dehaene et al. that number magnitude and its spatial representation is automatically activated from the presentation of Arabic numerals. (However, see Basso Moro, Dell'Acqua, & Cutini, 2018, for a recent examination of the SNARC effect and the conditions under which it is found. Their findings suggest that the root cause of the SNARC effect may be a combination of spatial-numerical associations and response-related processes.) Interestingly, developmental research has shown that the SNARC effect is found in preschool/kindergarten children (Hoffmann, Hornung, Martin, & Schiltz, 2013). Further, de Hevia, Girelli, Addabbo, and Macchi Cassia (2014) found that even 7-month-old infants preferred magnitudes increasing from left to right over magnitudes decreasing from left to right, suggesting an early predisposition to associate numbers with space.

The SNARC effect represents the semantic representation of number cognition being tightly linked to the physical dimension of left to right space, but subsequent research has demonstrated that this is based on an external frame of reference. In one of the Dehaene et al. (1993) experiments, they had half of their participants respond with their right and left hands (as in the other experiments) to a number magnitude task, but the other half of their participants crossed their hands to respond to the task. This allowed them to address the question of whether the SNARC effect arises from a hand-based frame of reference or an external frame of reference. They found that in the crossed-hand condition, small numbers were responded to faster by using the left-hand key, even though this key was now pressed with the right hand, and the opposite pattern was found with large numbers. These data indicate that number magnitude is not associated with a particular hand of response, but instead large numerosity is associated with the right side of external space and small numerosity associated with the left side of external space.

Crollen, Dormal, Seron, Lepore, and Collignon (2013) used Dehaene et al.'s (1993) number comparison task and borrowed their manipulation of hands in a regular position or hands crossed. Using this procedure, Crollen et al. were able to explore the developmental process of the mental number line, specifically addressing the role of vision in its acquisition. They hypothesized that if numerical cognition is grounded in sensorimotor abilities, this may develop from visual experience and the tactile experiences that stem from vision. For sighted individuals and blind individuals who developed blindness later in life (in this study, on average, after the age of 29), their visual–tactile experience early in life would result in an external coordinate system in space used for perception and action. This should mean that Dehaene et al.'s SNARC effect (faster responses when left-side response corresponds to small numbers and right-side response corresponds to large numbers) would occur with hands in both conditions, crossed or not crossed. However, for early-blind individuals, the lack of any visual experience should mean that they could not use of an external frame of reference, and they would have to use an anatomical frame of reference (i.e., their left and right hands) when performing the number magnitude task.

Crollen et al.'s (2013) findings exactly predicted this result: For sighted and late-blind participants, the SNARC effect was found on the number magnitude task for both the regular-hand condition and the crossed-hand condition, indicating that numbers are mapped onto an external or world-centered coordinate system. However, for the early-blind participants, the SNARC effect was found only in the regular-hand condition, and in the crossed-hand condition, a reverse SNARC effect was found—large numbers were responded to faster on the left and small numbers were responded to faster on the right, but of course this meant that responses were a function of the hand used to make the response, not the side of the body that the hand was on. Crollen et al. argued that the development of number cognition involves basic sensorimotor foundations that map magnitude to the left–right spatial dimension of one's body. For early-blind individuals, this mapping continues to be based on the anatomical reference point of their bodies.

Crollen et al. (2013) claimed that visual experience results in an automatic "remapping" of number and space that takes place developmentally as visual input is coupled with tactile experience, and numbers eventually become mapped onto an extra corporal (external to body) coordinate system (as evidenced by the crossed-hand condition's results). Interestingly, Crollen et al. suggested that similar to the mental time line, this SNARC effect may be a function of reading experience. Reading involves moving ones' eyes from left to right as one goes from beginning to end (in essence from small to large) and from start to finish (in essence from past to future). Reading experience would support the "spatialization" of the semantic representation of both numbers and time in both sighted and blind individuals, as Braille is also read from left to right. For blind individuals, the SNARC effect is due to this spatial correspondence with reading, but it stays hand based; for sighted individuals, reading, and thus the SNARC effect, is eye centered, resulting in an external frame of reference for numerosity.

Support for the contention that reading experience may play a significant role in the mental number line comes from one of Dehaene et al.'s (1993) experiments that showed that Iranian participants showed the opposite direction of the SNARC effect in the number comparison task—small numbers were responded to faster with their right hand and large numbers with their left hand. This result can be explained by the right-to-left writing and reading practice within the Iranian culture.

We have seen strong similarities between the representation of time and the representation of numerosity in that both seem to be grounded in the spatial dimension of the left/right axis. Interestingly, the direction of this spatialization of time and number appears to depend on culture and the direction of writing and reading within that culture. There is now strong neurocognitive support that suggests that both number and time are rooted in the same cortical networks that subserve spatial cognition (Bueti & Walsh, 2009; Cutini, Scarpa, Scatturin, Dell'Acqua, & Zorzi, 2014; Hubbard, Piazza, Pinel, & Dehaene, 2005).

Cutini et al. (2014) found robust activity in two different parietal areas as a function of the SNARC effect, and these areas, the bilateral intraparietal sulcus and the left angular gyrus, are also active in number-processing tasks as well as in spatial-orientation tasks that require left-versus-right key presses. Cutini et al. argued that their neurophysiological results rule out other explanations of the SNARC effect, such as response selection (Keus & Schwarz, 2005) or polarity correspondence (Proctor & Cho, 2006) and instead suggest a neurological basis for the number–space interaction.

Although certain neural pathways of the parietal lobe appear to be central to both the number–space interaction and the time–space interaction, some behavioral data do imply that there may be unique pathways for these representations. Bottini, Crepaldi, Casasanto, Crollen, and Collignon (2015) used the same paradigm as Crollen et al. (2013) to examine the role of vision in the development of the mental time line (instead of the mental number line as in Crollen et al.). Bottini et al. found that whether participants were sighted or not, and whether hands were crossed or not, responses were faster when the "past" key was responded to on the left (even if with the right hand) and when the "future" key was responded to on the right (even if with the left hand). Although Crollen et al. had found dissociation between sighted and blind individuals for the frame of reference used for the mental number line, Bottini et al.'s results suggest that the mental time line is always anchored in external space, even without visual experience. Because blind participants use different spatial frameworks for the mental time line and for the mental number line, this suggests that they may be representationally distinct. Recent evidence has further supported the independence of the representations of time and number (Hendricks & Boroditsky, 2015; Pitt & Casasanto, 2017). Future research will need to explore the differences in the mapping of these concepts onto a spatial dimension and the importance of factors such as visual experience, tactile experience, culturally determined writing and reading direction, and common spatial metaphors in the conceptualization of time and number.

Conclusions

This chapter is dense with different approaches to finding evidence that the body has a role in higher order cognition. There is clear developmental evidence that self-locomotion plays a critical role in the acquisition of cognitive skills such as understanding objects' permanence and for executive function and even memory processes. Few developmental psychologists deny the role of bodily action in developing cognitive function (see Adolph & Hoch, in press).

There is also evidence that the body plays a role in the representation of abstract concepts. Understanding free will, time, and numerosity clearly involves bodily effects, including chronic and acute bodily states and the frame of reference we use for the space around our bodies. Earlier theories of semantic knowledge would have difficulty accommodating these results because in these theories, there is no direct role of the body. Instead, bodily effects are the *consequence* of the activation of disembodied, symbolic knowledge—and yet there is little empirical evidence for this initial stage of disembodied knowledge. Instead, the data presented in this chapter can be explained within embodiment theory, in which the representation of abstract knowledge is multimodal and develops from sensorimotor functions, sharing neural pathways with sensory and motor actions.

Takeaway

- Sensorimotor systems that facilitate the acquisition of fundamental cognitive skills are tuned through action (Campos).
- Knowledge representations of abstract concepts such as time and numerosity are grounded in physical dimensions of space around the body as evidenced in both behavioral effects and in neural activity (Crollen, Cutini).

The Body's Role in Language Comprehension

5

Questions:

- What is the empirical support for an embodied approach to language comprehension?
- Is meaning grounded in bodily action such that action (or inaction) taken during text processing facilitates or impairs comprehension? Or does meaning come from mental simulations of prior sensorimotor experiences that are elicited during language processing?
- Is there any place for a hybrid, or pluralistic, model of language comprehension that involves both amodal, symbolic representations as well as modal, grounded representations of meaning?

The embodied cognition approach to language comprehension suggests that there is an essential link between bodily experiences and language. The argument of Glenberg and others (e.g., Glenberg & Kaschak, 2002; Kousta, Vigliocco, Vinson, Andrews, & Del Campo, 2011; Ponari, Norbury, & Vigliocco, 2018; Willems, Hagoort, & Casasanto, 2010; Zwaan, 2016) is that language comprehension uses neural systems that are established for perception, action, and emotion. In other words, language comprehension is "grounded in bodily action" because we use the same neural mechanisms for understanding language about action that we do for producing action.

http://dx.doi.org/10.1037/0000136-005

How the Body Shapes Knowledge: Empirical Support for Embodied Cognition, by R. Fincher-Kiefer

There is both behavioral evidence for this claim and evidence from neuroscience. This discussion concerning language comprehension is the perfect place to move from a "Glenberg-like" view that emphasizes how the body grounds abstract information in the systems used for perception and action planning (Glenberg, 1997) to a "Barsalou-like" view that claims that comprehension involves the simulation of past experiences, imaginations, or even observations of others, allowing us to derive meaning from abstract, arbitrary linguistic symbols (i.e., words, phrases, even syntactic templates; Barsalou, 1999, 2008a, 2008b). Of course it is difficult to separate the role of the body from the act of mental simulation because simulation involves a reenactment of that which the body has perceived, acted on, even simply imagined. This is why, as mentioned in Chapter 1, Glenberg and Barsalou's views are both embodied and are not contradictory but instead complementary. However, these views, although not theoretically disparate, do allow us to examine the empirical literature with a slightly different "lens" and learn how these different perspectives align to explain language comprehension.

Language Comprehension Is Grounded in Bodily Action

Traditional views of language comprehension proposed that language conveys meaning using abstract, amodal symbols called *propositions*, which are connected using syntactic rules (e.g., Chomsky, 1980; Kintsch, 1998; see also de Vega, Glenberg, & Graesser, 2008, for a thorough discussion of different approaches to establishing linguistic meaning). These theories of comprehension were quite complex, suggesting that understanding discourse may involve constructing levels of text representation, from a text-base level to a situation, or mental model, level of representation (Glenberg, 1997; Myers & O'Brien, 1998; Zwaan, Langston, & Graesser, 1995). However, this view of comprehension began to shift with Barsalou's (1999) proposal that situation model construction may involve modal symbol systems, or perceptual symbols, that represent knowledge. These perceptual symbols are derived directly from perceptual experiences. The perceptual symbol system framework contended that comprehension entails establishing an analogue relationship between the text and the reader's background knowledge. Thus, comprehension involves activating perceptual symbols, or simulating prior sensorimotor experiences. The use of perceptual symbols in reading facilitates the construction of a situation model, which is the level of comprehension that yields an interpretation of the text (Glenberg & Robertson, 1999).

There have been tests of the hypothesis that the construction of a situation model involves perceptual processing (Fincher-Kiefer, 2001). In this research, I demonstrated that readers holding a visual array in memory while concurrently reading a text showed impaired comprehension processes compared with readers holding a verbal array in memory. This interference effect supports the role of perceptual (in this case visual) processing during comprehension. However, a stronger view of embodied comprehension would suggest that bodily action plays a role in comprehension. For example, an embodied approach to language comprehension predicts that linguistic meaning is grounded in bodily action. Thus, action taken during the comprehension of a sentence should affect the processing and understanding of that sentence.

Glenberg and Kaschak (2002) tested the hypothesis that constructing meaning involves the recruitment of sensorimotor information (this theoretical perspective was first introduced as the *indexical hypothesis*; Glenberg & Robertson, 1999, 2000). Participants read sentences and made sensibility judgments to sensible and nonsensible sentences, such as, "Courtney handed you the notebook," and "Joe sang the cards to you." Notice that this sensibility judgment by itself has little to do with processing action, and making this judgment could occur with little consideration of the direction of the implied action. To make the yes/no sensibility judgment, Glenberg and Kaschak's participants were required to press a button on a box held on their lap. Participants rested their hand on the middle of three buttons. The placement of the "yes" button was the critical variable in this experiment. The "yes" button was either the button that required the participant to move their arm away from the body ("yes-is-far" condition), or the "yes" button was the button that required the participant to move their arm toward the body ("yes-is-near" condition). Participants read sentences that either implied action that was occurring toward their body ("Courtney handed you the notebook") or the action was occurring away from their body ("You handed Courtney the notebook"). Further, some of the sentences were *concrete transfer* sentences, such as these given previously that described physical transfer of objects, but other sentences were *abstract transfer* sentences that described nonphysical transfer (e.g., "The policeman radioed the message to you" or "You radioed the message to the policeman").

Glenberg and Kaschak (2002) found an action-sentence compatibility effect (ACE) in their sensibility judgment response times for all sentence types—understanding a sentence that implied action toward the body was faster when the motion made for that sensibility judgment was also toward the body ("yes-is-near" condition) compared with away from the body ("yes-is-far" condition), and the opposite pattern of response times was found for the sentences that implied action away from the body. These results suggested to Glenberg and Kaschak that mental representations of motor activity were automatically evoked when reading a sentence describing action. The fact that the same ACE was found for abstract transfer sentences as was found for concrete transfer sentences suggests that the meaning of transfer verbs, no matter how abstract (e.g., "delegate," "told") involves understanding the possibility for action or how action could occur. Glenberg and Kaschak suggested that although the sentences they used were closely associated with explicit action, other sentences that do not involve literal action (e.g., "The dog growled") may be understood in a rich context that would most likely entail some kind of action, thus meaning would typically be derived from representations of bodily action. They proposed that given the evolutionary basis of language to facilitate, plan, and coordinate action for survival, it is not surprising that comprehension shows an "observable remnant of that history" (p. 564).

There have been a number of studies that have extended Glenberg and Kaschak's (2002) findings and have supported their claim that we understand language because meaning is conveyed in the neural pathways that we use to plan and execute action (e.g., Lai & Desai, 2016; and van Dam, Speed, Lai, Vigliocco, & Desai, 2017). Zwaan and Taylor (2006) used a different kind of ACE procedure to examine online motor "resonance," or activation of action systems, during language comprehension. Participants in their experiments made sensibility judgments to sentences that implied action in the clockwise or counterclockwise direction (e.g., "Jenny screwed in the light bulb" and "Eric turned down the volume"). These judgments were made by turning a knob, and participants either turned the knob in the clockwise direction for a sensible judgment and counterclockwise for a nonsensible judgment or the opposite. Similar to Glenberg and Kaschak's ACE, Zwaan and Taylor found that manual rotations were made more quickly when the direction of the rotation for the sensibility judgment was in the same direction as the direction of the rotation implied by the sentence they were reading.

In one experiment in this series, Zwaan and Taylor (2006) changed the procedure somewhat to investigate the time frame of this motor resonance (activation) involved in language processing. Instead of asking for sensibility judgments, they simply had participants turning the knob in either the clockwise or counterclockwise rotation to present the sentences frame by frame, with each frame being a word or short phrase, and they measured reading time per frame. They found that reading times for the verb region of the sentences were faster when the rotation direction matched the implied direction in the sentence compared with when they mismatched the direction (another compatibility effect). This procedure allowed Zwaan and Taylor to conclude that comprehension of verbs involves motor resonance of the action associated with that meaning, and this comprehension is facilitated when that action is similarly engaged during comprehension.

Taylor, Lev-Ari, and Zwaan (2008) extended this result by using the same procedure with sentences that had ambiguous directional action (e.g., "The carpenter turned the screw"), but the sentence that followed disambiguated the direction (e.g., "The boards had been connected too tightly"). They found that any word that disambiguated the action, verb or not, induced the previously mentioned compatibility effect, indicating that motor activation is involved in comprehension of language as a whole, not simply for one word describing a specific action.

How specific are these motor representations that play a role in the construction of sentence meaning—are they literal and activate only the body parts mentioned in the sentence, or are they more global representations of the action described in the text? Masson, Bub, and Warren (2008) and Bub and Masson (2010) explored the specificity of the motor resonance that occurs during language comprehension. Masson et al. (2008) gave participants sentences such as, "The lawyer kicked aside the calculator." If motor activation was used to represent a literal depiction of the events described in the sentence, then there should be no activation of hand activity when comprehending a sentence such as this or a similar one with a noninteractive verb such as "looked at." To examine this hypothesis, participants in these studies were trained to use a device called the Graspasaurus that allowed participants to make a rapid hand gesture corresponding to either *functional* grasps (those that are used when using an object for its intended purpose, such as extending a finger in a poking gesture as would be done with a calculator) or *volumetric* grasps (those that are used for lifting or moving an object, such as a wide horizontal grasp used when lifting a calculator).

Sentences were presented to participants auditorially (comprehension was required as semantic probe questions were given on some trials), and the critical aspect of these experiments was that sentences referred to manipulable objects (e.g., calculators, thimbles, pistols), but verbs in the sentences either referred to attention being directed toward the object (e.g., approached or looked at) or referred to nonmanual but physical interaction (e.g., kicked or stepped on). Immediately after hearing the sentence, participants were presented a visual hand action cue (sometimes related to the object described, sometimes unrelated) and then required to make that same hand action using the Graspasaurus as quickly as possible. The dependent variable was response time to use the Graspasaurus, and the prediction was that participants' hand actions would occur more rapidly if the action had been activated on listening to the sentence.

Masson et al. (2008) found that participants processing sentences that had a word referring to a manipulable object (calculator) showed priming effects for functional hand actions, actions needed for that object's specific purpose, even though these sentences' verbs did not imply any manual interactions. In addition, sentences that used verbs denoting interactions (stepping on) also primed volumetric hand actions, or actions needed for manipulating the object (lifting), even though the sentence did not specifically concern manipulating the object with one's hands.

Masson et al. (2008) concluded that the motor activation automatically activated during comprehension of a sentence is not necessarily specific to the underlying meaning of the sentence. When understanding a sentence such as, "The lawyer kicked aside the calculator," although there may indeed be activation of motor areas associated with kicking (not measured in this experiment), perhaps more important is that there is also activation of sensorimotor activity associated with what it feels like to lift and move a calculator as well as activation of actions appropriate for its use. This means that motor activation during comprehension may be specific, if necessary, but also may be similar to that which is known about interacting with that object.

This behavioral evidence for the involvement of the sensorimotor system during language comprehension has also been supported and validated by evidence from neuroimaging and neuropsychological research. Initially, the examination of whether the sensory and motor systems were the neural correlates of meaning involved determining whether the understanding of action-related language led to activation in the appropriate motor areas of the brain. In one functional magnetic resonance imaging (fMRI) study, participants read verbs describing actions that involved the feet ("kick") and hands ("pick"), and the pattern of activation in the premotor cortex that occurred during reading was specifically similar to the pattern of activation that occurs when actually moving those body parts (Hauk, Johnsrude, & Pulvermüller, 2004). Others have extended this result beyond single word comprehension, finding differentially activated areas of the premotor cortex in response to comprehending sentences that described actions with the hands ("I grasp the knife") and the feet ("I kick the ball"; Aziz-Zadeh, Wilson, Rizzolatti, & Iacoboni, 2006; Tettamanti et al., 2005).

Perhaps even stronger evidence for the motor cortex providing meaning to action-based language comes from neuropsychological work with patients with motor deficits. Bak and Hodges (2004) found that motor neuron disorders (such as amyotrophic lateral sclerosis, or ALS), although supposedly affecting the motor system but keeping cognition intact, actually impair the understanding of action verbs more so than nouns. Grossman et al. (2008) similarly found that for ALS patients, cognitive judgments requiring knowledge of action (e.g., word–description matching) were significantly impaired compared with judgments requiring knowledge of objects. ALS patients' performance on measures requiring action knowledge correlated with the degree of atrophy in their motor cortex, but this correlation did not exist for performance on measures of object knowledge.

Fernandino et al. (2013) found that patients with Parkinson's disease, a disorder affecting the motor system, showed a selective impairment (slower reading times, poorer accuracy in making meaningful judgments) in processing action-related sentences compared with abstract sentences. Additionally, these patients also showed deficits in the comprehension of sentences that involved metaphoric action sentences (e.g., "The congress *pulled* their support for the plan"), supporting the view that the motor system plays a functional role in the processing of sentences involving literal action as well as figurative senses of action verbs.

Collectively, these data from patients with motor disorders imply that the brain areas responsible for producing action also provide a basis for conceptual knowledge about action. It seems that without full functioning of the body, there is disruption in the understanding of language concerning the body (see Willems & Casasanto, 2011, for a fuller discussion of research with patients with motor system impairments and limitations with those studies). The results of these studies are consistent with current theories that suggest that abstract and figurative language is processed in terms of embodied representations (Gallese & Lakoff, 2005).

Another empirical example of language dysfunction that occurs as a result of body impairment can be found in research using botulinum toxin-A (Botox). Havas, Glenberg, Gutowski, Lucarelli, and Davidson (2010) examined whether paralysis of the facial muscles used in expressing negative emotions (frown muscles—corrugator supercilii) would impair the processing of sentences describing those negative emotions. Women who were already scheduled to get injections of Botox for treatment of frown lines were asked to read happy, sad, and angry sentences at two different time periods. In the first session, the women read these sentences for comprehension, and reading times were measured. Following this, the women received their planned injections of Botox into their frown muscles. The same women returned 2 weeks later (to ensure the full effects of the Botox), had their check-up, and then read a new set of sentences with these same emotions. Figure 5.1 shows the reading times for angry, sad, and happy sentences in both sessions. It took significantly longer to read angry and sad sentences after the injections of Botox, but the reading times for happy sentences were not affected by the injection.

FIGURE 5.1

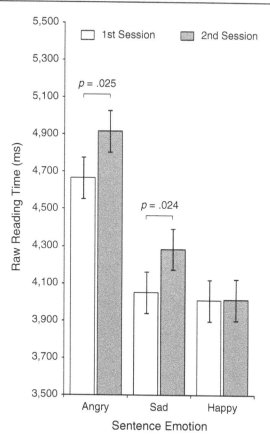

Mean reading times for sentences describing angry, sad, and happy situated before (first session) and after (second session) botulinum toxin-A injection in the corrugator supercilii. Error bars indicate ±1 *SEM*. Brackets indicate significant differences between sessions. From "Cosmetic Use of Botulinum Toxin-A Affects Processing of Emotional Language," by D. A. Havas, A. M. Glenberg, K. A. Gutowski, M. J. Lucarelli, and R. J. Davidson, 2010, *Psychological Science, 21*, p. 897. Copyright 2010 by Sage. Reprinted with permission.

These data demonstrate that blocking facial expressions selectively impairs the processing for sentences that invoke the emotion associated with that facial expression. Havas et al. (2010) argued that these results suggest a functional, not peripheral, role of bodily action (facial movement) in the comprehension of emotional language processing. The neural systems used for expressing emotions may also be used in understanding emotion in language. The fact that Botox impairs the comprehension of negative emotion sentences suggests a potential applied use of the drug for depressive symptoms.

As the facial-feedback hypothesis (Strack, Martin, & Stepper, 1988) would predict, negative facial posture produces negative mood, which activates negative thought patterns, and those augment negative mood. Havas et al.'s (2010) research suggests that if one cannot easily express a negative emotion with a facial posture, then the feedback system that tends to perpetuate negative affect will be broken. Finzi and Rosenthal's (2014) research using Botox injections into frown muscles of individuals with major depressive disorder has found support for this hypothesis.

Although this neuroscience support for the body playing a role in language comprehension seems compelling, a common critique is that the activation of specific motor cortex areas may simply be a "down-stream" consequence of spreading activation across amodal nodes of semantic knowledge. In other words, our knowledge representations may be symbolic and amodal, but after activating these representations, bodily action follows. This argument essentially refutes any functional role of grounded mental representations for meaning construction.

To counter this criticism, several researchers have used high-density magneto-encephalography (MEG) studies to demonstrate how rapid neural responses are to language cues. Pulvermüller, Shtyrov, and Ilmoniemi (2005) auditorily presented action words related to the face or to the leg to participants who were engaged in a distraction task, and neural activity was measured through MEGs. They found that face–word stimuli showed different spatio-temporal brain activity than leg–word stimuli, and these brain "signatures" for these action words occurred within 200 msec of the words being recognized as unique lexical items. Pulvermüller, Shtyrov, and Ilmoniemi argued that this fast activation of specific motor areas for different semantic meanings is inconsistent with the proposal that motor activation represents strategic reading effects or postcomprehension mental imagery; instead, it appears to be an essential part of the meaning representation for these words.

Despite this rapid activation of motoric areas when hearing or reading words, it is still not clear what the functional significance of this activity is for constructing meaning during language comprehension. Glenberg et al. (2008) and Pulvermüller, Hauk, Nikulin, and Ilmoniemi (2005) have used transcranial magnetic stimulation (TMS) to explore the causal role of motor activation in language comprehension. Glenberg et al. (2008) had participants reading concrete transfer sentences ("You give the papers to Marco"), abstract transfer sentences ("Anna delegates the responsibilities to you"), and nontransfer sentences ("You read the papers with Marco"). During the reading of each sentence, TMS pulses were delivered to the left-hemisphere motor cortex, specifically the region that controls action of the hand. These pulses evoke a motor response (motor evoked potential, MEP), and in this study, MEPs were measured from the opponens pollicis muscle of the hand, which is the muscle involved in grasping and transfer actions. The TMS pulses were delivered either 200 ms after the onset of the verb in these sentences or 200 ms after the onset of the last word. This delay was chosen on the basis of Pulvermüller, Shtyrov, and Ilmoniemi's (2005) finding that motor activation occurs as early as 150–200 ms after onset of written word stimuli.

Glenberg et al.'s (2008) prediction was that if understanding these transfer sentences involves modulation of motor system activity in the absence of real motor system activity, or movement of the hand, then there should be greater motor system activity (larger MEPs) during the reading of transfer sentences than of nontransfer sentences. Additionally, if online comprehension of the sentences involves motor activation, then there should be larger MEPs after the verb than at the end of the sentence. Glenberg et al.'s results supported these predictions: MEPs were indeed larger for transfer sentences than for nontransfer sentences, and there were no differences in MEPs between concrete and abstract transfer sentences. It is important to note that the MEPs were larger during the comprehension of the verb than they were at the end of the sentence, arguing against any postcomprehension process that uses mental imagery of motor actions.

These results indicate that the motor system is involved in the online comprehension of both concrete and abstract transfer sentences, replicating Glenberg and Kaschak's (2002) behavioral data. They also suggest that the motor activity occurring during comprehension is not simply an epiphenomenon that results from early sensorimotor associations with explicit language that refers to body parts. If that were the case, the abstract sentences that do not refer to hand or arm movement would not have shown the same motor activity effects as the concrete sentences.

Glenberg et al. (2008) argued that their data provide evidence for a general "transfer action schema" in the motor cortex. They argued that this schema develops early in life and is based on the infant's experience with reaching, grabbing, and transferring objects. This action schema (pattern of neural activity) is generalized over many experiences with moving objects to different locations and to different sources. Areas of the motor cortex become active when the action schema is needed to understand language about concrete or abstract transfer.

Glenberg et al. (2008) and Glenberg and Gallese (2012) argued that this action schema probably resides in the mirror neuron system (MNS), which was first discovered in the monkey premotor cortex (di Pellegrino, Fadiga, Fogassi, Gallese, & Rizzolatti, 1992). These sets of neurons are active when a monkey performs an action with their hand or mouth and are active when it observes the same or similar action done by another individual. The MNS is an execution–observation neural matching system (Tettamanti et al., 2005) that is considered to be responsible for understanding actions of others. Linking this system to language comprehension, Tettamanti et al. (2005) found activation in the MNS when participants were not observing action but were listening to sentences describing actions using the mouth, hands, and legs. Aziz-Zadeh, Wilson, Rizzolatti, and Iacoboni (2006) also found the MNS brain areas active when participants were reading short descriptions of these same actions. These data suggest that understanding language about action uses the same neural circuitry as that used in observing that action—presumably both involve the mental simulation, or reenactment, of the neural activity used in executing the action. Fascinating support for this contention is the fact that part of the MNS is located in Broca's area, a brain center long associated with language processing (Tettamanti et al., 2005).

So far in this chapter, the research discussed has focused on the direct effects that the body has on language comprehension. Evidence has been presented that demonstrates that bodily action during reading affects comprehension, at times facilitating the process and at other times impeding comprehension. Additionally, the inability to act, due to, for example, paralyzing agents such as Botox or motor neuron diseases, was also shown to affect language comprehension. Neuropsychological results provided further evidence that brain areas dedicated to motor activity are involved in comprehending language. This all represents one type of evidence that supports the contention that meaning is "grounded in the body."

Another type of evidence involves an indirect effect of the body, indirect in the sense that comprehension involves a reuse, or reenactment, of a prior experience that involved perception or action. The MNS research described previously provides us with neural evidence of a system specifically used to simulate an observed, listened to, or read experience. This reenactment constitutes a simulation, and in Barsalou's (1999) view, simulation is the core computational component of all thought. It is the reenactment of neural activity associated with the bodily experience that first formed that thought.

Language Comprehension Involves Sensorimotor Simulations

In addition to the neural evidence of simulation, there is strong empirical support from behavioral studies that demonstrate that the mental simulations we run when comprehending language are specific reenactments of sensorimotor experience. Zwaan and colleagues, as well as other researchers (Simmons et al., 2007; Stanfield & Zwaan, 2001; Zwaan & Pecher, 2012; Zwaan, Stanfield, & Yaxley, 2002), have found that mental simulations used during comprehension are sensitive to object properties such as shape, orientation, and color. The experimental paradigm often used to demonstrate the perceptual nature of mental simulations is a simple sentence-picture verification task (Stanfield & Zwaan, 2001). Participants read a sentence in which a visual dimension, such as the orientation of an object, is implied (e.g., "John put the pencil in the cup" or "John put the pencil in a drawer"). Immediately thereafter, a picture is shown of that object (pencil) in a certain orientation (vertical or horizontal), and participants have to press a key to indicate if the object shown was mentioned in the sentence. Figure 5.2 shows two of the pictures used in Zwaan, Stanfield, and Yaxley's (2002) investigation of the mental representation of shape for the sentences, "The egg was in the carton" and "The egg was in the pan."

What is important about this procedure is that the implied orientation or shape (or color in other experiments) is irrelevant to the task at hand, and in fact, participants could respond to the task without fully comprehending the sentences (they could just attend to the noun). However, if language comprehension entails mentally simulating the experience described in the sentence, then any measure of comprehension should be sensitive to whether the orientation or shape of the object in the picture matched or mismatched that described in the sentence.

The results of Zwaan et al.'s (2002) two experiments examining the mental simulations of shape are presented in Table 5.1. Reaction time data are shown for

FIGURE 5.2

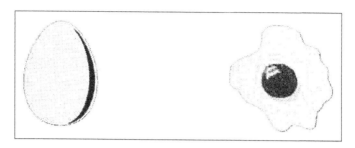

Different shapes of an egg: in a refrigerator versus in a skillet. From "Language Comprehenders Mentally Represent the Shapes of Objects," by R. A. Zwaan, R. A. Stanfield, and R. H. Yaxley, 2002, *Psychological Science*, *13*, p. 169. Copyright 2002 by Sage. Reprinted with permission.

Experiment 1's object recognition decisions for both the match and mismatch conditions, and for Experiment 2's picture-naming reaction times. These results are representative of the studies investigating the property of orientation as well—participants are faster to verify pictures that match what is implied by the sentences read than pictures that mismatch (see Zwaan & Pecher, 2012, for replication attempts with these studies).

Hoeben Mannaert, Dijkstra, and Zwaan (2017) have recently shown a similar matching effect with sentences that imply a color and the pictures shown are the correct color or a different color, but the correct color varied in the degree of saturation of the color. Matching effects were weaker when the saturation of the correct color was reduced, indicating that the simulations run during comprehension are perceptually

TABLE 5.1

Object Recognition Latencies and Accuracy in Experiment 1 and Picture Naming Times in Experiment 2

Measure	Condition		
	Match	Mismatch	Neutral
	Experiment 1		
Reaction time	697 (202)	761 (210)	—
Percentage correct	97 (6)	93 (7)	—
	Experiment 2		
Reaction time	605 (115)	638 (128)	617 (125)

Note. Standard deviations are given in parentheses. From "Language Comprehenders Mentally Represent the Shapes of Objects," by R. A. Zwaan, R. A. Stanfield, and R. H. Yaxley, 2002, *Psychological Science*, *13*, p. 169. Copyright 2002 by Sage. Reprinted with permission.

rich. Zwaan and Pecher (2012) argued that these results are not due to mental imagery that occurs postcomprehension.

Mental imagery is considered to be a conscious, resource-demanding process, whereas the mental simulation that occurs during comprehension is an automatic process that yields meaning. Zwaan and Pecher (2012) stated that if mental simulation was the same as mental imagery, then the size of the matching effect found in their series of orientation and shape studies would be correlated with mental imagery ability. When they examined participants' correlations between their matching effect sizes and their measured mental imagery ability, they found no such significant correlation. Zwaan and Pecher concluded that the matching effect found in their studies reflects the nonconscious mental simulation process that occurs during comprehension.

Kaschak et al. (2005) used a different paradigm to explore the specificity of the perceptual processing that occurs during the mental simulation of a sentence's meaning. They examined the visual processing that occurs during reading sentences that concern motion. Participants in Kaschak et al.'s study listened to sentences that described motion in a particular direction, for example, "The squirrel scurried away" and "The cat climbed the tree," and they had to make sensibility judgments. While listening to these sentences that implied direction either toward, away, upward, or downward, participants were simultaneously shown visual displays that depicted motion either in the same direction as that described in the sentence (the match condition) or motion in the opposite direction (mismatch condition).

Kaschak et al. (2005) questioned whether the sentences would be processed faster if the visual percept matched the motion described in the sentence, similar to matching effects in many other studies (e.g., Glenberg & Kaschak, 2002; Zwaan & Taylor, 2006). However, they also considered that the processing of the visual percept would use the same neural circuitry needed to understand the sentences that described visual motion and thus would interfere with sentence comprehension. Kaschak et al.'s data showed the latter; sensibility judgements took longer in the match condition than the mismatch condition, demonstrating an interference effect when processing sentences that imply motion in the direction that the comprehender was also visually processing.

The fact that the match condition showed slower sensibility judgments suggested to Kaschak et al. (2005) that there is a high degree of specificity in the perceptual mechanisms recruited for simulations constructed during language comprehension. This was not a general perceptual interference effect; slower response times only occurred in the conditions in which the motion being visually displayed was the same motion described in the sentences being processed. Kaschak et al. concluded that perception of motion engages those neural mechanisms specific to motion in that particular direction. When one constructs a simulation of events that involve motion in that same direction, this requires the identical neural mechanisms used in perception. If these events occur simultaneously, comprehension of the sentence will be impaired because construction of the visual simulation would be difficult (for other visual interference effects during reading, see Fincher-Kiefer, 2001; Fincher-Kiefer & D'Agostino, 2004; for evidence that this relationship between visual processes and simulation is bidirectional, see Meteyard, Bahrami, & Vigliocco, 2007, who found that comprehension of motion words interferes with perceptual detection of motion).

Kaschak, Zwaan, Aveyard, and Yaxley (2006) further examined the conditions for facilitation effects versus interference effects when processing perceptual stimuli and constructing simulations, and they concluded that when congruent stimuli are processed simultaneously, interference will occur due to competition for resources. However, when congruent stimuli are processed consecutively, typically due to one task following another, facilitation will occur because one process has primed another. Although further research is needed to examine the conditions responsible for either facilitation or interference effects, both can be explained by an embodied account of language comprehension that claims that perceptual simulations are integral to establishing meaning.

Neuroscience offers support for these conclusions concerning the nature and specificity of the mental simulations that occur in processing language. Willems et al. (2010) predicted that if understanding a word entails creating a mental simulation of the perception and action used when one experiences that thought, then these neurocognitive representations should differ for people who act on the world differently. For example, left- and right-handers should show different patterns of neural activity when exposed to the word *throw* because they have different brain regions controlling the actual action. Willems et al. gave left- and right-handed participants manual verbs (e.g., grasp, pick) and nonmanual verbs in a lexical-decision task and in a mental imagery task, all while in an fMRI scanner. They found that in the lexical-decision task, left- and right-handers showed contrasting patterns of activity in the premotor cortex contralateral to their dominant hand, but this was true for manual action verbs, not for nonmanual verbs.

They also found that the conscious mental imagery of manual action verbs is subserved by the contralateral motor areas of the brain responsible for planning and executing these actions. However, this body-specific pattern of activity was found in both the premotor cortex and the primary motor cortex during the mental imagery task and only in the premotor cortex during lexical decisions. This dissociation between the patterns of activity found in the lexical decision task and the mental imagery task suggests that the implicit simulation used in the semantic decision for the lexical decision is not the same as explicit mental imagery.

Willems et al. (2010) concluded that the action schema used in a simulation during language processing is probably less elaborated and less specific than that used in mental imagery. For example, the simulation of "throw" may involve a more general action plan that involves an action, actor, object, and target, whereas mental imagery of "throw" would have to involve a specific type of throw and a specific object's trajectory, and so forth. Willems, Labruna, D'Esposito, Ivry, and Casasanto (2011) followed up this fMRI research with a TMS study to examine whether a causal relationship exists between the motor activity found in the premotor cortex during the lexical decision task and the semantic analysis of the action word.

Using only right-handed participants, Willems et al. (2010) found that lexical decision times were faster to manual action verbs after stimulation of the hand area in the left premotor cortex compared with after stimulation of the hand area in the right premotor cortex. This pattern of differential facilitation for lexical decision response times did not occur for nonmanual action verbs, suggesting a functional role of premotor cortex activity in action–language understanding. It appears that people with different bodies perform actions in different ways, resulting in different neural pathways representing the meaning of action words.

One criticism of this experimental investigation of simulation that occurs during language comprehension is that typically the studies have focused on the grounding of single words or simple sentences. However, when we think about language comprehension, surely we are thinking about a more expansive view of language. Zwaan (2014) argued that making claims about grounded representations when text is decontextualized (as with single words or even individual sentences) is problematic because if we are to understand language comprehension, we really need to know whether symbolic representations and grounded representations play a role in extended discourse.

In addressing this criticism, research by Nijhof and Willems (2015) attempted to examine a richer representation of language comprehension. Nijhof and Willems examined the comprehension of discourse from the perspective of what type of language is used in the text, what different kinds of simulations might be involved in comprehension, and even what individual differences may suggest about the nature of the simulations used for understanding. To do this they used fMRI imaging to investigate individual differences in the comprehension of literary fiction. Three stories were broken into sections that were either high in action and visual content or were high in presenting the thoughts, beliefs, and intentions of the characters. These represented the two different types of simulations that could occur during reading—sensorimotor simulations, which occur when readers process text information about action or scenery, versus the simulation of another's thoughts and motivations, which has been referred to as *mentalizing* (Frith & Frith, 2006). Prior research has shown that while activation in the left and right motor cortices is associated with sensorimotor simulations (e.g., Speer, Reynolds, Swallow, & Zacks, 2009; Willems & Casasanto, 2011; Willems, Hagoort, & Casasanto, 2010), activation in the anterior prefrontal cortex, right temporoparietal junction, and precuneus occurs during mentalizing (e.g., Frith & Frith, 2006; Van Overwalle & Baetens, 2009).

While their participants were reading fiction, Nijhof and Willems (2015) found that there were strong individual differences in the types of simulations used during comprehension: Some readers showed high activation in the mentalizing areas of the brain (anterior medial prefrontal cortex) when reading about characters' goals and intentions, but low activity in the premotor cortices when reading about action or scenery. Other readers showed the exact opposite pattern—high activity in the premotor cortices when processing action or sensory text but low activity in the mentalizing areas when reading about the characters' thoughts. Nijhof and Willems argued that this online neural evidence indicates different reading preferences among individuals. Some individuals engage in literature by thinking about the characters' beliefs and goals, etc., whereas others engage by simulating the more concrete aspects of what they are reading, perhaps the sights, sounds, and actions being described.

This preliminary evidence from Nijhof and Willems' (2015) examination of extended text suggests that the types of simulations constructed during comprehension may vary depending on variables such as preferences, goals, expertise, even type of discourse. There is much to be explored in the investigation of simulations used to understand language, but the empirical findings to date suggest that these simulations will be neurological activity that represents reuse of prior perceptual, action-based, or even imagined experiences with the world.

Conclusions

When we ask if language is embodied, we are asking whether the body plays a role in the comprehension of the linguistic symbols we use to convey meaning. The body may play a role directly, as seen, for example, when we impair the body (by disease or injections of Botox) and find that language processing is impaired as well. Or the body may play a role indirectly, in that a reenactment of a prior bodily experience, called a *simulation*, allows us to give meaning to text. There is empirical support for both of these paths in language comprehension.

When we process the linguistic information, "kick," for example, comprehension of that verb entails recruitment of the motor system used to physically enact that action (e.g., Hauk, Johnsrude, & Pulvermüller, 2004), and when we read words and sentences involving emotion, understanding involves an internal simulation of that emotional state (e.g., Havas, Glenberg, & Rinck, 2007). There is now strong empirical evidence across behavioral studies as well as brain-imaging studies to support this claim that language comprehension involves sensorimotor simulations of previous bodily experiences.

There are two issues that require more attention as we move forward in our understanding of language comprehension. First, a challenge for embodiment theory has always been to explain how abstract language is grounded in the body. Action-based language has been an obvious test bed for the investigation of the role of the body in comprehension of linguistic symbols. It is more difficult to investigate body-action effects in abstract language, where there is no obvious linkage to the body.

The following chapters will address this challenge for embodiment theory and explain how the mental representations of abstract concepts are grounded in sensorimotor systems. Earlier discussion touched on this issue with abstract concepts that have to do with transfer, and evidence suggests that these abstract concepts are grounded in bodily action in the same way that concrete concepts about transfer are grounded. Vigliocco and colleagues (e.g., Kousta, Vigliocco, Vinson, Andrews, & Del Campo, 2011; and Vigliocco et al., 2014) have fascinating behavioral and neuroscience support for the contention that abstract concepts are grounded in emotion to even a greater extent than many concrete concepts. Chapter 8 also provides evidence that other abstract concepts may be grounded in sensorimotor systems through the linguistic device of metaphor, which establishes a link between an abstract concept (e.g., kindness) that has no direct link to the body, with a concrete concept (e.g., warmth) that does ("She is so warm").

The second issue to be addressed is whether grounded representations are sufficient to fully explain language comprehension. Zwaan (2014) argued for a pluralistic view of language comprehension that involves both symbolic representations of meaning as well as grounded representations. His argument is that there are times in which language is being processed where it is appropriate for grounded representations to be most available, for example, during demonstrations, where agents, objects, gestures, and other actions are all involved in the communication, and sensorimotor simulations are needed for comprehension. However, there may be other occasions, for example when reading highly abstract text such as philosophical arguments or scientific articles, where the initial representation of meaning may involve abstract symbols. Another factor involved in what form of representation best yields meaning may be expertise, such that experts processing language about their skill would have more sensorimotor experiences to call on than novices, yielding grounded representations for experts but either symbolic representations or impoverished grounded representations for novices. This may explain why novices have such poor understanding of language outside of their expertise. Other variables such as processing goals (how "shallow" can the comprehension be to suffice for understanding) and linguistic skills will determine the interplay between symbolic and grounded representations.

Zwaan argued that these two forms of representation are simultaneously active, but multiple factors will dictate which form of representation is dominate. Other investigators have also argued for an interaction between symbolic and grounded representations during text comprehension, especially as it pertains to connected discourse or more naturalistic language comprehension (Barsalou & Wiemer-Hastings, 2005; Bottini, Bucur, & Crepaldi, 2016; Lebois, Wilson-Mendenhall, & Barsalou, 2015; Louwerse, 2011; Taylor & Zwaan, 2009). Clearly, there is much more work to be done. However, a merging of more traditional, semantic networks of knowledge and grounded representations into a theoretical framework that considers when each are needed, will likely move us forward in understanding how we achieve meaning from language.

Takeaway

- The neural systems used for sensing and acting are the same systems used for understanding language.
- The words (symbols) in a language gain their meaning by being initially linked (developmentally, evolutionarily) to the systems used for perception, action, and emotion (Glenberg, Barsalou).

The Role of Simulation in Cognitive Judgments

6

Questions:

- What evidence supports the view that our perceptual knowledge and our conceptual knowledge share the same representational system?
- Does simulation, or the reenactment of prior sensory and physical experiences, constitute thinking?

The focus of the previous chapters in this book has been on the role of the body in cognition. This is a perspective that many embodied theorists have adopted, and the evidence to support this perspective is quite clear—bodily states play causal roles in some cognitive states, and bodily states are also the effects of some cognitive states (e.g., Glenberg, 1997).

Another perspective, and one that is not antagonistic to this body-centered perspective, emphasizes that cognition is the simulation of prior experiential states involving sensation, perception, motor activity, or introspection. This simulation, or reenactment of a previous experience, is dependent on the prior activity of the body and the mind—thus, these two perspectives are integrally related. This chapter and the next will present evidence that thought is represented in perceptual symbols; that is, that our knowledge is stored in the same neural systems that are active when the information was initially perceived (Barsalou, 1999). It will then be imperative to find evidence that

http://dx.doi.org/10.1037/0000136-006
How the Body Shapes Knowledge: Empirical Support for Embodied Cognition, by R. Fincher-Kiefer
Copyright © 2019 by the American Psychological Association. All rights reserved.

simulation, or the reuse of the neural pathways that perceived the information, is what constitutes thought—and that this may or may not involve one's physical body.

Barsalou's Perspective

Barsalou's (1999) seminal paper titled "Perceptual Symbol Systems" detailed his perceptual symbol systems (PSS) theory, which was a dramatic shift from the standard theories of cognition that tested an earlier hypothesis of knowledge representation called the *physical symbol system hypothesis* (PSSH; Newell & Simon, 1976). Simply put, this PSSH view was that memory consisted of physical symbols (often likened to memory cells in computers that store patterns of zeros and ones) that were amodal and had representational properties that "stood in" for real properties like color, emotion, or action. Collins and Loftus's (1975) semantic network theory of semantic memory discussed in Chapter 1 and represented in Figures 1.1 and 1.2 was one such PSSH model. These physical, abstract symbols were manipulated by rules, similar to if–then statements in computer languages, and importantly, they were arbitrarily related to what they referred to (e.g., just as a sequence of zeros and ones may be used in a computer to represent the concept *cat*, the mental symbol for cat would in no way sound like, look like, or act like a cat; see Glenberg, Witt, & Metcalfe, 2013, for a richer description of PSSH theories of cognition).

The problem with PSSH theories of cognition was that they worked well for computers, but they were not intuitively pleasing as a theory of human knowledge representation. Even prior to cognitive psychologists examining the theory of embodied cognition, non-PSSH models of knowledge were being constructed and were striving for representations of concepts that were at least traceable to referents in the world (i.e., were grounded; McClelland & Elman, 1986; Eich, 1985; Murdock, 1982). These models of knowledge were attempting to capture how representations of concepts could be likened to neural layers that responded to the outside world (again, the essence of being grounded) and could be structured in a way that made sense for semantic memory.

Barsalou's (1999, 2008a, 2008b) PSS theory was also a reaction to PSSH models, and it provided a very different view of knowledge representation. Barsalou defined the grounding of knowledge by proposing that concepts are represented in modality-specific perceptual symbols, not abstract symbols such as words or propositions, and these serve perception and action. Mental activity cannot be separated from the physical, bodily context in which those thoughts occurred. In fact, Barsalou (1999) stated that cognition is "inherently perceptual" in that a perceptual state arises with any sensorimotor activity. For example, when an experience occurs (his example is sitting in a chair), our brain will record a nonconscious neural representation of that physical experience that is multimodal. There may be a tactile experience of the chair's texture, a visual experience, a motor action from sitting in the chair, even an introspective record of comfort or lack thereof. There may also be an optional conscious experience that is associated with the perceptual state.

As Figure 6.1 illustrates, Barsalou (1999) claimed that some part of this perceptual state is "extracted" and results in a long-term memory representation. It is important to note that a critical aspect of this conceptualization is that the long-term memory is of the same representational format as the perceptual state, that is, neural activity that occurred during the original perceptual experience. This is the *analogue modal symbol*, and any time after this, when information about a chair needs to be retrieved, that perceptual symbol functions symbolically as a referent for conceptual knowledge about chairs. This perceptual symbol may be an extraction of all the relevant perceptual and sensorimotor features of the many chairs we have experienced.

Barsalou (1999) stated, "As collections of perceptual symbols develop, they constitute the representations that underlie cognition" (p. 578). In other words, all of our cognitive representations are at their core perceptual symbols. The core computational process of *thinking* is a simulation, or reenactment, of that neural activity that was associated with the sensorimotor formation of that thought. It should be pointed out that Barsalou stated that simulations do not necessarily fully recreate the experience at learning; in fact, most simulations are partial recreations of these initial experiences, and that is why the retrieval of knowledge often contains bias and error.

Barsalou argued that these perceptual symbols are multimodal (e.g., acoustic, haptic, visual), which counters more traditional models of semantic memory that argued for amodal symbol systems. Figure 6.2, also taken from Barsalou's (1999) seminal paper, illustrates another version of knowledge representation where the

FIGURE 6.1

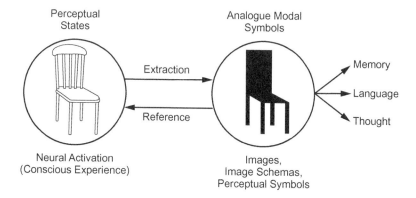

Perceptual Symbol Systems

The basic assumption underlying perceptual symbol systems: Subsets of perceptual states in sensory-motor systems are extracted and stored in long-term memory to function as symbols. From "Perceptual Symbol Systems," by L. W. Barsalou, 1999, *Behavior and Brain Sciences, 22*, p. 578. Copyright 1999 by Cambridge University Press. Reprinted with permission.

FIGURE 6.2

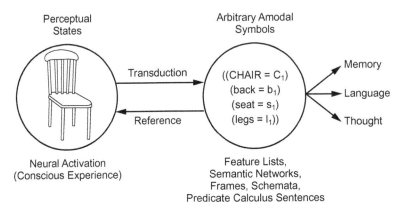

Amodal Symbol Systems

The basic assumption underlying amodal symbol systems: Perceptual states are transduced into a completely new representational system that describes these states amodally. From "Perceptual Symbol Systems," by L. W. Barsalou, 1999, *Behavior and Brain Sciences, 22,* p. 579. Copyright 1999 by Cambridge University Press. Reprinted with permission.

perceptual states that one initially experiences are then "transduced" into a different representational format. This is a *propositional,* or *amodal,* format, and these then form the representations of knowledge that are retrieved from memory when needed. These amodal symbols are linked arbitrarily to the perceptual states to which they refer; in other words, the word *chair* has no representational similarity to a physical chair. Semantic network theorists do not assume that words literally constitute the content of these amodal representations, but some linguistic form does (i.e., propositions). This is in direct opposition to the PSS view where the representation of a concept is constitutively identical to the perceptual state it is representing, with a linguistic label associated with it.

Barsalou (2008a) stated that it was only in the last 15 to 20 years that researchers began to rigorously test the earlier, widely accepted, PSSH view that knowledge is represented in amodal symbols. In general, the claims of that view were used to develop computer models of semantic memory, which often behaved in ways that appeared phenomenologically appropriate to human memory (e.g., J. R. Anderson's, 1974, fan effect, which was intuitively appealing as a memory effect and was supported in some experimental work). However, in the experimental tests of the semantic network theories, there has been an accumulation of evidence that questions the amodal or propositional representation of knowledge. Instead, the experimental work suggests that bodily states and simulations of those bodily states play a critical role in cognition, ushering in the theory of embodied cognition. Barsalou preferred the phrase *grounded cognition* to *embodied cognition* because, as he stated, the latter tends to emphasize the *necessity* of external bodily states to cognition, whereas the former recognizes that cognition may be represented in multiple ways. These could include bodily states but could also include internal states such as meta-cognition, introspection, and imaging—all simulations that can proceed independently of the body.

Evidence for Perceptual Symbol Systems

Evidence for PSS can be found in neuroimaging results that show that when conceptual knowledge about objects is processed or retrieved, brain areas that represent properties occurring during perception or action become active. Martin (2007) presented a wealth of neuroimaging results that demonstrate significant overlap in the neural pathways used for perceiving, acting on, and knowing about objects. When conceptual knowledge about objects is presented in a task, brain areas become active that represent their particular properties during perception (e.g., shape and color in the fusiform gyrus) and action associated with the object (e.g., grasping or kicking in the premotor and parietal areas). This supports the tenet of grounded cognition that object concepts are represented in the neural pathways used for perception and action (Barsalou, 1999, 2008a, 2008b).

Neuropsychologists have found evidence, using patients that have lesions to certain brain areas, for the claim that conceptual knowledge is represented in the same neural pathways used for sensorimotor processing of that knowledge. For example, the temporal lobes may be a critical site for stored representations about concrete objects as damage to the left posterior temporal cortex, responsible for auditory processing, results in a loss of conceptual object knowledge (Hart & Gordon, 1990; Martin, 2007). Additionally, specific object knowledge is often lost with other types of brain lesions (e.g., Cree & McRae, 2003; Gainotti, 2006; Humphreys & Forde, 2001).

For example, damage to visual areas (occipital lobes) increases the likelihood of loss of animal knowledge, presumably because visual processing is the dominate modality for interaction with this category. Damage to motor areas increases the likelihood of losing knowledge about tools, given motor processing is the dominate modality of interacting with these objects. This lesion evidence is consistent with the neuroimaging evidence that has been found when *processing* conceptual knowledge: When individuals read about, hear, or imagine animals, visual brain centers are especially active, but when people process information about tools and manipulable objects, motor areas are active (Bub & Masson, 2012; Chao & Martin, 2000). Similarly, when people process food information in the absence of eating, gustatory areas become active (Simmons, Martin, & Barsalou, 2005), and olfactory areas are active when people process words or objects that represent smell (González et al., 2006). Martin (2007) also described evidence that sensorimotor properties are often in different brain areas for different categories of knowledge. For example, different brain areas represent motion for animate versus inanimate objects.

These data suggest that concept knowledge is distributed across brain areas that represent different aspects of properties and actions associated with that concept. However, it has been argued that the brain activation found in these types of studies may be incidental to conceptual representations rather than a functional part of the conceptual representation (Mahon & Caramazza, 2008). Yee, Chrysikou, Hoffman, and Thompson-Schill (2013) argued that if sensorimotor representations are conceptual representations, then evidence should exist for a bidirectional relationship. This would mean conceptual knowledge should produce sensorimotor activity and sensorimotor activity should elicit conceptual knowledge. Thus, hearing the name of a manipulable object may activate the motor pattern associated with grasping, for example, but activating the motor pattern associated with grasping should also partially activate that object concept. Further, if for some reason it is difficult to activate the motor pattern associated with an object, then it should be difficult to think about that object. (Chapter 5 presents some data that support this prediction. Individuals who have motor deficiencies, for example, those with amyotrophic lateral sclerosis (ALS), do have difficulty retrieving concept knowledge that involves motoric actions.)

Yee et al. (2013) tested this hypothesis that sensorimotor activity should elicit concept knowledge by using an interference paradigm that blocked the motor actions used with certain objects. They predicted blocking certain motor actions would interfere with accessing concept knowledge. They also predicted that the extent to which a motor representation functionally represents a concept should depend on the amount of motoric experience one has had with that object. Therefore, the more experience one has with the object, the greater the impact of blocking the motor pattern on thinking about that object.

In Experiment 1, Yee et al. (2013) had participants making simple cognitive judgments about words presented on a screen ("Is this word concrete or abstract?"). Some of these words were objects that are frequently manipulated (e.g., toothbrush), whereas other words were infrequently manipulated objects (e.g., antenna). Although participants were making these cognitive judgments, they either performed a manual "patty-cake" task (these hand motions would be impossible to make while also making the motions associated with the presented word) or they performed a mental rotation task for abstract shapes. Participants also heard the concrete words again at the end of the experiment and indicated how much experience they had touching the object. Yee et al. found that when participants' hands were engaged in the manual patty-cake task, it took longer to think about those objects that are frequently manipulated (i.e., make quick, accurate, concrete/abstract judgments) compared with objects that are infrequently manipulated. Further, Yee et al. found that the amount of experience interacting with an object determined the degree of this interference effect.

Experiment 2 used the same interfering tasks of manual action or mental rotation, but changed the primary task from making concrete/abstract judgments, which entail an imagining of the object to make the decision, to a picture naming task, which bypasses the imaging stage of processing and more directly elicits the conceptual representation of the object. Yee et al. (2013) found that the manual task again interfered with the ability to think about frequently manipulated objects; specifically, it interfered with participants' ability to produce those objects' names. As in Experiment 1, the degree to which the manual task interfered with the picture naming was related to how much experience participants had touching the object.

Yee et al.'s (2013) results suggest that the motor activation found in previous studies is not merely incidental to the representation of knowledge about an object. Their studies show that engaging the motor areas associated with an object concept makes it difficult to think about the object. If processing "toothbrush" activates a motor area of the brain and if activating that same general motor area for a different purpose interferes with the processing of the concept "toothbrush," this bidirectional relationship indicates that the motor area activity is a functional part of the representation of the object concept.

The research presented to this point focuses on evidence that the same sensorimotor systems that initially processed any stimuli are the systems that also represent that information conceptually. Another aspect of this PSS view is that simulation is the core computational process of cognition. This means that although these representations of thought are grounded in our neural networks that were used in perception and action, they become available to us through the simulation, or reenactment, of the same processes used to create the representations. Evidence for simulation comes from quite disparate areas of psychological research.

Evidence for Simulation From Cognitive Tasks

Barsalou (1999) has argued that simulations are not only partial reenactments of the initial processing of a concept, but also componential, that is, not holistic. He claimed that simulations are not like video recordings of a past experience, but instead they contain many elements of a perceptual experience and sometimes these components are organized differently than other times. Although perceptual symbols can represent all modalities (vision, audition, touch, smell, action, emotion, etc.), they vary in accessibility from one thought to the next. Pecher, Zeelenberg, and Barsalou (2003) examined the hypothesis that if representations of concept knowledge are multimodal, then simulations of that knowledge may vary in terms of which modality is the focus of the simulation. For example, there may be situations where the visual aspect of a concept is most salient (e.g., cranberries are red), but other times the simulation may focus on the taste aspect of this concept (e.g., cranberries are tart).

To test whether conceptual representations are perceptual representations but vary by which modality is salient, Pecher et al. (2003) borrowed a paradigm from the perceptual literature that demonstrated that there are "costs" to switching between perceptual modalities (e.g., from vision to audition). Spence, Nicholls, and Driver (2001) had participants detecting a signal that was in one of three modalities: vision (a light), audition (a tone), or touch (a touch on a finger). Participants had to indicate whether these signals were presented on the right or the left of the participant, and sometimes consecutive signals were in the same modality and sometimes they were in different modalities. Spence et al. found that when the signals were presented consecutively in different modalities (e.g., a light was presented followed by a tone), there was a "cost" in processing—participants' reaction times for signal detection were slower than when the signals were presented consecutively in the same modality. Pecher et al. reasoned that if conceptual processing involves sensorimotor simulations, then using this Spence et al. paradigm, we may see that there are analogous "switching costs" in conceptual processing when moving from one modality to the next.

Pecher et al. (2003) gave participants a property-verification task. On each trial, participants had to respond "yes" or "no" to whether a property was true for a certain concept, and this property was in one of six modalities. For example, they had to verify whether a "blender was loud" (auditory modality) or whether "peanut butter is sticky" (touch modality). For some trials, the verification task had been preceded by a verification trial for a different concept but from the same modality, and on other trials, the trial that preceded the verification task asked for verification of a property from a different modality.

Pecher et al. (2003) predicted that if conceptual and perceptual processing behave similarly (because they are using the same representational system), there would be switching costs in conceptual processing when back-to-back trials concerned different modalities. Results supported this prediction: Response times were slower on trials in which the modality switched from one trial to the next compared with when the trials stayed in the same modality. Thus, switching modalities in conceptual processing incurred processing costs, just as did switching modalities in perceptual processing, suggesting that modality-specific brain areas represent properties of conceptual knowledge. Further, because the switching costs in this study occurred not with perceptual stimuli (lights and tones) but with linguistic stimuli (words), this indicates that linguistic processing elicits sensorimotor simulations, which are perceptual in nature.

Van Dantzig, Pecher, Zeelenberg, and Barsalou (2008) extended the findings of Pecher et al. (2003) by having participants perform a perceptual detection task ("Is the light/tone/vibration on your left or your right?") followed by a property-verification task ("Do leaves rustle?"). Results of this study demonstrated that this *modality-switch effect* found in Pecher et al. also occurs between perceptual and conceptual processing. Response times to the property-verification tasks were slower when the modality in that task was different from the modality in the perceptual detection task that preceded it compared with when both tasks were in the same modality.

Van Dantzig et al. (2008) suggested that their results indicate that perceptual processing (simply detecting perceptual stimuli) can affect the activation of conceptual knowledge. This supports the grounded cognition hypothesis that perceptual and conceptual processing are at least partially based on the same representational systems. This modality-switch effect reflects an interference effect: low-level perceptual processing needed for detecting a simple stimulus disrupted the construction of a mental simulation needed for the conceptual task of property verification. The activation of modality-specific brain areas to perform conceptual processing in the property-verification task is difficult to explain within an amodal symbol system that has typically explained property-verification response times through associative links between concepts (however, see Solomon & Barsalou, 2004, for boundary conditions for this effect).

Evidence for Simulation
From Memory Research

Evidence for multimodal representations of conceptual knowledge has come from memory research that demonstrates that during encoding, perceptual symbols may be stored in memory for a concept (e.g., for visual or auditory aspects). Later, when a similar concept is perceived, this will trigger the simulation of the perceptual states that were stored with the earlier memory. This leads to perceptual inferences, or perceptions that go beyond the perceived stimuli in interesting ways. For example, Hansen, Olkkonen, Walter, and Gegenfurtner (2006) found that when showing participants objects that had prototypical colors (e.g., yellow for banana), simulations of the object's natural color distorted the achromatic (i.e., gray) perception of the object toward the opponent color (i.e., a bluish banana). Similarly, when perceiving motion, viewers will simulate an object's trajectory beyond its actual trajectory (because of stored perceptual memories), and will then falsely remember that simulated motion (e.g., Stevens, Fonlupt, Shiffrar, & Decety, 2000). Even lexical knowledge produces simulations that result in speech perception effects, such as when phoneme gaps in sentences go unnoticed in speech perception due to the "phonemic restoration effect" (Warren, 1970). This classic result that has been interpreted as evidence for top-down knowledge effects may now be interpreted as the result of a simulation run due to prior experience with that phonetically incomplete word.

Barsalou (2008a) also suggested that implicit memory effects may be understood as simulations similarly to these perceptual inferences. Repetition priming for non-consciously processed stimuli may be explained by the fact that once a stimulus, for example, a face, is perceptually processed, then a simulation of that prior exposure occurs when asked to process that face again. This will result in responding to that second exposure quickly and accurately compared with a face that has not been processed perceptually (Schacter, Dobbins, & Schnyer, 2004). Further, repetition priming is strongest when the modality of the memory and the perceived stimulus match (e.g., Jacoby & Hayman, 1987), providing evidence of shared representational formats.

Explicit memory effects can also be seen as a function of PSS representations. Wheeler, Petersen, and Buckner (2000) used neuroimaging after a very simple learning experiment to find strong support for sensorimotor simulations in explicit memory. Wheeler et al. had participants learn a set of picture and sound items and then recall them while being scanned in a functional magnetic resonance imaging machine. Regions of the visual cortex were active when recalling what the pictures were, but regions of the auditory cortex were active when recalling the sound items. Thus, retrieval of learned information involves reactivation of the same sensory pathways that were used when initially perceiving that information. Additionally, Slotnick and Schacter (2004) found that it is possible to detect the "sensory signature" of a true memory and that true recognition of abstract shapes yielded greater visual cortical activity than false recognition of a visually similar lure.

Simulation also can explain some classic memory effects. An encoded stimulus will be represented in the modal area of the initial perception, and thus memory for that stimulus will be best if retrieved in that same modality than in a different modality (e.g., the encoding specificity effect; Tulving & Thomson, 1973). Further, reinstating actions performed at encoding during retrieval facilitates the memory for those actions (Engelkamp, Zimmer, Mohr, & Sellen, 1994), again demonstrating the benefit of overlap in the specificity of the sensorimotor representation generated at encoding and the simulation run at retrieval.

Evidence for Simulation From Developmental Literature

Evidence that infants' concept knowledge develops from bodily (motoric) actions, and that these simulations of prior motor routines are used in infants' decision making, can be found in typical errors infants commit. Rivière (2014) reviewed action choice errors in children and discussed *scale errors*, which is any error committed by children between 18 and 36 months of age where they try to fit their bodies into objects that are much too small for them. DeLoache, Uttal, and Rosengren (2004) found that scale errors are made spontaneously in the course of daily activity (e.g., trying to sit on a miniature toy chair) and are accompanied by true frustration and often despair when a child's action attempts are not successful. In Barsalou's (1999) terms, the simulation of the motor action associated with the perceptual symbol for the object (i.e., sitting in a chair) occurred automatically with the perception of the object, causing the action error (this is the kind of error that occurs with partial simulations). Giving an embodied explanation for this error, DeLoache et al. claimed that these action errors are due to a failure to inhibit the motor routine that would be successful with a full-sized version of the object.

Another common action error is referred to as the *A-not-B error*, committed by children between 7 and 12 months of age. This occurs when a child has successfully uncovered a hidden object (typically a small toy hidden underneath a slightly larger cloth) in an initial location (location A) but then the experimenter, in full view of the child, hides the object in a nearby location (location B). If given a short delay between hiding the object and allowing the child to search for it, the error that occurs is that the child continues to search in the old location despite the visual cues of the object being in the new location. Clearfield, Diedrich, Smith, and Thelen (2006) agreed with other developmentalists who argued that this common error is due to a stable motor pattern established from previous perceptual-motor activities in which reaching for objects was successful. As with scale errors, the reenactment of motor activity dictated the decision making in this task, but importantly, the motor activity also represents the child's understanding of location and object permanence.

Interestingly, when Clearfield et al. (2006) tracked infants' behavior on this A-not-B task on a monthly basis, they found that infants reached correctly at 5 months of age but made the error later in their development, beginning around 7 or 8 months. They suggested that reaching at the younger age was not well coordinated enough to establish a strong motor memory (pattern of neural activity), allowing this age to actually perform the search task correctly. This is evidence for the A-not-B error being due to an inability to suppress the simulation of prior motoric activity that was established in long-term memory.

Rivière (2014) presents one more action error that reflects embodiment in children's choices. The C-not-B error is a three-location search task that involves an experimenter showing a child a toy in his or her hand and then having that hand disappear under three cloths (A, B, and C). The experimenter releases the toy under the B cloth, which makes a visible bump, but continues to move his or her hand under the C cloth. Children around the age of 2.5 years tend to commit the search error of looking for the object under the last cloth that the experimenter's hand passed under, C, ignoring the visual information at location B. This C-not-B error has been explained by Rivière and Lécuyer (2003) as due to children applying a motor routine, or simulation, that represents their knowledge at that time that an object will be where its "container" (in this case, the experimenter's hand) was last seen.

In support of this explanation, Rivière and Lécuyer (2008) discovered that the error was not found when they placed small arm weights on the arms of the children during the task. They suggested that the success in the task with the arm weights resulted from the disruption of the automatic motor simulation that occurs when perceiving the hand movements of the C-not-B task. Other studies have also disrupted children's "normal" motor routine used in the C-not-B task by, for example, having children reach with a stick instead of with their arm, or by placing a see-through barrier in the path of the reaching movement so children have to reach over it. These changes, that presumably alter the simulation of the motor activity typically used for this task, have allowed children to perform successfully (Rivière & David, 2013).

Finally, Rivière and Lécuyer (2003) found that children with spinal muscular atrophy, a hereditary neuromuscular disorder that results in severe motor impairments, were significantly superior to age-matched control children on the A-not-B and C-not-B tasks. Rivière and Lécuyer claimed that children who have difficulty forming consistent motor memories, due to age or disability, are more likely to succeed on these action-based choices, strengthening the claim that the typical errors found in these developmental tasks are the result of simulations of prior motor actions inappropriately applied to these tasks.

Evidence for Simulation From Skilled Performance

Evidence that sensorimotor simulations are representations of thought, in other words, have *meaning*, can be found in interesting research with adults that explores the effects of skilled actions. Yang, Gallo, and Beilock (2009) chose the domain of typing to examine whether skilled typists would experience motor fluency for some letter sequences depending on the ease of actually typing the letters and whether this motor fluency (i.e., a simulation of typing) would constitute a mental representation. If so, what would be the consequences for memory of this motor fluency?

In their first experiment, Yang et al. (2009) had skilled and novice typists study a list of two-letter sequences (dyads) that were either easy to type (because the letters would be typed with a different finger) or difficult to type (because the letters would be typed with the same finger). The participants saw the dyads but did not type them; the instructions were only to indicate whether they "liked" them by responding with a verbal "yes" or "no." Following the presentation of the dyads, participants were given a surprise recognition test, in which they indicated whether a dyad was old or new.

Yang et al. (2009) found that for expert typists, recognition memory performance was influenced by how easy it would be to type the dyads even though no typing was involved (and participants were unaware that the study had to do with typing). Dyads that were easy to type were more often misrecognized as old compared with dyads difficult to type, but this effect only occurred with expert typists and not novices. This indicates that this motor fluency effect was due to an automatic simulation, developed through experience, of the motor plan for typing these dyads. That simulation resulted in a memory representation for that dyad. When other easy-to-type dyads were presented at recognition, the motor fluency prompted a partial simulation of the dyads presented and biased the participant to make an "old" response, even though the letters themselves had not been presented. This is another example of how a memory effect can be explained in terms of a simulation of prior bodily action (but no actual bodily action), and in this case, how partial simulations can explain biases and errors.

In a second experiment, Yang et al. (2009) tested the hypothesis that if this motor fluency effect on recognition was due to an online simulation of typing, then having participants perform another motor task right after the presentation of the dyad should interfere with the simulation and should reduce the effect. Further, the simulation that occurs with the presentation of the dyads would have to be very specific, so only a secondary task that uses the same fingers needed for typing should interfere with this covert simulation. Yang et al. gave expert and novice typists the dyads list, but this time, prior to the recognition test, one group of participants was given a motor task to perform that required the same fingers used for typing the dyads and another group was given a motor task that involved fingers that would not be involved in typing the letters. Yang et al. found the same motor fluency effect in recognition that occurred in their first experiment, but only in the condition in which the secondary motor task involved different fingers needed for typing the letters in the dyads. When the secondary task did involve the same fingers needed for typing the letters, the motor fluency effect in recognition was eliminated. These findings were found for expert typists, but novice typists showed no motor fluency effects in any condition in either experiment.

These results suggest that when simply perceiving these letter dyads, expert typists who have developed associations between letters and the fingers used to type them automatically simulate the actions involved in typing. This covert simulation produces motor fluency for these dyads, and this fluency impacts recognition judgments, in this case, false recognition of nonstudied items. This is an example of when the motor system affects memory by providing information about fluency in action even when no action had been explicitly involved. In other words, this is evidence for simulation without the involvement of the body itself.

Typing on a keyboard and typing on a cell phone has become a convenient action to examine in studies investigating simulations that activate mental representations. Topolinski's (2011) study used cell phones that, at that time, had keypads with digits and letters on the keys (see Figure 6.3). Given how ubiquitous typing text messages is, Topolinski wanted to examine whether typing sequences of numbers on a cell phone would activate the mental simulation of that sequence of associated letters, resulting in the activation of the meaning of a word (for example, 5683 and LOVE). Figure 6.4 is a picture of the cell phone used in the studies where only the digits were shown on the keys so that participants could not consciously recognize the words that were associated with the digit sequences they were typing.

Half of the participants in this study were asked to dial number sequences on the cell phone and immediately after doing so had to perform a lexical decision task on a computer screen in front of them. Some of the letter strings for this task corresponded to the words that would have corresponded to the digit/letter sequences that they had

FIGURE 6.3

Illustration of a cell-phone keypad. On cell phones, digits and letters are assigned to keys using an international standard, the E.161 assignment (International Telecommunication Union, 2001). From "I 5683 You: Dialing Phone Numbers on Cell Phones Activates Key-Concordant Concepts," by S. Topolinski, 2011, *Psychological Science, 22,* p. 356. Copyright 2011 by Sage. Reprinted with permission.

FIGURE 6.4

Cell phone used in the studies. So that participants would not consciously recognize the letter sequences that corresponded with the digit sequences they dialed, labels depicting digits only were pasted over the keys depicting both digits and letters. From "I 5683 You: Dialing Phone Numbers on Cell Phones Activates Key-Concordant Concepts," by S. Topolinski, 2011, *Psychological Science, 22*, p. 356. Copyright 2011 by Sage. Reprinted with permission.

typed but other letter strings were words not implied by that digit sequence. The other half of the participants typed the number sequence on the number pad of a computer keyboard, which has never had letters on the keypad. Results demonstrated that for the participants in the cell phone-dialing condition but not the computer-keyboard condition, words were responded to more quickly if participants had dialed that word's number sequence. It is important to note that during the debriefing, participants responded that they were unaware that the digit sequences implied words or that the letter sequences in the lexical decision task matched those words. Additionally, this response time effect was larger for "expert" text message typists or those participants who sent more text messages than other participants.

These results suggest that dialing numbers on that type of cell-phone keypad resulted in an "action effect" such that the associated letter sequence was mentally simulated, outside of conscious awareness, and integrated into a meaningful concept. Because this effect was related to expertise in typing text messages, this suggests that sensorimotor learning resulted in a consistent mapping of digits and letters, resulting in these simulated action effects. Another two experiments in Topolinski's (2011) study examined whether these simulations of letter sequences that come from dialing a digit sequence and result in the activation of a word's meaning also activate the emotional valence of those words. In Experiment 2, participants gave preference ratings for what they believed were random number sequences, and results showed that participants preferred dialing numbers that implied positive words (e.g., 373863, FRIEND) over dialing numbers that implied negative words (e.g., 26478, FEAR). (It should be noted that these are the English translations for the key-concordant German words used in this research.)

In a third experiment, Topolinski (2011) examined whether dialing numbers of key-concordant words that matched a dimension of a company (e.g., 25863, FLOWER for a florist) would shape participant's attitudes about that company. Results in fact did show that participants preferred companies with digit sequences that had letter sequences activating words that matched a dimension of the company. As in the other experiments, none of the participants reported a suspicion that the digit sequences were related to words or to any affective meanings. The results of these studies demonstrate that the mental simulation that automatically and nonconsciously occurs after typing digits on this kind of cell phone involves the activation of letters associated with those digits *and* the integration of those letters into a mental representation that has meaning (a word).

It also has been shown that the motor action of typing on a keyboard may influence our attitudes about words that we already know and may actually shape the meaning of new words (Casasanto, Jasmin, Brookshire, & Gijssels, 2014; Jasmin & Casasanto, 2012). Jasmin and Casasanto's (2012) research links some of the bodily effects presented in Chapter 3 concerning Casasanto's (2009, 2011) body specificity hypothesis (that body dominance determines emotional valence) with some of the simulation action effects of typing presented in this chapter. Jasmin and Casasanto explored how the frequency and popularity of typing language, a practice that began with the invention of the typewriter about a century and a half ago but increased dramatically with the availability of computers and the Internet into people's homes (roughly 1990), has changed the meanings of some words.

Jasmin and Casasanto (2012) examined the form of words and the meanings associated with those forms. They discovered that on average, words typed with more letters on the right side of the QWERTY keyboard (so named because of the arrangement of those letters in the top left row of all keyboards) were rated as more positive in meaning than words with more letters on the left side. Jasmin and Casasanto call this the QWERTY effect, and it has been shown in different languages (English, Spanish, and Dutch) and also for phonologically possible nonwords. Casasanto predicted this result based on his research that shows body dominance determines emotional valence (consistent with an embodied perspective on emotions). Therefore, for right-handers, right is "good" and left is "bad," an association represented in many colloquial phrases such as "my right-hand man" and "my two left feet." Thus, this QWERTY effect can be explained by the fact that because the majority of people are right-handers, words that are spelled with more letters on the right side of the keyboard will be found as more positive in meaning than words with more letters on the left side.

These data provide evidence of simulation because when one is thinking about the meaning of a word, it is not clear that form or its "typeability" is important. However, an automatic simulation of the action required to type the word occurs, producing the QWERTY effect. Jasmin and Casasanto (2012) found that this effect was strongest in new words that were adopted after the QWERTY keyboard was invented, providing strong support for the contention that the way words are typed actually shapes their meaning.

Casasanto, Jasmin, Brookshire, and Gijssels (2014) replicated the QWERTY effect in five experiments and found that it extends to Portuguese and German. They also discovered the very curious finding that the QWERTY effect is found in names given to babies. Not only have the first names that Americans have given to babies changed over time, with names given to babies postpopularization of QWERTY (roughly, 1990) having more right-side letters than names given to babies pre-QWERTY, but also names coined after 1990 have significantly more right-side letters than any of the previous 3 decades. These results support Casasanto's earlier work that body dominance plays a role in determining emotional valence, but they also suggest that simulation of motor actions acquired from experience with language, in this case from typing, occur when thinking about words' meaning.

Evidence for Simulation Without Body Involvement

One of the most important issues that embodiment has to address to be a complete theory of knowledge representation is how people are able to understand concepts that have never been physically experienced. Abstract concepts such as justice, integrity, or honesty are difficult to explain within a theory that says that conceptual knowledge is grounded in sensorimotor activity that occurred when that knowledge was acquired. A strong version of embodiment would require that even knowledge about abstract concepts comes from bodily experiences.

A less body-driven view would suggest that knowledge about abstract concepts can be represented by "scaffolding," or using analogical expressions that are based on other more experience-based domains (e.g., Boroditsky, 2000; Lakoff & Johnson, 1980). In a later chapter concerning metaphor (Chapter 8) this perspective will be fleshed out to explain how linguistic expressions that connect concepts that do have representations of sensorimotor experiences to concepts that do not can provide meaning to abstract concepts. However, even in the absence of a linguistic convention like metaphor, abstract concepts may be understood through a connection with another concept that does have a representation built up through physical experience.

For example, Boroditsky and Ramscar (2002) tested the hypothesis that the abstract domain of time is understood through an individual's experiences in the concrete domain of space. They tested the claim that an individual's representation of time is dependent on their experience with space to the degree that even every-day spatial activities, like waiting in line for lunch or arriving at an airport after a flight, will influence their conceptualization of time. They predicted that contrary to the strong view of embodiment, abstract thinking may not depend on the physical experience one finds oneself in at a particular moment. Instead, abstract thinking may depend on the representation of a concrete concept (e.g., space) that has been constructed based on prior experiences, and that concrete concept may provide a context for understanding the abstract concept. For example, if the representation of time is tied to the representation of space, then when people think about space in a specific way, it should influence how they think about time—independent of how their own body is situated in space.

In a series of experiments, Boroditsky and Ramscar (2002) had participants fill out a questionnaire that included one critical question: "Next Wednesday's meeting has been moved forward two days. What day is the meeting now that it has been rescheduled?" In their first study, this question was preceded by one of two spatial primes, shown in Figure 6.5. The top spatial prime (Figure 6.5a) was intended to get participants to think about themselves moving through space in an office chair, which was intended to prime the idea of their body moving forward in time (i.e., moving into

FIGURE 6.5

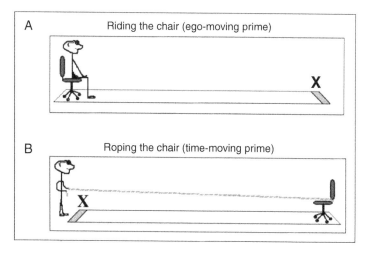

The ego-moving (a) and time-moving (b) priming materials used in Study 1. The instructions began, "Imagine you are the person in the picture. Notice there is a chair on wheels, and a track." From "The Roles of Body and Mind in Abstract Thought," by L. Boroditsky and M. Ramscar, 2002, *Psychological Science, 13*, p. 186. Copyright 2002 by Sage. Reprinted with permission.

the future). The bottom spatial prime (Figure 6.5b) was intended to get participants to think about an office chair coming toward them, which was intended to represent "time passing them by" (or time moving toward and eventually past them).

Boroditsky and Ramscar (2002) called the first spatial perspective the "ego-moving" perspective and the second spatial prime the "time-moving" perspective. They found that if participants had been primed with the ego-moving perspective, they answered the "Wednesday" question in the previous paragraph more often with the response "Friday," but if they had been primed with the "time-moving" perspective, they answered more often with a "Monday" response. This suggested to Boroditsky and Ramscar that participants' thinking about time was tied to their spatial thinking.

Boroditsky and Ramscar (2002) continued to examine this ego-moving perspective versus time-moving perspective for participants in more naturalistic settings. In a second study, they asked participants the Wednesday question when they were waiting in a long line at a cafeteria for lunch. Figure 6.6 shows the percentages of responses for the ego-moving response of "Friday," which should occur when participants have experienced more forward movement (they were closer to getting

FIGURE 6.6

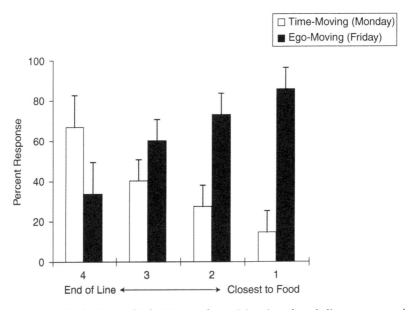

Results of Study 2, in which 70 people waiting in a lunch line answered the ambiguous time question. From "The Roles of Body and Mind in Abstract Thought," by L. Boroditsky and M. Ramscar, 2002, *Psychological Science, 13*, p. 187. Copyright 2002 by Sage. Reprinted with permission.

their food), and for the time-moving response of "Monday," which should occur when participants have experienced little movement and feel that time is "passing them by." The results shown in this figure demonstrate that as one moves through space from the end of a line to the beginning, one's spatial perspective determines their time perspective: The response of "Monday" is given when you are at the end of the line, but "Friday" is the response when you are at the point of being close to the food.

In Boroditsky and Ramscar's (2002) final experiment, individuals riding a train were asked this Wednesday question. Although all individuals were asked while the train was moving (i.e., their bodies were experiencing the same forward movement), their response was dependent on where they were psychologically in their train journey. If they were at the beginning of their trip or if they were about to get off the train, they were more likely to give the ego-moving response of "Friday." However, if they were in the middle of their trip, and therefore not really thinking about their destination, they showed equal likelihood for the "Monday" or "Friday" response. Boroditsky and Ramscar interpreted these findings as suggesting that thinking about time is not about how one's body is moving through space, but instead, how one is thinking about the consequences of their motion. They claim that thinking about abstract domains, time in this case, is built on representations of experience-based domains (space) that are functionally separable from the sensorimotor experiences occurring at that moment (bodily movement). Thus, our representation of time may be less about what our body is experiencing and more about how we are thinking about, or simulating, spatial motion at that moment.

In a final example of how simulation may not directly involve the body, Witt, South, and Sugovic (2014) conducted a study in which they explored the question: When one observes another's behavior, in this case playing a video game, does that elicit a simulation of the observed person's behavior *or* a simulation of one's own behavior as it would be in that particular context? This study was an extension of Witt and Sugovic's (2012) prior research where participants played a video game similar to the game "Pong," where "balls" come across the computer screen at diagonals and the participants use a joystick to control the "paddles" that are on the sides of the screens. The paddles are used to block the balls before they go off the screen. Witt and Sugovic had participants play this game and attempt to block the balls using different-sized paddles (white rectangles that varied in length). Participants were then asked to make speed estimates for the balls going across the screen. Witt and Sugovic found that the balls appeared to move slower when participants had been successful at blocking the ball and when the paddle was bigger. They claimed that this was an "action-specific" effect, similar to that seen in much of Proffitt's work (discussed in Chapter 2) where visual perception is affected by one's personal abilities of acting in their world (e.g., Bhalla & Proffitt, 1999; Witt & Proffitt, 2008). In this case, perception of speed is influenced by personal success in the game, whether personal or due to bigger paddles. Witt, Tenhundfeld, and Tymoski (2017) replicated this "Pong effect," and their studies ruled out nonperceptual explanations of these data, such as participants guessing the experimenter's hypothesis about paddle size.

Interestingly, Witt, Sugovic, and Taylor (2012) found that ball speed estimates in this Pong game were similarly affected when participants were watching another participant play the game. This suggests that it is not only the perceiver's ability to act that influences perception; observing another person's ability to act also affects perception. This result poses a problem for the action-specific account of perception in that when observing another perform, where is the role of one's own body in the perceptual experience? The central claim of the action-specific perspective is that perception is affected by how one's own body can act on the environment and thus plan future actions. But how is it adaptive to see the world in terms of someone else's ability?

Witt, South, and Sugovic (2014) tested the hypothesis that "other-based" action-specific effects could still reflect the perceiver's perceptual bias from the influence of their own abilities. They examined whether participants simulated their own abilities when observing another person performing a familiar action or if they perceived the observed person's abilities as if they were their own. This observation–action link suggests a form of mirror-neuron activity similar to that discussed in prior chapters; however, what was questioned in the Witt et al. (2014) study was whether the observation of another's performance leads to a direct simulation of that performance, or instead, to a simulation of one's own personal performance.

Witt et al. (2014) grouped participants, who were couples involved in another study examining romantic relationships, according to whether their ability in Pong was better or worse than their partner's abilities. They then had participants both playing and also observing their partner playing, and participants made speed estimates for the balls in both conditions. This allowed the researchers to examine whether perceived speed of the ball was a function of the participant's own abilities or their partner's abilities. If speed perception was a function of the participant's own abilities, those who were better at the game (more effective at blocking the ball with the paddle) than their partners would observe their partner's lesser play but still see the ball as moving slow. However, if speed estimates were influenced by the perception of how the other person playing the game was doing, then participants who were better blockers than their partners should observe their partner's play and see the balls as moving fast.

The data from this study support the action-specific account of perception from the participant's personal perspective: Witt et al. (2014) found that participants who were better blockers than their partners perceived the ball to be moving slower, both when estimating speed after they had played and after observing their partner play. It appears that when observing another person play this game, one simulates the activity of playing the game, and perception of speed (and paddle size) is influenced by one's personal abilities. Witt et al. claimed that these results suggest that the motor simulation that underlies this effect is not a mirror simulation, or a direct simulation of that which is being observed, but instead a self-projection mechanism by which the observer's own actions and presumably thoughts are simulated as if they are in the same situation as the person being observed. This demonstrates that simulation does not have to involve one's body directly; it can involve reenacting a bodily experience, in this case a perceptual judgment, when observing another person's behavior.

Conclusions

Collectively, these results provide support for the PSS account of knowledge representation—knowledge is represented in multimodal perceptual symbols that are developed at encoding and then are reactivated when that knowledge is needed for cognitive tasks or memory. Evidence for shared representations of perceptual and conceptual knowledge is found in neuropsychological results that have shown that when individuals think of a concept, brain activity occurs in those sensorimotor areas that are used for processing the properties of that concept. This is distributed activity across modal systems that are associated with the various properties or actions that constitute a concept.

Another central tenet of the grounded cognition view is that thinking about a concept means simulating the sensorimotor activity that underlies the very representation of the concept. Evidence for this can be found in many different areas of research. One example is found in studies demonstrating that conceptual processing shows the same "costs" that occur in perceptual processing when one modality has to switch to a different modality in consecutive cognitive judgments. Thinking proceeds smoothly when processing multiple concepts that are represented within the same perceptual modality.

Classic explicit and implicit memory effects can be explained by simulation; from the encoding specificity effect to repetition priming, simulating processes used at encoding during retrieval can account for many memory phenomena. Common developmental action errors can also be explained by a simulation of prior motoric actions that are erroneously applied in a new context. Additionally, nonconscious simulations of skilled and overused actions will result in interesting cognitive effects. The QWERTY effect reflects how the meaning of language can be shaped by the simulation of skilled motor actions.

Simulation does not have to require bodily activity, however. Simulation can take the form of imagining where one's body would be in a particular context even if the body is experiencing something different (e.g., physically moving forward but not thinking about moving forward, as in the train experiment in Boroditsky & Ramscar, 2002) or imagining how one's own body would experience something that is only being observed (e.g., Witt et al.'s, 2014, evidence of simulation when making perceptual judgments about another person's behavior).

These data are difficult to explain within a theory that posits conceptual knowledge is represented in amodal symbols and sensorimotor activity is simply the downstream consequence of thinking about concepts. The evidence provided in this chapter suggests otherwise. The next chapter presents data concerning simulation and social cognition that suggests that simulation that occurs when observing another person but simulating your own abilities (as in the Pong studies described previously) is a way in which we come to understand another person's goals, intentions, and motivations.

Takeaway

- The core computational process of thinking is the simulation of prior sensorimotor and emotional experiences (Barsalou). Therefore, the body cannot be extricated from how knowledge is represented in the brain.

The Role of Simulation in Emotion

7

Questions:

- What is the evidence to suggest that our conceptual representations of emotions are distributed across modality-specific areas of the brain?
- Does understanding another's emotion require the ability to emotionally reenact that emotion concept?
- If embodiment can explain how we understand others' emotions, can it explain how we understand others' actions?

This chapter presents both behavioral and neuroimaging evidence to support an embodied view of emotion that has as its core assumption that emotions are neurophysiological states derived from prior experiences of sensory, perceptual, and motoric events. These states (perceptual symbols) are reenacted, or simulated, when we process emotional stimuli and understand the emotions of others. This perspective on emotion is consistent with a wealth of empirical evidence that suggests a strong link between emotion and bodily action.

Traditional models of how our conceptual knowledge of emotion may be represented in the brain are symbolic, amodal, semantic network models (e.g., Bower, 1981; Rosch, 1973; Russell, 1991) that suggest that basic emotions (joy, sadness, etc.) are central organizing nodes in a hierarchical network

http://dx.doi.org/10.1037/0000136-007
How the Body Shapes Knowledge: Empirical Support for Embodied Cognition, by R. Fincher-Kiefer

of concept nodes. When an emotion is activated by some external or internal stimulus, activation spreads throughout the network, which includes associated behavioral and physiological events. For example, an event that elicits happiness may activate other cognitions related to happiness and would also likely lead to an increase in heart rate and activation of the zygomaticus smile muscle. This semantic network model of emotion has allowed psychologists to test the structure and content of emotional knowledge. However, the argument that knowledge about emotion is represented in symbolic concept nodes that are related to other concept nodes falls prey to Harnad's (1990) "symbol merry-go-round" problem discussed in Chapter 1, in that we neither understand the nature of the mental representation of emotion (i.e., what is a concept node?) nor do we understand what the referents are for those basic concept nodes. Further, this semantic network model of emotion has not been successful in explaining recent data suggesting a tight link between emotion and bodily action.

Embodied emotion theorists, on the other hand, claim that our understanding of different emotions is found in their associated behavioral patterns such as facial expressions or bodily reactions (e.g., Gallese, 2003; Lambie & Marcel, 2002; Niedenthal, 2007; Niedenthal, Barsalou, Winkielman, Krauth-Gruber, & Ric, 2005). Niedenthal, Wood, and Rychlowska (2014) argued that representations of emotions are distributed across modality-specific areas of the brain, so that an emotional experience involves multiple systems that include cognition, behavior, facial expression, bodily posture, and the limbic system (specifically, the amygdala). Barrett (2006a, 2006b) similarly claimed that emotions are categorizations of conceptual knowledge developed out of sensory, motor, and interoceptive (internal feedback) experiences.

Barrett (2006a, 2006b) argued that when a neurophysiological state is experienced at some developmentally early time (e.g., a physiological state for anger—increases in heart rate, blood pressure, respiration), this occurs in a particular valence (negative) and at some intensity (adrenaline increases arousal). In parallel, this state is accompanied by a context that also includes sensory, motor, and interoceptive states (loud noises, face flushing, muscles tense, fight or flight feelings) that will come to be associated with that neurophysiological state. Typically, the entirety of this experience will be labeled by another person at that time ("You are so *angry!*"), and that label is then taken on as part of the conceptual representation for that neurophysiological state. These "situated conceptualizations" that occur become perceptual symbols (Barsalou, 1999) for that emotion.

Emotional Simulation and Comprehension of Emotional Language

Gallese (2005) argued that there is a strong interaction between emotion and action. The coupling of emotion and facial action is evidenced in Adolphs, Damasio, Tranel, Cooper, and Damasio's (2000) research investigating the cognitive and emotional consequences of certain areas of brain damage in over 100 brain-damaged patients. Surprisingly, patients who suffered damage to the sensory-motor cortices, those brain areas responsible for sensation and motor planning, were those who also scored most poorly on the rating and naming of basic emotional expressions on human faces. Adolphs (2002) suggested that the sensory-motor cortices appear to be necessary for the recognition of emotional expressions because these cortices are needed for the production and sensory feedback involved in the bodily state for these emotions. In essence, one cannot recognize an emotion in another that one cannot easily produce. When we speak of "feeling" an emotion, we may be expressing our ability to simulate that emotion, or reuse the neural pathways that are used in the physical (facial) expression of that emotion.

If the recognition of emotion is dependent on the ability to simulate that emotion, then blocking that simulation should disrupt or interfere with understanding the emotion. Preliminary evidence has already been found for this prediction with Havas, Glenberg, Gutowski, Lucarelli, and Davidson's (2010) research discussed previously in Chapter 5 demonstrated impaired comprehension of negative sentences for women who had received injections of Botox into their frown muscles. In other work examining the comprehension of emotional language, Havas, Glenberg, and Rinck (2007) had participants read pleasant sentences such as, "You and your lover embrace after a long separation," and unpleasant sentences such as, "The police car rapidly pulls up behind you, siren blaring." During reading, Havas et al. covertly manipulated the participants' facial action (postures) so that they either matched or mismatched the emotional state described in the sentence. Using Strack, Martin, and Stepper's (1988) procedure described earlier in Chapter 3, Havas et al. had readers holding a pen between their lips (to produce a frown) or between their teeth (to produce a smile), and they measured sentence processing times to make valence and sensibility judgments.

Havas et al. found an emotional congruency effect such that comprehension judgments were facilitated in the conditions in which the emotional facial posture matched the emotion portrayed in the sentence. These data suggest that emotion simulation plays a role in comprehension. Adopting a facial posture (nonconsciously) of a particular affective state enhances the simulation of that emotion, which is used to comprehend a sentence that describes that emotional state. Havas, Glenberg, and Rinck's (2007) and Havas et al.'s (2010) research suggests that the ability to produce facial postures of emotion plays a causal role in the comprehension of language about emotion.

Baumeister, Rumiati, and Foroni (2015) also investigated of the role of facial action, or as it is often referred to, "facial motor resonance," in both the encoding and the retrieval of emotional language. In their experiment, participants first took part in an encoding phase in which they categorized a series of words as emotional or not (words presented were either related to disgust, happiness, or fear, or were neutral words). Participants then had an hour break before a retrieval phase in which they were presented with an unexpected memory task. The critical manipulation was that half of the participants in each phase wore a facial mask that hardened and blocked the movement of the participants' facial muscles, and the other half wore a creamy facial mask that did not impair facial movement. Participants were told that the masks were intended to change "skin conductance" and the experiment was investigating the effects of that change on word processing.

The accuracy data on the encoding task is shown in Figure 7.1 where Baumeister et al. (2015) computed a sensitivity index, *d'*, to reflect the participants' ability to discriminate between emotional words and neutral words. These data demonstrate that blocking the facial muscles significantly impaired the ability to discriminate between emotional and neutral words, and this was true across all three of the emotion word types. Although this replicates Havas et al.'s (2010) finding that blocking facial motor resonance impairs the encoding or initial comprehension of emotion language, Baumeister et al. also found that blocking facial motor resonance impairs the memory for emotional language.

Figure 7.2 depicts the impaired memory accuracy, again as reflected in *d'* scores that represent the ability to discriminate between words presented at encoding (i.e., old words) and new words for each of the emotional word types. Baumeister et al. (2015) found that this memory impairment seen in this figure for the blocked condition compared with the free condition occurred in all conditions in which the mask

FIGURE 7.1

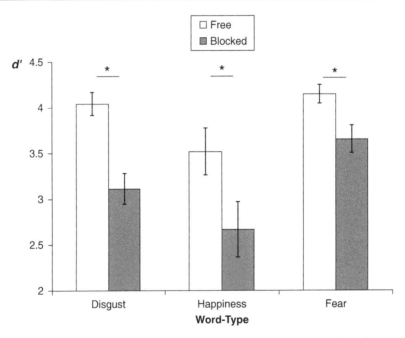

Classification task. Accuracy of word classification expressed in *d'* as a function of word type (disgust vs. happiness vs. fear) and encoding condition (free vs. blocked). Error bars represent ±1 *SE*. **p* < .05. From "When the Mask Falls: The Role of Facial Motor Resonance in Memory for Emotional Language," by J.-C. Baumeister, R. I. Rumiati, and F. Foroni, 2015, *Acta Psychologica*, *155*, p. 33. Copyright 2015 by Elsevier. Reprinted with permission.

FIGURE 7.2

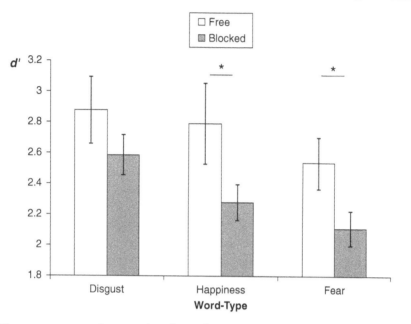

Memory accuracy for emotional words expressed in *d'* as a function of word type (disgust vs. happiness vs. fear) and condition (free vs. blocked). Error bars represent ±1 *SE*. **p* < .05 (one-tailed). From "When the Mask Falls: The Role of Facial Motor Resonance in Memory for Emotional Language," by J.-C. Baumeister, R. I. Rumiati, and F. Foroni, 2015, *Acta Psychologica*, *155*, p. 33. Copyright 2015 by Elsevier. Reprinted with permission.

was on the participants: during encoding, during retrieval, or during both. They argued that these results demonstrate that facial motor resonance is essential to both the initial and later stages of processing emotional language.

Emotional Simulation and Comprehension of the Emotion of Others

Beyond language, does understanding the emotion of others similarly require a facial simulation for that emotion? Perhaps the perception of another's facial expression leads to a recreation of the motor activity used to produce that facial expression in our own body, just as processing emotion language appears to require an emotional simulation. In fact, there is evidence that individuals observing a facial expression automatically reenact it, showing electromyographic (EMG) activity in emotion-relevant facial muscles (Carr, Iacoboni, Dubeau, Mazziotta, & Lenzi, 2003; Krumhuber, Likowski,

& Weyers, 2014; Rychlowska et al., 2014). This facial mimicry occurs even when the faces are perceived nonconsciously and when the emotional expression is not relevant to the task at hand (Dimberg, Thunberg, & Elmehed, 2000; T. W. Lee, Dolan, & Critchley, 2008).

It has been argued that facial mimicry is responsible for emotion recognition in others, evidenced by the fact that blocking or reducing facial mimicry impairs our expert skill in identifying the facial expressions of emotion. Rychlowska et al. (2014) used a mouthguard procedure to investigate how limiting facial movement would affect judgments of the genuineness of true and false smiles. In their first experiment, Rychlowska et al. found that participants watching videos of true and false smiles showed greater EMG activity in the zygomaticus major muscle when viewing true smiles than false smiles, demonstrating facial mimicry that was sensitive to subtle differences in the meaning of facial expressions. However, participants wearing mouthguards showed significantly reduced activity in the zygomaticus muscle (as expected) and, more important to the hypothesis tested, no difference in activity when viewing true and false smiles. This confirmed what the researchers had hoped—that the mouthguard could be used to interfere with the process of facial mimicry. Rychlowska et al.'s next two experiments showed that while watching the videos of true and false smiles, participants wearing mouthguards were less able to discriminate between true and false smiles compared with participants not wearing mouthguards. They concluded that facial mimicry must be used to facilitate the detection of subtle differences in an emotional expression's meaning.

In support of this finding, A. Wood, Lupyan, Sherrin, and Niedenthal (2016) also explored how facial movement plays a role in making perceptual discrimination judgments for faces along an angry–sad continuum. A. Wood et al. (2016) found that participants who had on a gel facemask that restricted facial movement showed significantly poorer ability to discriminate between angry–sad facial expressions but little difficulty discriminating between nonface control stimuli. Control participants who had on lotion that did not limit facial movement showed equally strong performance in the face discrimination task and the control task. The gel facemask appears to alter sensorimotor processes used in emotion *perception* just as the mouthguard altered the processes used in emotion *recognition* (Rychlowska et al., 2014).

If facial mimicry is used to understand others' emotions, then limiting that mimicry early in life may have long-term consequences for emotional development. Niedenthal et al. (2012) tested both male and female children that had used pacifiers for varying amounts of time, and they measured their emotional competence later in their life in terms of empathy and emotional intelligence. Their data can be found in Figure 7.3a, b, and c. Figure 7.3a shows that the longer the pacifier use in males, but not females, the less spontaneous facial mimicry they produced (at an average age of 7 years). Figure 7.3b demonstrates that pacifier use in males was associated with poorer scores on an empathy measure that required the test taker (average age 20 years) to imagine the situation of another person. Figure 7.3c also shows that, again for males only, the longer the pacifier use, the lower their scores on the emotional intelligence measure (average age 20 years).

FIGURE 7.3

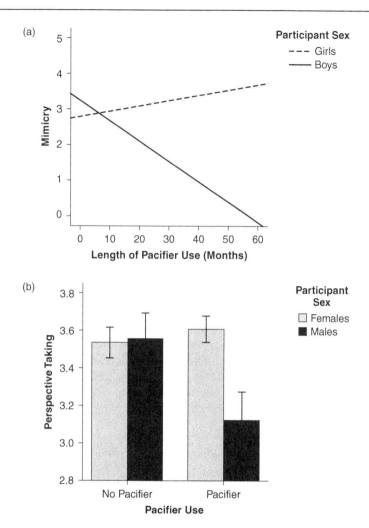

(a) Mimicry as a function of participant gender and length of pacifier use in Study 1. *Note:* The lines represent predicted values that were estimated at the mean of the covariates. (b) Perspective taking as a function of participant sex and pacifier use (coded yes/no) in Study 2.

(continues)

FIGURE 7.3 *(Continued)*

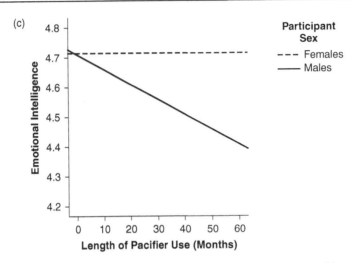

(c) Emotional intelligence as a function of participant sex and length of pacifier use in Study 3. *Note:* The lines represent predicted values that were estimated at the mean of the covariates. From "Negative Relations Between Pacifier Use and Emotional Competence," by P. M. Niedenthal, M. Augustinova, M. Rychlowska, S. Droit-Volet, L. Zinner, A. Knafo, and M. Brauer, 2012, *Basic and Applied Social Psychology, 34*, pp. 390–392. Copyright 2012 by Taylor & Francis. Reprinted with permission.

This sex difference in the link between pacifier use and emotional competence may mean that to understand emotions, boys in their early years need the sensorimotor simulation of facial mimicry more so than girls. Perhaps girls are more emotionally expressive in other social forms than facial mimicry, allowing them to develop emotional competence from multiple sources. However, boys tend to be socially and culturally limited in their expressions and discussions of emotions, and thus they are more vulnerable to disruption of facial mimicry. This repeated inhibition of facial muscles in young boys who use pacifiers appears to disrupt the automatic facial mimicry that is used to develop an understanding of emotion in others.

This research clearly suggests that understanding others' emotions requires simulation of the facial activity used to experience that emotion. However, facial mimicry may only be part of the sensorimotor simulation that occurs during processing others' emotions. A. Wood, Rychlowska, Korb, and Niedenthal (2016) argued that emotion recognition involves the subthreshold reenactment of both the primary motor processes involved in producing the facial expression and the premotor, somatosensory system that supports the expression. This latter neural system may involve a facial feedback loop that provides information about the congruence or incongruence of one's own facial expression relative to the one being observed.

Both of these neural systems are part of the sensorimotor simulation involved when observing another's facial expression, and under certain conditions, one of these systems may be more active than the other. For example, facial mimicry may not be essential to the sensorimotor simulation despite the research findings that blocking facial mimicry impairs emotion recognition. It is possible that this impairment is not due to the primary motor system being disrupted, but instead is due to the somatosensory neural system that provides facial feedback information. A. Wood, Rychlowska, Korb, and Niedenthal (2016) claimed that the impaired emotion recognition could be a function of the fact that when facial mimicry is blocked, the feedback from this sensorimotor loop would be negative and surprising because the facial posture of the perceiver and the facial posture of the observed are incongruent. This mismatch, or disfluency, could by itself cause disruption in emotion recognition.

Others have also argued that facial mimicry may reflect and enhance sensorimotor simulation, but it may not mediate the emotion recognition process (Korb, With, Niedenthal, Kaiser, & Grandjean, 2014). Mimicry may be absent because it is constrained by social and cultural influences, but that does not necessarily indicate the absence of internally simulated emotional expressions (A. Wood, Rychlowska, Korb, & Niedenthal, 2016). For example, mimicking another's facial response to an anger cue could be physically dangerous as well as socially inappropriate. Thus, facial mimicry may not be essential in the simulation process, but it is still a marker of the emotional simulation that plays a causal role in understanding the emotions of others (see Hess & Fischer, 2014, for a review of the conditions needed for mimicry to occur).

Perhaps the most convincing evidence that understanding others' emotions occurs through emotional simulation comes from Tamietto et al.'s (2009) research showing that both facial and body postures perceived nonconsciously elicit facial mimicry, representing an emotional simulation. Tamietto et al. investigated facial mimicry in two individuals who had lesions to the visual cortex of one of their cerebral hemispheres. This type of brain damage results in "blindsight" in one visual field, meaning these individuals report no visual experience on one side of their visual world but have normal visual experience in their intact visual field (e.g., a patient with damage to the visual cortex of the right hemisphere will be functionally blind in their left visual field, or the left side of each eye). These patients were shown pictures of happy and fearful expressions to both their intact visual fields as well as to their blind visual fields.

When these facial expressions were presented to the blind visual fields, the patients reported that they could not see the image. However, in guessing, they correctly recognized the expressions on a 2-item forced-choice face recognition test significantly above chance, and their recognition performance was not significantly different than when the face was presented in their sighted visual field. Further, EMG activity was measured during picture viewing in both their zygomaticus major muscle (used in smiling) and in their corrugator supercilii (used in frowning). Evidence of facial mimicry was found in these patients even when the image was shown to their blind visual field. For happy faces shown to the intact and to the blind visual field, there was more EMG activity in the zygomaticus muscle and inhibition in the corrugator supercilii, but for fearful faces shown in both visual fields, the opposite pattern of EMG activity occurred.

To test the hypothesis that these two cortically blind patients could have been automatically mimicking facial expressions that they "saw" at an unconscious level, Tamietto et al. (2009) also showed these patients images of happy and fearful body positions that would provide emotional cues without providing the information needed for facial imitation. They found that the EMG activity in the zygomaticus major and the corrugator supercilii was the same pattern after exposure to the body postures as it was after viewing the pictures of the faces. This indicated that these individuals were not just imitating the motor pattern in the stimuli, but were also simulating the affective *meaning* that is represented in both face and bodily gestures. Whether it is a happy face or a happy body position, even nonconscious exposure to these stimuli elicits facial action that represents the emotional simulation of "happiness," presumably for the purpose of understanding that emotion in others.

Taking this evidence even further, de Groot et al. (2015) found that not only does the nonconscious perception of "happy" facial and body positions elicit an emotional simulation of that emotion, but exposure to bodily odors (chemosignals) associated with emotions (in this case, happiness) also elicits simulation of that emotion. De Groot et al. found that participants who smelled the sweat of happy "senders" produced more Duchenne smiles (considered "real" smiles) in "receivers" than receivers who smelled the sweat of neutral or fearful senders. This suggests that bodily cues perceived by an observer, whether they are facial, body, or olfactory cues, elicit a simulation of that same cued emotion in the observer, allowing for what de Groot et al. referred to as a "synchronization" of emotion between sender and receiver. This process appears to be the basis of our ability to understand others' emotions.

Facial mimicry is not just evidence of the emotional simulation that leads to understanding others' primary emotions, as evidence has also been found for the role of facial action when understanding "social" emotions and judgments. Calder, Keane, Manes, Antoun, and Young (2000) found that an individual with neural damage to the insula and putamen, areas in which functional magnetic resonance imaging (fMRI) studies have consistently shown to be involved in processing facial expressions of disgust, demonstrated impairment both in experiencing and recognizing disgust in others. Calder et al. found that this patient, when shown pictures of facial expressions of the six basic emotions (anger, fear, happiness, sadness, surprise, and disgust), was selectively impaired in recognizing expressions of disgust and also showed impairment in recognizing social signals of disgust (nonverbal emotional sounds such as retching). It is important to note that when given disgust-provoking scenarios and asked for reactions to each in a questionnaire, this patient again showed significantly lower scores on the intensity of disgust experienced compared with control participants. This could not be explained by a semantic impairment for the concept of disgust as the patient showed no difference with control performance in identifying disgust from pictures (e.g., a filthy toilet). These findings support the conclusion that the neural substrates in the anterior insula and putamen may be used for experiencing a specific emotion and may also be used in recognizing that emotion in others.

Another brain center that appears to be critical for recognizing social emotions as well as more complex social judgments is the amygdala. Adolphs, Tranel, and Damasio (1998) found that subjects with bilateral damage to their amygdala were impaired in judging trustworthiness and approachability in the faces of others compared with control subjects, and this impairment was only present when making these social assessments from faces, not from verbal descriptions.

Adolphs, Baron-Cohen, and Tranel (2002) also tested individuals with unilateral or bilateral damage to the amygdala and had them perform matching tasks on face stimuli (both whole face and eye only) with labels for basic emotions and for complex social emotions (arrogant, guilty, admiring, and flirtatious). Compared with control individuals, amygdala damage led to significantly worse performance matching social emotions than matching basic emotions. Of particular interest is the fact that for the eye stimuli, the individuals with the amygdala damage were significantly worse in matching the stimuli with the labels for the social emotions than the control individuals, but the two groups did not differ significantly when matching the eye stimuli with the labels for the basic emotions. Interestingly, these impairments in the amygdala-damaged group were not due to a broader impairment in recognizing all complex mental states, because they were not impaired in the matching tasks for faces and labels on expressions that would not be considered social emotions (interested, scheming, thoughtful, quizzical, and bored). Adolphs et al. concluded that the amygdala is important for recognizing social emotions from faces, suggesting that this brain center may be grounding representations of knowledge concerning complex social emotions.

The specific impairment of recognizing complex social emotions from the eye region from amygdala damage is a pattern that is similar to the impairments seen in individuals with autism (Baron-Cohen et al., 1999). This result, as well as other findings, has suggested that the often severe impairments found in the social behaviors of autistic individuals may in part be due to damage in the neural circuitry of brain areas that include the amygdala (Baron-Cohen et al., 2000). It is possible that the impaired recognition of social emotions for individuals with autism spectrum disorder is a reflection of the inability to experience those complex social emotions and that may require a fully functioning amygdala.

Emotional Simulation and Understanding Others' Actions

So far we have addressed how embodiment explains how we understand the emotions of others. Now we need to explore the research that examines how we understand the actions, intentions, and motivations of others.

How we derive meaning from the actions of others is traditionally thought of as social cognition. Many theoretical perspectives have claimed that when we perceive the actions of others, we automatically make inferences about their goals, desires, and beliefs (e.g., Jones & Harris, 1967; Uleman, 1987). In other words, we perceive others acting, and without conscious awareness, we recognize and understand the meaning of those actions (not that this is foolproof; we often make errors). The question for experimental psychologists interested in social cognition is: How does this happen? Embodiment theory has provided a neurobiologically plausible explanation, and it involves the same system used to understand language about others' actions and beliefs—the mirror neuron system.

Gallese (2003, 2005) and colleagues (Gallese, Keysers, & Rizzolatti, 2004) argued that the discovery of mirror neurons in the parietal-premotor cortical networks of both monkeys and humans reveals that the observation (simple perception) of an action by another leads to activation in the same neural network used to actually execute that action. Simply stated, just as in facial mimicry, this means that observation of action leads to the neural simulation of that same action. This *mirror mechanism*, found in the anterior insula and ventral premotor cortex brain regions, may serve as the basis of understanding others' actions (Gallese, 2003, 2005; Gallese & Sinigaglia, 2011; Rizzolatti & Sinigaglia, 2010). Gallese and Sinigaglia (2011) claimed that this mirror mechanism is a reuse, or simulation, of one's own mental state or processes to functionally attribute them to another. If this were the case, then one's ability to interpret another's actions or emotions may be dependent on the ability to act or experience emotions.

Children and adults with autism do have impaired motoric actions, which is part of the etiology of the disorder, and this offers an opportunity to examine this hypothesis that the ability to act may affect the ability to interpret others' actions and emotions (Di Cesare et al., 2017). Recent studies exploring autism in children have suggested that the motor atypicalities seen in this disorder may impact the ability to simulate "typical" motoric actions, limiting the understanding of others' actions (see Cook, 2016, for a review of this research). This could explain some of the issues with difficult social interactions for autistic individuals: If these individuals have unusual motor patterns in their own behavior, this predicts that they will be impaired in perceiving, recognizing, and understanding others' behavior (because they cannot simulate that behavior). This further predicts that this lack of motor synchrony will cause even more disruption in "interpersonal sense-making" for autistic individuals (Cook, 2016).

Di Cesare et al. (2017) had children with autism spectrum disorder (ASD) and "typically developing" children attempt to recognize social aspects of different motor actions. All children were shown video clips of arm actions (move a bottle, a jar, a can) by actors whose faces were not shown (to ensure perception of motor actions and not facial expressions). These actions were at eight different "velocities," meaning the movements ranged from being either very fast or very slow. The children were immediately asked to make a verbal judgment concerning the action by responding to a 5-point Likert scale that ranged from *very rude* to *very gentle* (with *so-so* in the middle).

Autistic children, even as young as 8 years, were significantly different from typically developing children in categorizing the social aspect of these motoric actions. The autistic children had particular difficulty categorizing the less extreme actions. Although the most rapid movements were perceived as *very rude* by both the ASD and the typically developing children, the middle-range speeded movements were categorized differently for ASD children than typically developed children (autistic children used all scale points, whereas typically developing children used the middle *so-so* scale points).

Di Cesare et al. (2017) claimed that these results suggest that ASD involves an impairment in perceiving the social interaction aspects of actions—and that these form the basis of social judgments that allow for understanding and relating to others. They also suggested that the reason for this is that children with ASD show motoric atypicalities in their own social interactions—they manifest less engagement with others (Cattaneo et al., 2007; Hobson & Lee, 1998). This could suggest that to understand the social aspects of actions, one needs to be able to execute those actions.

In support of this, Di Cesare et al. (2016) used the same stimuli with the actions that could be perceived as "rude" or "gentle" and had adults (none were autistic in this study) watch these video clips while in an fMRI. They found activation in the dorso-central insula, suggesting a mirror mechanism in this brain center for a specific aspect of action that Di Cesare et al. (2014) referred to as "vitality form." The term *vitality form* was introduced by Stern (2010) to represent the social interaction aspect of an action; it reflects "how" the action took place (not the "what" or the "why"). Neuroimaging studies have demonstrated that this is a unique aspect of understanding actions. Di Cesare et al. (2014) found that when participants were in an fMRI observing actors performing actions with objects and were asked questions concerning "what" action was taken versus "how" these actions were taken, the tasks activated different brain regions—occipito-temporal areas for "what" questions but dorso-central insular cortex for "how" questions. (This is also a different brain area than that involved in processing emotional information, signifying the distinction between emotion and vitality forms.) Di Cesare et al. (2016) suggested that unlike the similar mirror mechanism found in the parietal and frontal brain areas specialized for action goal understanding (Rizzolatti & Sinigaglia, 2010), this mirror mechanism in the dorso-central insula may serve to express vitality forms in actions and to understand the vitality form in others' actions.

This suggestion that the social difficulties in ASD stem from a broken mirror neuron system in the dorso-central insula has recently been called into question by Cracco et al. (2018). In a large sample study of participants with ASD, Cracco et al. found no difference in the automatic imitation of behavior between autistic participants and control participants, an indicator of processing self–other information. Cracco et al. concluded that ASD is not specifically associated with impairments in imitating others or in imitative control, implying that their self–other processes are not the source of the disorder. However, the fact that the amount of automatic imitation is similar for autistic and control participants does not necessarily indicate that imitation is normal in ASD. Prior research has found that healthy participants showed stronger automatic imitation in prosocial contexts than antisocial contexts, but ASD participants did not show this difference (Cook & Bird, 2012). Further, eye contact affects automatic imitation in control participants, but it does not affect imitation in ASD participants (Forbes, Wang, & de C. Hamilton, 2017).

Cracco et al. (2018) argued that their results are in strong disagreement with the embodied, self–other theories of autism that would suggest imitation is a critical component of ASD. Instead, their findings suggest that the self–other processes in ASD individuals are intact, and it is more likely that these individuals process or interpret social cues in an atypical fashion. However, Cracco et al. did acknowledge that self–other impairments in ASD may exist for specific representations. Deschrijver, Wiersema, and Brass (2017) found that ASD individuals' difficulties in distinguishing self from others may be restricted to somatosensory processing. Using an electroencephalogram paradigm, Deschrijver et al. compared the brain activity of ASD adults with control adults when both were observing another person's hand touching a surface while they were experiencing a taplike tactile sensation that either matched or mismatched the tactile consequence of the observed movement. They found that brain activity in ASD individuals was diminished compared with controls in the matched conditions. They reasoned that sensory difficulties may be linked to social impairments in ASD because of deficits in self–other representations that are focused on touch. In fact, ASD individuals do often self-report severe sensory difficulties in addition to their social difficulties. Clearly, more research is needed to understand the role of self–other processing in autism.

This research examining autistic populations suggests that when some motor program does not exist in a person's repertoire of motoric activity, or when motor resonance for the observation of someone else's activity is not fluently accomplished, then understanding the observed person's behavior is impaired. This nonfluent processing of another's behavior may also result from an effortful simulation process for unfamiliar behavior.

There is neurophysiological evidence to support the contention that when simulating an unfamiliar, as opposed to familiar, action, this requires more effortful processing in the mirror neuron system. Petroni, Baguear, and Della-Maggiore (2010) provided evidence that when observing another person, perception of unfamiliar actions requires higher neural energy demands in the mirror neuron system (MNS) than perception of familiar actions. Further, Liew, Han, and Aziz-Zadeh (2011) also found higher energy demands at the MNS site when Chinese participants were observing American participants using unfamiliar hand gestures during communication compared with when they were using familiar hand gestures (a thumbs-up).

Finally, Soliman, Gibson, and Glenberg (2013) used a behavioral measure similar to that used by Proffitt (2006) to examine this hypothesis that effortful simulation occurs for processing unfamiliar behavior in others. Soliman et al. borrowed Proffitt's distance judgments measure that has shown that individuals inflate perceived distance judgments for targets that require more effort to reach, such as when one is walking toward something wearing a heavy backpack (this research is discussed in Chapter 2). Soliman et al. found that individuals judging physical distances away from other individuals who were either outgroup or ingroup members (based on their cultural similarities) judged outgroup members to be further away than ingroup members. This supported their cultural motor-effort hypothesis that suggests that thinking about (simulating) social interactions with others who are not similar is more effortful, and less fluent, than thinking about interactions with those who are similar. Just as the body informs perception, the body informs social judgments—simulations "run" to determine distance from another person involve using a bodily scale that is affected by cultural or social effort to the same degree that it is affected by physical effort (a heavy backpack).

This cultural motor-effort hypothesis is another example of a cognition (conceptual knowledge about cultural similarities/dissimilarities) and action (bodily effort) link that is one of the hallmarks of embodiment. Soliman et al.'s (2013) data suggest that processing information about others, even how far away they are, involves simulations of bodily experiences. As Gallese and Sinigaglia (2011) argued, these simulations occur to understand another's actions. When simulations fail because the observer has not had those bodily experiences or because dissimilarities between the observer and the observed make the simulations effortful, comprehension of another's behaviors are impaired or errorful (e.g., Di Cesare et al., 2017; Soliman et al., 2013).

One final example of how culture, and cultural differences, may moderate the role of emotion simulation in understanding another's emotion can be found in research cited in A. Wood, Rychlowska, Korb, and Niedenthal (2016). These authors discuss the role of culture in emotional expressiveness and therefore as a factor in mimicry and the sensorimotor simulations used in recognizing facial expressions. Cultural variation in facial expressiveness has been explored by Jack, Garrod, Yu, Caldara, and Schyns (2012). Jack et al. found emotional expressions were not as universal as previously thought and were strongly influenced by culture. Western culture individuals represent the six basic emotions (happy, surprise, fear, disgust, anger, and sad) with distinct facial expressions that are easily recognizable within the culture. However, Eastern culture individuals do not use these same facial expressions, instead having distinct eye movement patterns that represent the intensity of an emotion.

When investigating these cultural differences, Rychlowska et al. (2015) discovered a fascinating predictor of emotional expressiveness—the migratory immigration history of a country. Figure 7.4 shows a map of historical heterogeneity of long-history migration that predicts emotional recognition accuracy (found in A. Wood, Rychlowska, & Niedenthal, 2016). When measuring social norms for individuals from countries that historically had migratory patterns that led to heterogeneous populations (darker countries on the map), Rychlowska et al. (2015) found preferences for emotional expressiveness across the six basic emotions. This was presumed to be due to a history of not having cultural commonalities among the people, and therefore there would be some pressure to use emotional expression for ease in interacting. Individuals from these countries also produced facial expressions that were readily recognized by other cultures (A. Wood et al., 2016). Individuals from countries that historically had more internal long-history migratory patterns (lighter countries on the map) that led to homogenous populations reported preferences for the attenuation of emotional expressions. Again, this presumably indicates that in these cultures' history, emotional expressions were less important as signals to

FIGURE 7.4

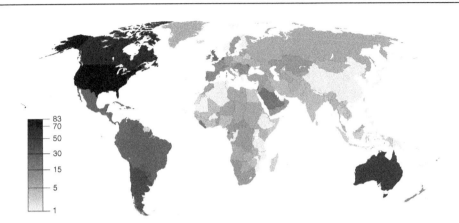

Map of historical heterogeneity. Darker countries are more hetero-geneous, meaning their present-day populations originate from a greater number of source countries (values on legend refer to number of source countries). Map generated at http://gunn.co.nz/map and based on data from World Migration Matrix (http://www.econ.brown.edu/fac/louis_putterman/world%20migration%20matrix.htm). From "Heterogeneity of Long-History Migration Predicts Emotion Recognition Accuracy," by A. Wood, M. Rychlowska, and P. M. Niedenthal, 2016, *Emotion*, *16*, p. 415. Copyright 2016 by the American Psychological Association.

facilitate interaction with others. These individuals, who preferred less emotional expressivity, also produced facial expressions that were more difficult to recognize (A. Wood et al., 2016).

How do these data support the contention that emotion simulation is used in emotion recognition? Because variables such as migratory history affect emotional expressivity, and how emotionally expressive an individual is can predict the accuracy of recognizing others' emotions. Apparently, emotional simulation is more difficult when expressions are ambiguous, limiting one's ability to recognize emotion in others. Other variables that play a role in the sensorimotor simulation of an emotion are more specific to the observer in the moment: the social constraints of the perceiver/observed interaction, the gender match of perceiver and person being observed, the motivational goals and intents of the perceiver, as well as personality characteristics of both individuals. A. Wood, Rychlowska, Korb, and Niedenthal (2016) argued that emotion simulation is on a continuum, and the degree to which one simulates another's emotional expression is a function of many of these variables. This continuum may flow from a partial reenactment of the observed emotion expression, which would include some actions and cognitions, to a full reenactment or simulation that "spills over" to facial mimicry as an indication of the completeness of this simulation.

Conclusions

An embodied account would suggest that the conceptual underpinning of emotion is the neural activity in the perceptual and sensory systems used for the bodily expression of emotion. In other words, representations of emotions are grounded in the brain areas responsible for producing them, and we are able to recognize them in others through the reuse, or simulation, of those same brain areas. When embodied theorists claim that the representation of emotion is multimodal, this means that emotion is represented in facial activity, bodily postures, even chemosignals—all of these are what Barsalou (1999) referred to as *perceptual symbols*. Further, the grounding of emotions allows for these perceptual symbols to be reenacted, or simulated, when perceiving and recognizing emotional expressions of others and when comprehending emotional language.

In applying an embodied perspective to understand social cognition, or the actions, motivations, and goals of others, the discovery of mirror neurons provided a neurobiological account for the possibility that social cognition at least starts at a primitive level of motoric action and planning. That allowed for some of the same questions to be asked as in the primary emotion research—can we understand another's actions if we cannot fluently express or experience that same action?

There is evidence to support a simulation account of social cognition from the research concerning those with motoric difficulties, autistic individuals, and their impairment in understanding social emotions of others and making social connections as well. It seems that disfluency in understanding others' behaviors may stem from an inability to "tune" one's motor system to behaviors that are unfamiliar, making the processing of any information about another person effortful (Soliman, Gibson, & Glenberg, 2013).

Gallese and Sinigaglia (2011) argued that even when available, simulation does not guarantee making sense of others' behavior because there could be higher level factors at play—sociocultural factors that are outside of our own experience. Instead, their proposal is that embodied simulation provides an initial attempt at making sense of others. There is much research left to be conducted to determine which aspects of social cognition start with mirror neuron activity and then what cognitive processes take over for more complex social processes.

Takeaway

- Emotion is represented in the perceptual and sensory system used in the bodily expression of emotion.
- To understand others' emotions, the MNS provides a neurophysiological mechanism that simulates a similar emotional reaction in the perceiver (Gallese).

The Role of Metaphor in the Representation of Abstract Concepts

8

Questions:

- How are concepts that have never been physically experienced represented conceptually?
- Can conceptual metaphor theory add to our understanding of embodiment theory?

The theory of embodiment has a problem that needs to be resolved theoretically and experimentally if it is going to be a viable theory of knowledge representation. The problem is this: Embodied cognition proposes that our conceptual knowledge is represented in the sensory and motor neural networks that were involved in our initial experience with a concept. If so, how do we represent concepts that we have never physically experienced (i.e., concepts that are abstract)? Barsalou (1999) claimed that simulation of prior sensory and motor experiences constitutes thinking, but how would we simulate a concept such as *power* or *love*?

Some theorists have argued that any role that the body plays on cognition is simply peripheral or epiphenomenal, and they see this abstract concept problem as insolvable for the theory of embodiment (e.g., Dove, 2009; Mahon & Caramazza, 2008). However, others have proposed that the solution to this problem can be found in language—language reflects the structure of how abstract concepts are represented. Specifically, *metaphors* are integral to how

http://dx.doi.org/10.1037/0000136-008
How the Body Shapes Knowledge: Empirical Support for Embodied Cognition, by R. Fincher-Kiefer

we understand the world (Lakoff, 1993; Lakoff & Johnson, 1980), and their structure demonstrates that we "scaffold" or map abstract concepts onto concrete, familiar knowledge to think abstractly (Jamrozik, McQuire, Cardillo, & Chatterjee, 2016; Williams, Huang, & Bargh, 2009). Although Lakoff and Johnson's (1980) original work was about language, their conceptual metaphor theory is a theoretical account concerning the structure of our abstract conceptual knowledge.

A metaphor is a linguistic device—it is a figure of speech that although not literally true, allows one to understand one difficult concept by applying a word or phrase representing another simpler concept. In their seminal book, *Metaphors We Live By*, Lakoff and Johnson (1980) argued that the English language is filled with metaphors that we typically do not even notice but shape our communication and, importantly, determine the way we think and act.

The structure of a conceptual metaphor is that there are two conceptual domains involved: a *target domain*, which is the domain that is abstract and, by itself, difficult to understand (i.e., *love*), and a *source domain*, which is typically a concrete domain that brings clarity to the abstract concept (i.e., *journey*). Thus, when the target domain is mapped onto the source domain (e.g., *love is a journey*), this allows for a particular understanding of the target domain within the context of the language used at that time (i.e., loving relationships develop over time; there are critical points "along the way" in a relationship that are notable, etc.). There may be many conceptual mappings for a particular concept (e.g., *love is a battlefield; love is a roller coaster*), each representing a different aspect of meaning. Which metaphor is used for a concept and how it is used is intended to shape the way we think and how we should act. For example, if *police are guardians*, then law enforcement may be viewed as protecting individuals with strength and bravery; but if *police are warriors*, then law enforcement may be conceptualized as aggressive and potentially violent (Thibodeau, Crow, & Flusberg, 2017). These different conceptualizations will direct our thinking and our behavior at any given time.

There are many different types of metaphors, but one important distinction is that between conceptual metaphors and idiomatic metaphors. Conceptual metaphors are not always commonly used in speech and language. Instead, they are the over-arching mappings between abstract and concrete concepts that take concrete, bodily experiences and map them onto abstract concepts. Metaphors such as *morality is cleanliness* (Schnall, Haidt, Clore, & Jordan, 2008) or *weight is importance* (Jostmann, Lakens, & Schubert, 2009; Schneider, Rutjens, Jostmann, & Lakens, 2011) are not by themselves part of our everyday speech, but they allow us to make inferences about abstract concepts. There is a body of evidence that is summarized in this chapter that indicates these conceptual metaphors underlie our thinking about abstract concepts and organize our conceptual knowledge.

The conventional or idiomatic metaphors that do permeate our everyday speech are often representations of these conceptual metaphors, such as *that was a heavy topic*, or *her thoughts were pure*. These idiomatic metaphors also have a concrete source concept, such as the physical state of sweetness, with an abstract target concept, such as revenge (e.g., *revenge is sweet*).

Hellmann, Echterhoff, and Thoben (2013) claimed that the difference between conceptual and idiomatic metaphors is that for idiomatic metaphors, the associations between the target and source concept are less strong and unidirectional (i.e., revenge is sweet but sweetness does not always elicit negative affect such as that associated with revenge). Thus, for idiomatic metaphors, both source and target concepts must be sufficiently activated for the source concept to be mapped onto the target concept, thereby guiding thought and action (Hellmann, Thoben, & Echterhoff, 2013).

However, conceptual metaphors guide cognition even when only one of the concepts is activated because one concept spontaneously activates the other (Barsalou, 2003). In a conceptual metaphor, the relationship is bidirectional, indicating that the abstract concept and the source concept are represented together conceptually. For example, if the abstract concept of the *future* is mapped onto the source concept of *bodily movement in a forward direction*, reflected in the metaphoric expression *the future is ahead of us*, then thinking about one's future should automatically elicit forward movement, and forward movement should elicit thoughts of one's future. This should remind you of Chapter 4, which provided experimental evidence for this exact bidirectional relationship between abstract concepts relating to time (past, future) and source concepts relating to spatial dimensions (forward, backward; Casasanto & Boroditsky, 2008; Miles, Nind, & Macrae, 2010).

Behavioral evidence for the representation of abstract concepts in conceptual metaphors can be found using the metaphoric transfer strategy (Landau, Meier, & Keefer, 2010). This involves investigating an idiomatic expression such as "That was a dirty move on his part," in which the conceptual metaphor being expressed is *morality is cleanliness*. The metaphoric transfer strategy looks for evidence for both a cognition (morality) affecting behavior (cleanliness) and for the opposite as well—behavior (cleansing one's hands) affecting cognition (moral purity; Zhong & Liljenquist, 2006).

Data that suggest a bidirectional relationship for metaphor-consistent cognition and behavior provide particularly strong support for the view that metaphors are reflections of how knowledge is represented in prior sensorimotor, or bodily, experiences. If the relationship were only unidirectional, for example, if the thought of morality influenced one's cleanliness, it could be that this effect was simply the result of semantic priming. The concept of morality may be semantically associated with concepts of being "good," which may be linked to concepts of purity and cleanliness. However, a priming effect cannot easily explain how the opposite might occur, that an act of cleanliness would bias moral judgments.

These concepts of physical cleanliness and morality are, on the surface, too dissimilar to be explained by priming effects. A better explanation for this bidirectional relationship is the one that conceptual metaphor theory provides—that the linguistic structure of the metaphor reflects that the meaning for one concept is "grounded" (shares neural pathways) in the representation of the other concept. That would result in a shared or common representational space; those concepts are integrally linked, with one concept activating the other.

Lakoff and Johnson's (1980) conceptual metaphor theory proposes that the concrete concepts that are mapped onto abstract concepts are concepts that refer to bodily experiences involving space, time, movement, and other core elements of physical and neural experiences. The embodied aspect of conceptual metaphors is that the mappings between these target (abstract) and source (concrete) domains is assumed to correspond to neural mappings, such that thinking about an abstract concept shows neural activity representative of the concrete domain involved in the metaphor (Gallese & Lakoff, 2005). In this way, all concepts are grounded in bodily experiences, just as Glenberg (2010) has proposed, and the conceptual metaphor itself is simply a linguistic reflection of the simulation run (Barsalou, 1999). Evidence for this conceptual metaphor theory should be found in neurological support for the mappings between abstract concepts and concrete domains in addition to the behavioral evidence from the metaphoric transfer strategy.

Before looking at this evidence, there are two other types of evidence for conceptual metaphor theory worth considering. These come from the universality of metaphors across different languages and the prevalence of many different types of metaphors to express abstract knowledge.

The Universal Nature of Metaphors

A primary tenet of conceptual metaphor theory is that metaphors are not just linguistic conventions but reflections of how we represent abstract knowledge. If this is the case, then metaphor use should be found in all languages and across all cultures. There is a large body of research showing that many cultures share the same conceptual metaphors (Gibbs, 2011; Kövecses, 2003). For example, there are many idiomatic expressions in English that represent the conceptual metaphor that *the mind is a living thing or a body*. Expressions such as *my mind was racing* and *I see what you are saying* represent this target (mind)/source (physicality) mapping—living things move and living things perceive. These same metaphoric mappings are found in Chinese (e.g., translated: *train of thought*, and *way of looking at things*; Yu, 2003). Gibbs (2011) argued that the abstract concept of *thinking* is represented metaphorically in similar embodied ways across cultures because it is an abstraction shared by all people, thus the associated source concepts are also shared human experiences, as in moving, perceiving, and manipulating objects.

It is also possible for two cultures to have different metaphors for a particular abstract concept when there are very different cultural views of that concept. Again, this supports the proposal that metaphors are more than idiosyncratic expressions passed down over generations, but instead are expressions that stay prevalent because they reflect meaning with embedded cultural values (Yu, 2008). For example, both English and Japanese have metaphors to represent their conceptual representation of the abstract concept of assertiveness. In Western cultures, getting attention and being assertive is generally viewed positively, so the idiomatic expression *the squeaky wheel gets the grease* represents the cultural directive to speak out and be heard. For Asian cultures, being assertive is not particularly positive, and the conventional expression found in Japanese language that reflects their view of assertiveness (and similarly, of individuality) is (translated) *the nail that stands out gets hammered down first*.

Despite the linguistic differences in these cross-cultural idiomatic expressions, the conceptual metaphor being represented is similar in that it is linking assertiveness (target concept) to a physical act (source concept). In general, the extensive analysis of metaphors across different languages supports the contention that many conceptual metaphors are universal, especially when the metaphors are based on bodily experiences. Differences in the way cultures metaphorically express certain abstract concepts reflect differences in how those cultures think about those domains (Yu, 2008). These analyses support the contention that metaphors provide meaning across language users for concepts that by themselves have not been physically experienced but when attached to a concrete concept can be understood.

Categorizations of Metaphors

Others have provided a far richer categorization of metaphors and have described their role in thought (e.g., Gibbs, 1994; Lakoff & Johnson, 1999; Landau, Robinson, & Meier, 2014), so this will only cover a few different types of metaphors that have been studied empirically in psychological research. This is just a brief taxonomy to demonstrate metaphor's influence on cognition.

There are many different types of metaphors. Metaphors can be categorized by their syntactic category, such as *nominal* metaphors, which are figurative extensions of nouns and typically of the form, *an X is a Y* (e.g., *time is a thief*). Cognitive and neuropsychological research has tended to focus on this category of metaphors, but adjectives can also be used metaphorically (e.g., *close* relationship, or a *loose* cannon), as can verbs (e.g., *drove* the point home).

Metaphors can also be categorized by conceptual type, such as *structural* metaphors, where one concept is described in terms of another (as in the previously mentioned *love is a journey*, and *time is a thief*), versus *orientational* metaphors, which have been widely studied because of how ubiquitous they are in organizing a number of concepts in relation to one another and are found across many languages (Kövecses, 2003). The most prominent of these orientational metaphors is the *good is up* metaphor, which is associated with power (*upward mobility*, or *went up a notch or two in his pay grade*), mood (*things are looking up*, or *I'm feeling down*), morality (*taking the high ground*, or *that was so low*), and religiosity (*God is up in heaven*, or *the devil is down in hell*; Meier, Hauser, Robinson, Friesen, & Schjeldahl, 2007; Meier & Robinson, 2004, 2005; Schubert, 2005).

The *good is up* orientational metaphor maps positive and negative concepts onto a vertical dimension of space, and this is not arbitrarily determined. An embodied perspective on metaphor use would suggest that this metaphor reflects that because our bodies are in upright positions when we are healthy and mobile, *good* IS *up*. The same is true when we are in powerful positions. Power is typically physically represented by being on top (*he is at the top of the heap* vs. *he is the low man on the totem pole*), and when our bodies are in a prone position, we are physically vulnerable (*don't take it lying down*; Schubert, 2005).

The *up* metaphor is particularly pervasive with mood, and happiness and sadness are regularly associated with upright versus slumped physical postures. Lindeman and Abramson's (2008) theory of the causal mechanisms of depression suggests that depression is conceptualized metaphorically as powerlessness and motoric incapacity (e.g., *I'm so down I can hardly move; I'm sinking lower and lower*). They claim that because of this conceptualization, when in a depressive state, individuals simulate the experience of motor incapacity, which results in physical lethargy. A simulation of motor inaction would also involve an inability to alter events or take control, which would explain why depression is sometimes described as *spinning out of control*.

This theoretical perspective of depression suggests that one way to change this mood state is to alter the metaphorical mapping between the abstract concept of depression and the concrete physical state of motor inaction. This implies that physical activity and changes in bodily posture could alter one's cognitions, affecting mood, power, and personal agency. In fact there is some evidence that physical actions that move depressed individuals forward and require upright bodily postures are as effective in relieving some symptoms of depression as pharmaceutical interventions. Bodin and Martinsen (2004) found that even one session of martial arts exercises significantly improved feelings of self-efficacy and positive affect in depressed individuals compared with control individuals. However, riding on a stationary bike did not alleviate any symptoms of depression. Consistent with a metaphor perspective, riding a stationary bike is a simulation of "going nowhere," but martial arts simulate activity of "fighting back" and being powerful.

A prediction of Lindeman and Abramson's (2008) metaphor simulation model of depression is that the conceptualization of depression as "being down" or being in a state of motor incapacity yields feelings of powerlessness and hopelessness. Therefore, any activity that changes this simulation of motor inefficacy and allows an individual to reconceptualize their mental state as "moving forward"—dancing, running, even gardening—should have therapeutic benefits. This model also suggests that any condition associated with motoric difficulties, such as obesity, aging, and/or chronic disease, could cause depression.

There are other examples of how metaphors represent meaning in ways that might suggest clinical interventions. Clinicians have reported that having patients reconceptualize ways in which to understand themselves or others by changing metaphoric representations can be effective for at least some time (e.g., Loue, 2008; McMullen, 2008). The research concerning metaphor is extensive and multifaceted, much of it focusing on how pervasive metaphoric expressions are in the English language and how different types express specific forms of meaning intended for particular contexts (Gibbs, 1994; Kövecses, 2010; Lakoff & Johnson, 1980, 1999).

These data concerning the universality of metaphors and the different types of metaphors that appear to guide both thought and behavior are clearly supportive of conceptual metaphor theory. However, perhaps the strongest support for the embodied perspective of conceptual metaphor theory comes from the metaphoric transfer strategy that looks for bidirectional relationships between the abstract and concrete linkages in metaphors, and from neuroscience showing brain activity in sensorimotor pathways consistent with the metaphors used to describe abstract concepts.

Behavioral Evidence for Conceptual Metaphors

Landau et al. (2010) argued that the traditional view of conceptual knowledge proposes that concepts are understood as part of *schemas*, or abstract mental structures that organize knowledge about categories of information, including social information (e.g., gender) and cognitive information (e.g., importance). Spreading activation is the process by which concept nodes within a schema become activated, and associative links between those concepts are strengthened when frequently used in decisions and judgments. Of course theories of embodied cognition argue that instead of spreading activation, thinking about a concept involves a sensorimotor simulation that reenacts processes used when initially experiencing that concept.

Landau et al. (2010) claimed that metaphors reflect the sensorimotor simulations that occur when we are interpreting and evaluating information related to abstract concepts. What differentiates metaphors from schemas is that metaphors link superficially dissimilar concepts—one abstract and one more concrete—and these links are so unique that it would be very unlikely for them to be found within a schema. The metaphoric transfer strategy is an empirical strategy that is used to determine if metaphors do indeed offer more to our understanding of the representation of conceptual knowledge than schemas alone. This strategy involves experimentally manipulating the psychological states related to one concept in a metaphor to determine if that alters the way we process information about the other concept in the metaphor.

Following are just a few examples to demonstrate how the strategy yields evidence that metaphors represent abstract concepts differently than schemas; first, some research that has examined the conceptual metaphor linking the abstract concept of personality traits (e.g., generous, caring, or unsocial, aloof) with the concrete concept of physical temperature (e.g., *she has such a warm personality*, or *he acts very cold toward his father*). Williams and Bargh (2008) asked participants to hold either a warm cup of coffee or an iced coffee for an experimenter while the experimenter was recording participants' demographic information. The participants were then asked to read about Person A, and the description was intended to be socially neutral by emphasizing qualities such as determined, skillful, and practical. After reading the description, all participants rated the individual on a 1 to 7 (*cold* to *warm*) personality scale as well as a number of other scales pertaining to other personality dimensions (some semantically related to the warm/cold dimension, some not). Williams and Bargh found that those participants holding the warm cup rated the described person as significantly "warmer" than participants holding the cold cup. It is important to note that no participants claimed to be aware of the purpose of the manipulation. Further, the temperature manipulation did not affect other scale judgments, demonstrating that this result was a metaphor-consistent effect and not simply a "halo" effect for all positive personality traits.

Williams and Bargh (2008) argued that both in this experiment and in a second that replicated the effect, the physical sensation of warmth gave rise to feelings and cognitions of psychological warmth, which would include traits such as trustworthy and generous. They suggested that this likely takes place in the brain's insular cortex, which has been shown to be active during both physical and psychological aspects of warmth information (Meyer-Lindenberg, 2008). These neural pathways in the insular cortex that provide sensory information also appear to "ground" conceptual knowledge about psychological warmth, and this linkage is presumably developed early in life. Harlow's (1958) classic studies on maternal–infant bonding in primates demonstrated that physical warmth could be a more critical determinate of attachment than even nourishment.

Bowlby (1977) extended Harlow's conclusions to suggest that early childhood experiences of physical warmth from caregivers is critical for the normal development of interpersonal warmth and the detection of this attribute in others. Thus, as Lakoff and Johnson (1980) stated, a metaphor such as *she has such a warm personality* is not simply a linguistic convention that has no meaningful basis—the basis for the metaphoric expressions linking physical warmth and personality traits is bodily experiences established through early interactions with the world. As the link between physical warmth and psychological warmth (i.e., feeling attached, protected, loved) strengthens with repetition, these neural pathways serve dual representational functions, one sensory, one conceptual (Lakoff, 1993).

Landau et al. (2010) argued that prior to Williams and Bargh's (2008) results, there would have been little reason to suggest that physical warmth would be part of the schema concerning traits such as trustworthiness. Further, there is no a priori reason to believe that holding a warm cup would likely lead to a simulation of trustworthiness. However, an embodied perspective can account for these findings by suggesting that metaphors serve as a reflection of the conceptual representational structure that links an abstract concept that cannot be physically experienced, such as a personality trait, with a bodily experience, in this case, physical warmth.

Zhong and Leonardelli (2008) also examined the conceptual metaphor linking personality trait and physical temperature, but they examined the "other direction" of this relationship. Instead of exploring how temperature elicits a personality assessment consistent with the metaphor, Zhong and Leonardelli examined how the activation of the abstract concept of a personality trait would affect the bodily experience of temperature. They examined the *cold and lonely* metaphor that links the physical experience of being cold to the abstract concept of loneliness. Zhong and Leonardelli hypothesized that because Williams and Bargh (2008) found that the physical experience of holding a cold drink elicited thinking of others as "cold," then the opposite should occur as well, and thinking of instances of social exclusion should elicit the sensory simulation of feeling cold.

In their first experiment, Zhong and Leonardelli (2008) found that participants who recalled a past experience of being socially excluded reported the ambient temperature of the room they were in to be colder than those participants who recalled a past experience of being socially included. In Experiment 2, half of the participants were in a social exclusion condition in which they played a virtual ball-tossing game on a computer and were passed the ball very infrequently, and the other half of the participants were in a control condition in which they played the same computer game but were passed the ball a random number of times. Both groups of participants then took part in a supposedly unrelated marketing survey and rated their liking of five different products. Figure 8.1 presents the average desirability ratings for products that varied in temperature from being warm (coffee and soup) to cool (Coke and an apple) or neutral (crackers). This figure demonstrates that participants preferred warm food when they experienced social exclusion, implying that they had experienced a simulation of being physically cold.

These data confirm the "other" direction of this conceptual metaphor—activating the abstract concept of a personality trait, loneliness, elicited the simulation of the concrete concept of physical temperature, cold. Zhong and Leonardelli's research combined with Williams and Bargh's studies suggest a bidirectional relationship between physical temperature and certain personality traits, such that when one of these concepts is activated, the other may become accessible as well. This provides support for the embodied perspective that these concepts share representational space, and metaphors develop to reflect that representational linkage.

Slepian, Weisbuch, Rule, and Ambady's (2011) research provides another example of how social-category information is embodied, or grounded, in a bodily experience and reflected in a metaphor that links abstract information (gender) with a physical experience (tactile information of hardness). They chose the concept of gender to examine as it is often metaphorically aligned with sensory feedback from

FIGURE 8.1

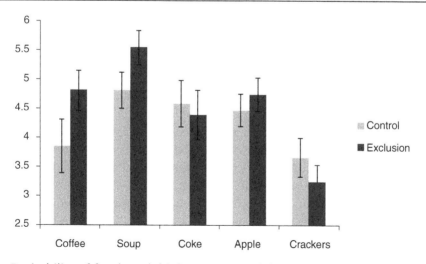

Desirability of foods and drinks among participants in the exclusion and control conditions in Experiment 2. From "Cold and Lonely: Does Social Exclusion Literally Feel Cold?" by C.-B. Zhong and G. J. Leonardelli, 2008, *Psychological Science*, *19*, p. 840. Copyright 2008 by Sage. Reprinted with permission.

hard (tough) or soft (tender) tactile experiences. One of the most common ways to metaphorically describe trait differences between males and females is with language about proprioceptive sensory feedback—males are *tough* and involved in *rough and tumble* play, where females are *tender* and *soft* and typically play *gently* with one another (Feingold, 1994). Slepian et al. hypothesized that this sensory experience of tactile information may ground gender representations. It is easy to imagine the developmental basis of this metaphor as infants being held by postpregnancy mothers would experience soft sensory feedback compared with the less soft bodies they would experience when held by their fathers. Because of the experiential basis for the metaphor, Slepian et al. expected that a physical experience of toughness (or tenderness) could affect gender categorization.

In Experiment 1, Slepian et al. (2011) had participants squeeze either a hard ball or a soft ball while they categorized sex-ambiguous faces as male or female. They found that faces were categorized as male more often by participants squeezing the hard ball, supporting their hypothesis that gender category representations include tactile information about toughness. Experiment 2 replicated this effect by having participants pressing either hard or pressing gently on pieces of paper to choose the gender categories for the same sex-ambiguous faces shown in Experiment 1. Faces were categorized as male more often when participants had to press hard on the paper than when they pressed gently. These data are difficult to reconcile with a schema approach to knowledge representation (except with a post hoc explanation) because there is no a priori reason for a schema for gender to include tactile sensory experiences. However, these data do support a metaphor-enriched perspective for the representation of abstract concepts such as gender. This perspective suggests that the metaphors we use (e.g., *He's such a tough guy!*) elucidate the abstract to concrete concept link that reflects embodied conceptual knowledge. At least part of the representation of gender may share neural pathways with the representation of sensory information about "hardness."

Slepian, Rule, and Ambady (2012) further examined whether person perception was grounded in proprioception by investigating whether this embodied effect for gender extended to socially constructed categories such as political party affiliation. Slepian et al. first determined that participants use metaphoric descriptors such as *hard* and *soft* to describe politicians, with Republicans referred to more often as hard than Democrats. Also, academic disciplines were assigned these same metaphoric descriptors, with natural science disciplines referred to as hard but social science (e.g., sociology) and history referred to as soft. Slepian et al. then conducted an experiment that had participants squeezing either a hard ball or a soft ball while viewing faces, similar to the Slepian, Weisbuch, Rule, and Ambady (2011) study, but this time participants categorized the faces as Republican or Democrat. They found that participants squeezing the hard ball categorized more faces as Republican than participants squeezing a soft ball.

In another experiment, Slepian et al. (2012) found that when participants were categorizing faces as belonging to professors either in physics or in history, participants squeezing the hard ball identified more faces as physicists than participants squeezing the soft ball. Thus, across these experiments, the sensory/tactile experience of hardness influenced person perception across multiple social categories. Again, to have schemas that organize knowledge about political parties or academic disciplines include tactile information about hardness does not seem likely. However, the metaphor enriched perspective suggests that metaphors that describe a political party or an area of academia (e.g., *Scientists are hard-nosed* or *Democrats are soft on crime*) reflect the embodied nature of conceptual knowledge—knowledge is grounded in the sensory experience that is reflected in the metaphor.

Finally, in one last experiment, Slepian et al. (2012) examined the bidirectional nature of this metaphoric relationship between social category and proprioceptive feedback. They claimed that if Barsalou (1999) was correct that sensorimotor modalities are part of the representation of even abstract concepts (political party), then when thinking about (or simulating) the abstract concept, this would include its perceptual symbol (hardness). The simulation of this abstract concept should bias the judgment about the physical features, or hardness, of an object. Slepian et al. (2012) had participants write a short narrative about a typical meeting that either a Republican or a Democrat might have concerning a hot-topic issue. After 3 minutes of doing this, participants were asked to pick up a ball that was filled with latex, making it neither hard nor soft, and they had to make a scale judgment about how hard or soft the ball was. Results showed that participants who wrote about a Republican judged the ball to be harder than participants who wrote about a Democrat. Evidence for this bidirectional relationship (e.g., if hard, then Republican; if Republican, then hard) suggests that the representation of abstract social categories such as political affiliation is at least partially embodied in the sensory feedback system for tactile information.

The metaphoric associations of "hardness" or "roughness" are also aligned with the concept of difficulty, specifically in terms of social interactions (e.g., *That was a rough conversation we had.*) Ackerman, Nocera, and Bargh (2010) asked participants to put together a five-piece puzzle, and for half of the participants, the pieces were covered in rough sandpaper (rough condition) and the other half of the participants handled pieces that were uncovered (smooth condition). After completing the puzzle, participants read a passage describing an ambiguous social interaction and were asked to answer questions about this interaction. Results indicated that the participants in the rough puzzle condition rated the social interaction as more difficult and "harsh" than participants in the smooth condition. Further, this roughness manipulation did not affect questions concerning other aspects of the social interaction, such as relationship familiarity. Ackerman et al. concluded that the tactile feedback led to a simulation of "social coordination" consistent with common metaphors about roughness, suggesting that this abstract concept of difficult social interactions may be neurally connected to the sensory pathways used for experiencing touch.

There are many other studies that provide behavioral evidence of abstract concepts grounded in concrete experiences in metaphor-consistent ways (Landau et al., 2010, provided a comprehensive review of the research). For example, the concept of importance is metaphorically associated with "having weight," and the evidence that this is more than a linguistic convention is that participants holding a heavy clipboard judged items on that clipboard to have greater value than participants judging the same items that are on a light clipboard (Ackerman et al., 2010; Jostmann, Lakens, & Schubert, 2009). Additionally, if participants believed that a USB-stick (portable hard drive) holds important tax information, they judged that small device as heavier than when they believed the USB-stick holds less important or no information (Schneider, Parzuchowski, Wojciszke, Schwarz, & Koole, 2015). Interestingly, research has suggested that knowledge of the material that is being judged by weight may affect the use of the metaphor. Chandler, Reinhard, and Schwarz (2012) found that a book was considered more important when it weighed more but only when participants had knowledge about the book (having read it before or at least read a synopsis). More research is needed to investigate the boundary conditions for the accessibility of metaphoric knowledge.

Other conceptualizations for abstract concepts have been found to be embodied within physical sensations: time, embodied in forward and backward movement (Miles, Nind, & Macrae, 2010); moral purity, embodied in physical cleanliness (S. W. S. Lee & Schwarz, 2010; Schnall, Benton, & Harvey, 2008; Zhong & Liljenquist, 2006); relationship stability, embodied in physical stability (Forest, Kille, Wood, & Stehouwer, 2015; Kille, Forest, & Wood, 2013); and many more discussed elsewhere (Lakoff, 2014; Landau et al., 2010; Landau et al., 2014). But this behavioral evidence for metaphor-consistent behavior needs to be supported by neurological evidence showing activity in brain centers responsible for the sensorimotor concepts linked to the abstract concept in the metaphor.

Neurological Support for Conceptual Metaphors

Lakoff (2014) posited that metaphors are neural circuits that link two brain regions, a source (concrete concept) region and a target (abstract concept) region. But is there research to back this up? Schaefer, Denke, Heinze, and Rotte (2014) examined the neural evidence for the conceptual metaphor linking hardness with social interactions by employing the procedure used by Ackerman et al. (2010). Schaefer et al. told participants that they would be participating in two separate experiments while lying in a functional magnetic resonance imaging (fMRI) scanner. In one, they would be touching different surfaces to investigate the neural correlates of touch. In another, they would be making judgments about passages describing social interactions to investigate the neural correlates of social judgments.

While lying in the scanner, participants received tactile stimulation (rough, smooth, or no touch), and this was followed by a screen describing an ambiguously valenced social interaction. Following the short text, participants responded to two sets of questions. One set addressed the social coordination aspect of the interaction (was the interaction friendly or adversarial), and the other set addressed relationship familiarity (was the interaction businesslike or casual). After the scanning, participants were probed for any suspicions concerning the relationship between the "two experiments," and none of the participants reported any knowledge of the experimental hypothesis.

The behavioral results are shown in Figure 8.2 and replicate Ackerman et al.'s (2010) results. The rough tactile condition led to significantly lower scores on the social coordination scale compared with the smooth tactile condition and the no-touch condition. There were no effects of the tactile manipulation on the relationship familiarity questions, suggesting that the tactile priming led to simulations of social interactions that were harsher and more adversarial but did not make the scenario seem generally negative or impersonal (i.e., the results were metaphor consistent). The critical results in this study come from the brain responses during these different phases of the study.

First, brain responses while participants received the touch stimulus did not differ between rough and smooth touch, with both, unsurprisingly, activating areas in the somatosensory cortex. Second, brain responses did differ between the rough, smooth, and no-touch conditions during the time participants were judging the social interaction (and touch was not involved). Schaefer et al. (2014) found that activation in the somatosensory cortex, hippocampus, amygdala, and premotor cortex was

FIGURE 8.2

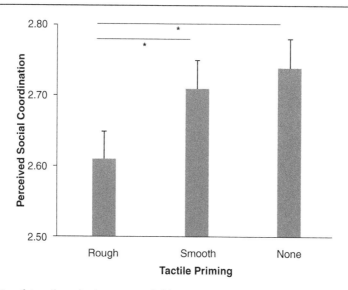

Effects of tactile priming on social impressions. Perceived social coordination was significantly lower when participants were primed with a rough stimulus (sandpaper) compared with a smooth prime (paintbrush) or no prime. From "Rough Primes and Rough Conversations: Evidence for a Modality-Specific Basis to Mental Metaphors," by M. Schaefer, C. Denke, H.-J. Henize, and M. Rotte, 2014, *Social Cognitive and Affective Neuroscience, 9*, p. 1655. Copyright 2013 by M. Schaefer, C. Denke, H.-J. Henize, and M. Rotte. Reprinted with permission.

greater during the reading of the ambiguous scenario when it followed the rough tactile experience condition than when it followed the smooth or no-touch tactile experience conditions. Additionally, somatosensory activation correlated highly with the degree to which participants judged the social interaction as difficult. Thus, the brain activation was closely aligned with the roughness metaphor. The activation in this network of brain areas was specific to the issue of social coordination and was not involved when participants were judging the relationship familiarity of the interaction.

Schaefer et al. (2014) concluded that their results strongly support embodiment theory, which proposes that processing conceptual meaning in the form of metaphorical knowledge involves a simulation of sensory experiences. These sensory experiences appear to ground the knowledge that roughness is associated with concepts of harshness or difficulty. The activation in the hippocampus and amygdala during the text processing may indicate emotional processing (amygdala) and retrieval of related memories (hippocampus). When addressing why conceptual representations of concepts relating to social interactions are so closely aligned with tactile experiences, Schaefer et al. surmised that touch may be the first sense to develop, used to both acquire information and to manipulate the environment. As such, it may be especially important in scaffolding the development of conceptual and metaphorical knowledge, especially in terms of early social bonds and then later social inferences. They concluded that their results suggest that activation in the primary somatosensory cortex may include higher order cognitions such as the roughness metaphor.

Critics of embodiment have argued that fMRI data, with its low temporal resolution, cannot be used to distinguish between early brain effects of automatic sensorimotor activation when accessing word meaning from later, more strategic effects that arise from conscious mental imagery (Mahon & Caramazza, 2008). Therefore, other researchers have used event-related potentials (ERPs) as a real-time measure of brain function associated with numerous aspects of language. For example, Zanolie et al. (2012) examined both behavioral and ERP evidence for attentional shifts consistent with the power metaphor. Schubert (2005) argued that the idiomatic metaphors for power, such as "She looked *up* to her boss" and "Those workers were the *under*lings in the company," involve the vertical dimension in space.

To test whether understanding the concept of power activates the up–down (verticality) spatial dimension, Schubert (2005) presented pairs of stimuli in clear power-differential positions, such as *master* and *servant,* simultaneously on a computer screen, one above the other. When participants were asked to detect the powerful or powerless member of the pair as quickly as possible, Schubert found that responses were faster to identify the powerful word when it was presented on top and faster to identify the powerless word when it was presented on the bottom. In another experiment where participants were asked to make power decisions to words (e.g., defeats vs. obeys), participants were faster to respond to powerful words when they appeared at the top of the screen and faster to respond to powerless words when they were at the bottom of the screen.

Zanolie et al. (2012) used ERP responses to test the automaticity of the activation of the vertical spatial dimension in the processing of power metaphors. Zanolie et al.'s first experiment employed a behavioral paradigm used by Meier and Robinson (2004) that protects against a response bias explanation for results such as Schubert's (2005). In prior studies concerning the *good is up* metaphor, the spatial relationship assumed to be embedded in the positive/negative concepts could have been noticed by participants and then used strategically to improve their performance (Lebois, Wilson-Mendenhall, & Barsalou, 2015). Zanolie et al. had participants make power decisions to words denoting powerful (dictator) or powerless (maid) people, but in this procedure, unlike Schubert's, the words were presented in the center of the screen.

Following each decision, a target letter (p or q) was presented in the upper or lower visual field of the screen. Participants were required to identify the letter as quickly and accurately as possible. If the up/down vertical dimension is activated automatically with the presentation of the word, then spatial attention should be directed to the part of the visual field that was simulated when making the power decision immediately preceding this letter identification.

Figure 8.3 shows the reaction times for the target letter identification in Zanolie et al.'s (2012) first experiment. Participants were faster to respond to the letter

FIGURE 8.3

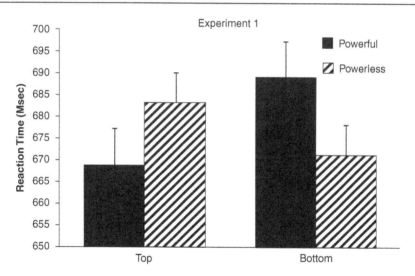

Reaction times and error rates (in proportions) for the target letter identification task (*p–q* judgment) in Experiment 1. Error bars represent standard errors of the mean difference between adjacent bars. From "Mighty Metaphors: Behavioral Evidence and ERP Evidence That Power Shifts Attention on a Vertical Dimension," by K. Zanolie, S. van Dantzig, I. Boot, J. Wijnen, T. W. Schubert, S. R. Giessner, and D. Pecher, 2012, *Brain and Cognition*, *78*, p. 53. Copyright 2011 by Elsevier. Reprinted with permission.

identification at the top of the screen when it was preceded by a powerful word, but they were faster to respond to the letter identification at the bottom of the screen when it was preceded by a powerless word. Replicating Schubert (2005), this result suggests automatic activation of the vertical dimension of space when thinking about the abstract concept of power. It is unlikely this spatial attention effect can be explained by a response bias because the identity of the target letter was not related to the position of the prior word or its meaning.

In a second experiment, Zanolie et al. (2012) wanted to use ERP evidence to explore a more detailed observation of the time course of this spatial attention shift that occurs when making a power decision. They predicted that a shift of attention consistent with the power metaphor should be indicated by a larger amplitude response in ERP activity (specifically, an N1 response, which is a component sensitive to attention directed to a visual target). This should occur when the spatial location of the target was congruent with the powerful or powerless word compared with when it was incongruent.

Their results supported their prediction: Modulation of the N1 component was affected by congruency between the direction of the vertical dimension elicited by the power metaphor and the spatial location of the target. Zanolie et al. (2012) argued that the spatial shift of attention found in this study could only be due to the meaning of the power word and not due to any explicit spatial stimulation because the words were presented centrally. This ERP data provides important neural evidence that the spatial up–down dimension is activated when the concept of power is activated, causing an attentional shift in the direction implied by the power word.

Other research that has investigated the neural basis of metaphorical mappings has compared brain activity during the processing of literal meaning with brain activity during the processing of metaphoric expressions. Bardolph and Coulson (2014) examined event-related brain responses to visually presented words that either literally represented movement in the up/down direction (e.g., descend and ascend) or metaphorically represented the same direction of movement (e.g., agony and delight). These words were presented to participants on a screen while they were concurrently performing a movement task that had them making upward and downward movements with their arms. These movements were either congruent with the movement direction suggested by the word or they were incongruent. Participants' ERP data was collected from a cap worn that collected data from the motor and premotor cortex of the participants' brains.

Consistent with their prediction from an embodied perspective, Bardolph and Coulson (2014) found that words whose verticality was literal showed more positive ERPs within 200–300 ms after their onset in the incongruent condition than in the congruent condition (called the "congruency effect"). They suggested that this congruency effect reflects greater activity in the motor or premotor cortex because of the incompatibility of the hand movements with the meaning elicited by the word. It is important to note that effects of movement congruency did not affect words whose meaning was metaphorical until more than 500 ms after word onset. By 700–1,100 ms after word onset, both literal and metaphorical words showed the ERP congruency effect.

Bardolph and Coulson (2014) argued that the early congruency effects for the literal words strongly support embodiment theory that suggests that words that elicit meaning about movement automatically activate motor cortex areas. The 200-ms onset of the congruency effect is consistent with other data that suggests that during that postword onset interval, semantic processing occurs that influences action responses (e.g., Hauk, Johnsrude, & Pulvermüller's, 2004, data showed similar ERP responses with activity in the motor and premotor cortex after reading action verbs such as "kick").

The fact that the metaphoric congruency effects occurred later argues against the strongest version of embodiment theory that would suggest literal meaning and metaphoric meaning similarly evoke sensorimotor processing (Gallese & Lakoff, 2005). However, the late congruency effects for the metaphorical words suggest that participants are sensitive to the connection (or as Lakoff would describe, the metaphoric circuitry) between an abstract concept and the spatial dimension consistent with the *good is up* orientation metaphor. Although these data are not consistent with a strong embodied model for conceptual metaphor, a more tempered model would suggest that while sensorimotor simulations of a metaphor's meaning take longer than that which occurs for literal meaning, they do occur but are perhaps constrained by context and task demands (Lebois et al., 2015; Louwerse & Jeuniaux, 2008).

Conclusions

The studies discussed in this chapter offer empirical support for the conceptual metaphor theory (Gibbs, 1994; Lakoff & Johnson, 1980). This theory suggests that abstract concepts' conceptual structure comes from concrete domains of experience, and through the process of metaphorical mapping, these abstract concepts become grounded in sensorimotor processing. This view emphasizes that metaphors are not just linguistic conventions, but instead a reflection of mental representation. Therefore, we not only speak in metaphors, we think in metaphors (Gibbs, 2011; Lakoff, 1993).

There are a number of different paths that researchers have followed to find evidence for conceptual metaphors reflecting the representation of abstract knowledge. Some have argued that the universality of conceptual metaphors in all languages and across all cultures is testament to the proposal that these linguistic devices represent physically rooted knowledge (Gibbs, 2011; Kövecses, 2003). The ubiquity of metaphors in the English language and the number of different categorizations of metaphors is supportive of the fact that abstract knowledge is understood in multifaceted ways and always as a function of the context in which it is found (Lakoff & Johnson, 1980, 1999). If one is describing time as *the days are dragging on*, we understand time very differently than when it is described as *flying by*. Although both idiomatic expressions represent the conceptual metaphor that links time with physical motion, meaning is derived from the specific metaphor used within a context.

Empirical evidence for conceptual metaphors representing abstract knowledge can be found in both behavioral experiments and in neuropsychological studies.

Landau et al. (2010) discussed the Williams and Bargh (2008) and Zhong and Leonardelli (2008) studies as one example of how behavioral evidence can be found with the metaphoric transfer strategy that demonstrates there is a bidirectional relationship in the metaphor linking physical temperature and personality assessments. This evidence indicates that in thinking about an abstract concept, the concrete concept is automatically activated, and the opposite occurs as well. Zhong and Leonardelli's studies suggest that the physical experience of coldness is an integral part of the experience of social rejection. Slepian et al.'s (2011, 2012) data suggests that tactile stimulation (e.g., experiencing sensory resistance) may simulate a social category, and thinking about a social category may simulate a tactile experience.

Finally, neuroscience is extending our understanding of conceptual metaphor theory. Schaefer et al. (2014) concluded that the demonstrated metaphor-specific impact of rough tactile priming that lead to interpretations of difficult social interactions rely on a network of brain regions typically involved in sensorimotor processing. Although support has been found for the neural circuitry involved in abstract to concrete concept mappings of metaphoric expressions (Zanolie et al., 2012), others have cautioned that the neuroscience results suggest a more tempered view of embodied conceptual metaphors. In this view, the recruitment of brain areas responsible for sensorimotor processing may be immediate for words that literally evoke physical properties such as movement, but metaphorical expressions may be somewhat delayed, perhaps suggesting time needed to process the mappings between abstract and concrete concepts.

Takeaway

- Language has evolved in systems of perception and action.
- The linguistic device of a metaphor reflects the embodied nature of conceptual knowledge because the linkage between an abstract concept and a concrete concept represents the body-driven, possibly neural, mapping between these two concepts (Lakoff).

Reactions to the Theory of Embodied Cognition

The degree to which cognition is thought to be "grounded" in systems for perception and action has been debated by cognitive psychologists, cognitive neuroscientists, and cognitive scientists when trying to construct a theory of the mind. The issue has been whether grounded or embodied cognition can effectively replace the older, more traditional, modular views of the mind, in which cognition operates on symbolic, abstract, conceptual representations that are structurally autonomous from sensory and motor processes (e.g., Collins & Loftus, 1975; Fodor & Pylyshyn, 1988; Newell & Simon, 1972; Smith, Shoben, & Rips, 1974). This debate has generated significant interest both theoretically and experimentally.

Most theorists acknowledge that these older theories cannot account for the wealth of evidence supportive of this new perspective (e.g., Barsalou, 2016; Glenberg, 2015). However, many have argued that current versions of the theory of embodied cognition lack precision and do not adequately specify the relationship between the body and cognition (e.g., Gentsch, Weber, Synofzik, Vosgerau, & Schütz-Bosbach, 2016; Goldinger, Papesh, Barnhart, Hansen, & Hout, 2016; Mahon & Caramazza, 2008; A. D. Wilson & Golonka, 2013). In this chapter, general reactions to embodiment theory will be presented followed by discussion of some of the more specific criticisms of embodiment research. What is important for the reader to know is

http://dx.doi.org/10.1037/0000136-009
How the Body Shapes Knowledge: Empirical Support for Embodied Cognition, by R. Fincher-Kiefer

that to date, there has not been a new theory of knowledge representation presented to counter the theory of embodied cognition. There are different philosophical versions of the theory (as presented in Chapter 1), and these are detailed in other texts (e.g., Chemero, 2009; Shapiro, 2011, 2014). However, within experimental cognitive psychology, those interested in how knowledge is represented in the brain either examine and test the traditional, modular, view of semantic representations of knowledge, or they investigate the theory of embodied cognition and explore the role of the body in building conceptual knowledge.

Current Status of Embodiment Theory

As embodiment theory has developed, there have been a number of frameworks and categorization schemes put forth (e.g., Gentsch et al., 2016; Philbeck & Witt, 2015; A. D. Wilson & Golonka, 2013), and predictably, there have been some strong critiques of the theory (e.g., Firestone, 2013; Firestone & Scholl, 2017; Goldinger et al., 2016; Mahon, 2015). There are complex and often highly philosophical reactions to the theory, and sometimes the critiques are specific to an area of empirical research. To simplify these ongoing debates, I argue that much of the reaction to embodiment theory focuses on the nature or strength of the relationship between the body and cognition.

Some claim that the body, or neural representations of what the body has physically experienced, is what constitutes knowledge. Others contend that what the body has experienced, or the perceptual symbols that come from that, partially represents knowledge, but there is a role for other forms of knowledge representation as well. These other forms are "abstractions," such as categorical knowledge or schematic knowledge, and they could take the form of traditional symbolic representations (Goldinger et al., 2016; Mahon, 2015). However, Barsalou (2016) and others (e.g., Dove, 2016; Zwaan, 2016) argued that even these abstractions are not amodal representations with abstract symbols such as propositions; instead, they are multimodal, neural networks that have "compressed" or organized detailed knowledge. Barsalou (2016) maintained that these abstractions (neural networks) are distributed across brain areas that are not necessarily sensorimotor, but converge with these other sensorimotor representations in a way that is highly compatible with grounded approaches to cognition.

The extent to which cognitive processes involve more than sensorimotor representations of knowledge is what determines the nature and the strength of an embodied relationship. A. D. Wilson and Golonka (2013) proposed that if cognitive psychologists accept the definition of embodied cognition as the interplay between perception, action, and the environment on cognitive processes and representations, then the more traditional views of cognition must be replaced by quite different processes and representations that are perception–action couplings and little more. This version of embodiment is what Shapiro (2011) has referred to as the *replacement hypothesis*, which essentially represents the strongest view of embodiment, one that questions the need for internal representations at all. A. D. Wilson and Golonka make the claim that this version of embodiment is necessary to truly differentiate this theory from the standard theories of cognitive psychology.

However, the replacement hypothesis version of embodiment was not tested in the cognitive research presented in this book because it is not a perspective that is considered possible for complex human cognition. It is a view that is more appropriate for cognitive scientists to consider as they test embodiment through modeling and robotics. Robots are built without concern for validating what internal human knowledge representation looks like. In fact, robots are indeed capable of some fascinating behaviors such as locomotion and mate selection and do so without any explicit representation of those behaviors in their operating system (see A. D. Wilson & Golonka, 2013, for a summary of embodiment research in both the robotics and animal literature). However, this most radical view of embodiment may "work" better for robots and animals than for humans.

If we move away from the strongest view of embodiment where the body fully constitutes thought and internal representations of knowledge may not even be needed, how do we characterize the constitutive relationship between the body and cognition? A constitutive relationship is a dependent relationship that can vary from strong to weak (see Gentsch et al., 2016, for this type of categorization of different theories of embodiment). What is critical in a constitutive relationship is that one process may be necessary for another (e.g., action may be essential to perception), but the second process may also involve other constituents (e.g., perception may involve other processes as well). Therefore, "weaker" or more flexible views of embodiment acknowledge that sensorimotor representations may partially constitute thought, but they allow for the possibility of other forms of knowledge representations to be involved (Barsalou, 2008a, 2008b, 2016).

Barsalou's (1999) original perceptual symbol systems theory proposed a full constitutive relationship between action and cognition. If cognition is essentially a reenactment of sensorimotor processes, perhaps supported by a mirror neuron system, then in this view, action and perception share the same representational states and therefore are fully constitutive. An example of evidence for such a view is found in a study that tests patients who have severe impairment with locomotion (paraplegia) and examines the consequences of that impairment on the perception of human locomotion. Arrighi, Cartocci, and Burr (2011) found that patients with severe spinal injury showed a significant reduction in detecting and discriminating the direction of biological motion in the perception of point-light walkers compared with healthy control patients. These results suggest interdependence between producing and perceiving motion, implicating shared neural mechanisms, or a constitutive relationship between action and perception.

Similarly, Grossman et al. (2008) demonstrated that patients with amyotrophic lateral sclerosis, a disease of progressive degeneration of motor tracts, showed more impairment for concepts of actions than for concepts of objects, and this was specifically associated with the patients' atrophy of their motor cortex. This type of evidence indicates that an intact motor cortex may not only be necessary for the detection of motion, but may also be necessary for intact *conceptual* knowledge of action, suggesting, again, a constitutive relationship between bodily action and cognition.

However, in his recent conceptualization of the current state of embodied cognition, Barsalou (2016) argued that the constitutive relationship between the body and cognition may be partial rather than full. This view suggests that knowledge is represented conceptually by partially reusing the same modality-specific brain areas that were used in the initial sensorimotor experience of that information. This "neural reuse" is *simulation*, but it may not be complete in any cognitive act because it will vary as a function of context and task demands. However, cognition always involves the partial reuse of the modality-specific pathway that was used during the initial perception, action, or internal state (i.e., emotion, imagining) concerning that thought, but this may be coupled with other mechanisms needed to completely understand that thought. For example, this may include activation of neural pathways that represent linguistic information such as metaphoric relationships. These are not amodal symbols (e.g., propositions) however; they are still multimodal representations.

Zwaan (2016) fleshed this argument out a bit further in the context of how sensorimotor representations play a role in language comprehension. Zwaan proposed that language comprehension may begin with activation in distributed linguistic representations, which are characterized as words activating other words via semantic associations. However, these are not amodal symbols in propositional networks as in traditional models, but instead, perceptual representations of concepts (words) in multimodal neural networks organized by meaning (this is one form of the abstraction "compression"). Zwaan claimed that these linguistic representations interact with the sensorimotor representations of what is being read bidirectionally, with these "layers" of representation constraining each other to produce fluency in comprehension (Zwaan & Madden, 2005).

The degree to which sensorimotor representations are used in language comprehension is variable and due to context. For example, some abstract concepts connect to sensorimotor representations immediately given how they are presented in the discourse and the reader's knowledge (imagine a physics expert reading a physics text), but other abstract concepts may initially need linguistic representations (a physics novice may only be able to comprehend a physics word because it is semantically related to another word that they do understand). These linguistic, more symbolic, representations may stand in as a "placeholder" in working memory until sufficient context allows for a richer, grounded, representation of what is being read.

Zwaan's (2016) view of these distributed linguistic representations is that they can be used to perform some cognitive tasks quickly and effectively, but they result in a level of comprehension that is less than when using multimodal perceptual simulations. Others have similarly argued that these kinds of more symbolic representations may be needed for certain task demands that require quick responses and shallow processing, but they would not be sufficient for tasks that demand richer levels of comprehension (Barsalou, Santos, Simmons, & Wilson, 2008; Lebois, Wilson-Mendenhall, & Barsalou, 2015; Solomon & Barsalou, 2004).

Some evidence has been presented that is not consistent with a strong version of embodiment theory but may be compatible with this more flexible, or "weak," version of the theory. A strong view of embodiment would predict that even non-conscious priming of spatial words (e.g., up, down) would yield action compatibility effects similar to those found in Glenberg and Kaschak (2002) during comprehension (i.e., reading language that implies movement in one direction primes how the reader moves in that direction and vice versa). This is because in the strong version, the meaning of a word is a sensorimotor representation, and whether that word is consciously or nonconsciously presented, a simulation of that representation will occur (Glenberg & Gallese, 2012; Pulvermüller, 2013). However, Bottini, Bucur, and Crepaldi (2016) found that the sensorimotor processing that occurs during language comprehension requires conscious processing. Bottini et al. found that subliminal priming of spatial words did not lead to the typical spatial congruency effects with bodily action that was found with conscious priming. These data require a flexible view of embodiment that can account for data in conscious priming conditions as well as in nonconscious priming conditions.

Mathôt, Grainger, and Strijkers (2017) also tested a strong versus a weak version of embodiment when they examined whether word meaning by itself could trigger an involuntary response—pupil constriction. They tested the hypothesis that if word comprehension involves sensorimotor simulations, or activating brain areas responsible for processing nonlinguistic information such as light information, then understanding words that convey meaning about brightness or darkness should result in appropriate pupillary responses (constricting for brightness, enlarging for darkness).

In their experiment, Mathôt et al. (2017) measured pupillary responses when participants read or listened to single words in four categories: words conveying brightness, words conveying darkness, neutral words, and animal names. Participants were asked to press the space bar on a computer whenever they saw or heard an animal name. Mathôt et al. found that their participants' pupils were smaller when both reading and listening to words that were semantically related to brightness (e.g., sun) than when they read or listened to words related to darkness (e.g., night). This response did occur slowly, peaking between one and two seconds after the presentation of the word.

These data suggest that word meaning alone can trigger a mental simulation that produces a sensory response largely beyond voluntary control. However, the fact that these pupil responses occurred late in the comprehension process, peaking about a second after readers had processed the word's meaning, suggests that this involuntary response is likely not essential to comprehension. This could support a weaker view of embodiment where a type of linguistic representation may have preceded the sensorimotor representation of the words.

However, Mathôt et al. (2017) argued that even if word representations are not strongly embodied (i.e., they may be accompanied by sensorimotor simulations instead of consisting of sensorimotor representations), the fact that word meanings trigger mental simulations that lead to physiological responses suggests a "profound" interaction between language and sensory systems. They propose that in this case of semantic pupillary response, the automatic sensorimotor simulation that occurs with language comprehension may be a preparatory action response—adjusting pupil size to have optimal perception of something just comprehended. This language–action link may be removed enough from the immediate comprehension of a word to be less "embodied" than a strong view of embodiment would require, and yet it is a reflection of what the sensorimotor simulation involved in language comprehension does—prepare for actions and perceptions that may be forthcoming.

Critics have suggested that these weaker views of embodiment are not sufficiently different from the traditional, amodal views of language to be meaningful (Mahon, 2015; Mahon & Caramazza, 2008). They want to see that embodied responses are automatic (i.e., nonconscious and immediate) for the theory to offer a radically different perspective on knowledge representation. However, others have suggested that when we see that some bodily responses take time, this does not necessarily suggest that cognition is not grounded in systems of perception and action. Van Dantzig, Zeelenberg, and Pecher (2009) argued that it may not be necessary for cognitive concepts to be mapped directly onto the lowest levels of sensorimotor representations (e.g., at the muscle activation level). In a dynamic system, concepts may be mapped onto perceptual and motor systems at a higher level of action representation—even at the level of goals and motivations. Van Dantzig et al. stated that these higher level representations are more abstract and complex than the lower level representations and may take longer to develop, but they are still a function of perception and action.

By allowing some flexibility concerning where in the hierarchy of a sensorimotor system actions play a role in cognition—in their most rudimentary form (neural activity in the motor cortex) to their most abstract form (meeting intentions, goals, and motivations)—this permits cognition to be embodied all along that hierarchy. Van Dantzig et al.'s (2009) claim is that cognition embodied in higher order sensorimotor representations allows humans to move beyond simply responding in reflexive ways, which would occur with only low-level sensorimotor representations. To claim that embodiment must occur at the lowest level of sensorimotor representations (immediate event-related potentials [ERPs] or pupillary responses) would be ignoring the essential role that these sensorimotor representations play in human cognition.

Where are we now in understanding embodiment theory? Theory and research have demonstrated that knowledge is constructed through bodily processes—our perceptual, motoric, and emotional experiences shape our representations of conceptual knowledge. Whether the body constitutes thought may be a question of degree—theories of embodiment vary in whether the body fully or partially constitutes thought. The complexity of this debate is beyond the scope of this chapter (see Barsalou, 2016; Glenberg, 2015; Goldinger et al., 2016), but undeniably, future behavioral and neuroscience research is needed to help us understand such processes as neural reuse and if and when any other types of abstract representations of knowledge are needed.

Specific Criticisms of Embodiment Research

Although a number of studies exploring embodiment have been criticized, the area of embodiment research that has perhaps been most hotly debated is that concerning embodied perception and the many findings supporting Proffitt's (2006) view that perception serves action (see Schnall, 2017). There are numerous results that suggest that a person's action capabilities (a body's morphology, physiology, and behavior) change the perception of spatial properties such as slant, distance, size, and weight (e.g., Proffitt & Linkenauger, 2013; Witt, 2011), but other research has been conducted that suggests that these findings are the result of postperceptual processes (see Durgin et al., 2009; Durgin, Klein, Spiegel, Strawser, & Williams, 2012; Firestone, 2013).

Postperceptual processes include demand characteristics, in which participants guess how the experimenters want them to respond, and response biases, in which participants respond in the direction consistent with their body's current state. Thus, these effects would not be "perceptual" effects, but decision-level effects that occur at output, or after perception. This is an impassioned controversy, with strong views that are backed by empirical work on both sides of the argument (see Philbeck & Witt, 2015). However, recent studies have effectively ruled out demand characteristics as an explanation for many of the effects of one's bodily state on perception. For example, Zadra, Weltman, and Proffitt (2016) found that glucose consumption in athletes affects distance perception such that higher glucose drinks yield shorter distance judgments than no-glucose drinks, even when taste differences are empirically ruled out. Despite these data, arguments persist that participants in these studies consciously or nonconsciously comply with the experimenter's expectations that the body affects perception.

One way to discount criticisms such as those by Durgin et al. (2012) that action–cognition effects are laboratory phenomenon would be to find evidence of Proffitt's (2006, 2013) economy of action model of perception in everyday behavior. Proffitt's model predicts that subgroups that have resources depleted (overweight, aged, and encumbered people) should perceive stairs to be steeper than those with more resources and would therefore "economize" their action by avoiding stairs. Eves (2014) reported observational data from 11 studies examining behavior at shopping malls and from over 20 studies examining behavior in travel settings and found that women, overweight individuals, elderly individuals, and people carrying multiple shopping bags or heavy luggage avoid stairs (the manmade equivalent of steep hills) more than their counterparts, opting for escalators.

Further, in a follow-up study to this observational study, women, older individuals, and those who were heavier and shorter were stopped in a shopping mall and asked to judge the steepness of the mall's stairs. These groups all reported staircases to be steeper than their comparison groups (Eves, Thorpe, Lewis, & Taylor-Covill, 2014). The finding that women are in this category may be not as intuitive as the other subgroups, and the exact physiological reason for women's action capabilities being lesser than men's may be due to a number of factors. It may be that women have lower centers of gravity, making steep inclines more difficult to ascend, or a greater percentage of body fat, or possibly less leg strength than men. Whatever the cause, the consistency of this demographic, as well as the others, both naturally avoiding a resource-demanding activity and also reporting the stairs to be steeper, supports Proffitt's (2006, 2013) contention that perception is a function of both the spatial layout of the environment and the energetic costs of behaving in that environment.

Despite the convergence of laboratory and naturalistic data suggesting the role of bodily influences on perception, it is clear that there is no immediate end to this debate, and it is difficult to imagine how even neuropsychology could resolve the controversy (Teufel & Nanay, 2017). Critics of the embodied perception account may continue to believe that "pure" perceptual processes remain informationally encapsulated and modular (Firestone & Scholl, 2017; Fodor & Pylyshyn, 1988), and these embodied perception effects are not about perception at all but instead about environmental and bodily effects on thinking.

Of course there are other daunting empirical issues for embodiment theory that go beyond demand characteristics. The research in this area is young enough that many studies have yet to be replicated, thus the validity and the reliability of numerous results will depend on that process and its findings. We already know that Papesh (2015) failed to replicate the findings of Glenberg and Kaschak (2002), and Carney et al.'s (2010, 2015) power-pose data have had replicability difficulty as well (see Simmons & Simonsohn, 2017, but also see Cuddy, Schultz, & Fosse, 2018, for a rebuttal and supporting evidence concerning the effects of postural feedback). As failed replications of embodiment effects are found, some have questioned whether these published effects are "false positives" or perhaps the result of questionable research practices (see Bohannon, 2014; Ebersole et al., 2016; Johnson et al., 2016). Further, as Mathôt et al. (2017) claimed, there are no large-scale meta-analyses of embodiment effects at this time, which would allow for a more careful examination of published data's p values and effect sizes. For example, a meta-analysis of an effect might show that many of the studies conducted were underpowered, which would be true, for example, if p values tended to fall between .025 and .05. If the results showed significance levels of $p < .01$, however, this would suggest a replicable effect. Further, if results of studies examining an embodied effect were associated with large effect sizes, this also would predict a reliable and replicable finding. Discussions of power and effect sizes in embodiment research have been limited.

Others have argued that another way to think about inconsistent findings in the embodiment literature is to understand that the variability across studies suggests theoretically relevant moderating variables that have yet to be identified (Noah, Schul, & Mayo, 2018; Petrova et al., 2018; Zestcott, Stone, & Landau, 2017). Noah, Schul, and Mayo (2018) argued that human behavior is complex and variable, and the context in which this behavior occurs is similarly variable, so it should not be surprising that a replication attempt, which can never be exact, would fail. Noah et al. and others claimed that the strategy of showing that a replication effort may depend on identifying a moderator is rare in the replication literature but crucial to advancing science and enhancing continued scientific creativity (Brainerd & Reyna, 2018; Luttrell, Petty, & Xu, 2017). Finally, Noah et al. emphasized that psychology is a cumulative science and, as such, no single study can be the end-all for any hypothesis or phenomenon.

Thus, although caution may be appropriate for overinterpreting embodiment results, extreme skepticism is uncalled for given the accumulation of data supporting the theory (Mathôt et al., 2017). Certainly the findings supporting embodiment need to be replicated with high power and precision, and careful and deliberate method-ological and statistical practices need to always be followed. However, inconsistent findings across studies should trigger theoretically driven investigations of boundary conditions and contextual moderation. There is much to be learned about embodiment, and these types of studies will be essential to advancing the theory.

Applications of Embodiment Theory

One promising aspect of embodiment research is that although few empirical studies in cognitive psychology get translated into applied research, some of this embodiment work has. Glenberg and colleagues' (2004, 2011) Moved by Reading intervention for early readers teaches children how to map abstract words and phrases onto current as well as remembered bodily experiences. In the primary manipulation stage of this intervention, children read simple texts about activities (e.g., a farm scenario), and using toys that are in front of them, they physically manipulate the toys to represent the action that the sentence is describing (e.g., a farmer taking hay to a horse). Following the primary manipulation stage, this intervention teaches children to use a similar imaginary manipulation strategy to comprehend sentences. The critically important aspect of this intervention is having children use their bodies (and later imagine doing so) to connect abstract symbols (words) to bodily action. Glenberg and his colleagues have found that early readers who used these stages during reading showed significantly superior comprehension scores compared with children who read the same text but were simply told to reread critical sentences in the text (see Glenberg, Goldberg, & Zhu, 2011; Glenberg, Gutierrez, Levin, Japuntich, & Kaschak, 2004).

In similar applied research, Kaschak, Connor, and Dombek (2017) tested the efficacy of Enacted Reading Comprehension (ERC), an intervention aimed at improving the comprehension of a wide range of texts, such as those involving the abstract notion of opposing forces. Kaschak et al. have found that third- and fourth-grade students who learn to use gestures to represent opposing forces in concrete settings (while reading texts that describe movement of tectonic plates) can use those same gestures to facilitate the comprehension of texts describing opposing forces in abstract settings (texts that describe different sides of an argument or the internal conflicts that arise in people faced with moral dilemmas).

Several researchers have also examined the gestures used during both the learning and the teaching of mathematical concepts and ideas, and these gestures have been taken as evidence that mathematical knowledge is embodied (e.g., Alibali & Nathan, 2012; Irving, 2015). A prime example of this is the universal use of fingers to count and solve mathematical problems (Fischer & Brugger, 2011). Research on mathematical education has shown that learners' actions also influence how they think arithmetically. Students that use manipulatives (objects that can be interacted with by sliding, flipping, or turning, or digital versions of these objects in video games) are able to connect these concrete objects with abstract concepts, allowing for better conceptual understanding of mathematical concepts. New approaches, both digital and nondigital, that encourage the "scaffolding" of knowledge by linking concrete and abstract through bodily action are being used to support learning in science, technology, mathematics, and engineering (see DeSutter & Stieff, 2017, and Tran, Smith, & Buschkuehl, 2017). Finally, Lozada and Carro (2016) have similarly shown that embodied "action" improves complex cognition in children: Having children enact typical Piagetian conservation tasks helped them recognize quantity invariance in a higher proportion than children who were passive observers.

Glenberg and Hayes' (2016) embodied approach to memory can also be applied to explain infantile amnesia and childhood amnesia because it depends on the sophistication of self-locomotion. In addition, this approach implies that there may be interventions for protecting episodic memory formation in the elderly. Their interventions support the link between brain and body by encouraging aging individuals to follow the common advice to remain active to prevent memory loss. Anderson-Hanley et al. (2012) found data to support this suggestion. These researchers randomly assigned older participants (average age 78.8 years) to a condition in which they rode stationary bicycles in a virtual reality context so that they experienced a simulated environment (tours through different landscapes) or to a condition in which participants simply rode the stationary bicycles for the same period of time as the other group. Despite the similar effort and physical activity between the two groups, the virtual reality cyclists showed larger increases in an important neurochemical (BDNF, brain-derived neurotrophic growth factor) thought to be responsible for exercise-induced neural growth. These elderly cyclists also showed significantly greater cognitive functioning on several measures compared with the traditional cyclists. Repetto, Serino, Macedonia, and Riva (2016) also argued that virtual reality could compensate for the decrease of spontaneous mobility in the elderly and provide the same benefits by simulating active navigation, presumably activating the same brain circuitry that is needed to support episodic memory and other cognitive functions.

These applications of embodiment theory simply speak to the breadth of influence that the theory may have on the discipline of psychology. What is most important is what this book presents—empirical backing from well-conducted studies that suggest that the body shapes the mind. What follows after that is where good basic research goes—to applied research.

Conclusions

Theories evolve over time, and embodiment theory is still young. There is much work to be done. Replications and extensions of research reported in this book and other research in multiple areas of cognitive psychology, as well as psychology's other subdisciplines, will be critical to theory development. New advances in technology will further elucidate the neural underpinnings of cognitive processes, and the questions of whether the body fully or partially constitutes thought will be thoroughly addressed. The theory will need to be able to explain and account for classic cognitive phenomenon, from perceptual effects to memory effects. It will also need to be the impetus for experimental work that goes beyond demonstration experiments to empirical investigations that test the newest model of embodiment. The fact that this basic research in embodiment may make contact with real-world phenomenon and suggest applications of the theory would be, metaphorically, icing on the cake. Eventually, the body of evidence will build, and we will be able to determine whether embodiment theory is no longer the theory that simply competes with the traditional theories in cognitive psychology but is now the dominant theory of human knowledge representation.

References

Ackerman, J. M., Nocera, C. C., & Bargh, J. A. (2010). Incidental haptic sensations influence social judgments and decisions. *Science, 328*, 1712–1715. http://dx.doi.org/10.1126/science.1189993

Adolph, K. E., & Hoch, J. E. (in press). Motor development: Embodied, embedded, enculturated, and enabling. *Annual Review of Psychology, 70.*

Adolphs, R. (2002). Neural systems for recognizing emotion. *Current Opinion in Neurobiology, 12*, 169–177. http://dx.doi.org/10.1016/S0959-4388(02)00301-X

Adolphs, R., Baron-Cohen, S., & Tranel, D. (2002). Impaired recognition of social emotions following amygdala damage. *Journal of Cognitive Neuroscience, 14*, 1264–1274. http://dx.doi.org/10.1162/089892902760807258

Adolphs, R., Damasio, H., Tranel, D., Cooper, G., & Damasio, A. R. (2000). A role for somatosensory cortices in the visual recognition of emotion as revealed by three-dimensional lesion mapping. *The Journal of Neuroscience, 20*, 2683–2690. http://dx.doi.org/10.1523/JNEUROSCI.20-07-02683.2000

Adolphs, R., Tranel, D., & Damasio, A. R. (1998). The human amygdala in social judgment. *Nature, 393*, 470–474. http://dx.doi.org/10.1038/30982

Alibali, M. W., & Nathan, M. (2012). Embodiment in mathematics teaching and learning: Evidence from learners' and teachers' gestures. *Journal of the Learning Sciences, 21*, 247–286. http://dx.doi.org/10.1080/10508406.2011.611446

Alsmith, A. J. T., & de Vignemont, F. (2012). Embodying the mind and representing the body. *Review of Philosophy and Psychology, 3*, 1–13. http://dx.doi.org/10.1007/s13164-012-0085-4

Anderson, D. I., Campos, J. J., & Barbu-Roth, M. A. (2003). A developmental perspective on visual proprioception. In G. Bremner & A. Slater (Eds.), *Theories of infant development* (pp. 30–69). Oxford, England: Wiley-Blackwell.

Anderson, D. I., Campos, J. J., Witherington, D. C., Dahl, A., Rivera, M., He, M., . . . Barbu-Roth, M. (2013). The role of locomotion in psychological development. *Frontiers in Psychology, 4*, 440. http://dx.doi.org/10.3389/fpsyg.2013.00440

Anderson, J. R. (1974). Retrieval of propositional information from long-term memory. *Cognitive Psychology, 6*, 451–474. http://dx.doi.org/10.1016/0010-0285(74)90021-8

Anderson, J. R. (1983). *The architecture of cognition.* Cambridge, MA: Harvard University Press.

Anderson-Hanley, C., Arciero, P. J., Brickman, A. M., Nimon, J. P., Okuma, N., Westen, S. C., . . . Zimmerman, E. A. (2012). Exergaming and older adult cognition: A cluster randomized clinical trial. *American Journal of Preventive Medicine, 42*, 109–119. http://dx.doi.org/10.1016/j.amepre.2011.10.016

Arrighi, R., Cartocci, G., & Burr, D. (2011). Reduced perceptual sensitivity for biological motion in paraplegia patients. *Current Biology, 21*, R910–R911. http://dx.doi.org/10.1016/j.cub.2011.09.048

Aziz-Zadeh, L., Wilson, S. M., Rizzolatti, G., & Iacoboni, M. (2006). Congruent embodied representations for visually presented actions and linguistic phrases describing actions. *Current Biology, 16*, 1818–1823. http://dx.doi.org/10.1016/j.cub.2006.07.060

Azouvi, P., Samuel, C., Louis-Dreyfus, A., Bernati, T., Bartolomeo, P., Beis, J.-M., . . . the French Collaborative Study Group on Assessment of Unilateral Neglect (GEREN/GRECO). (2002). Sensitivity of clinical and behavioural tests of spatial neglect after right hemisphere stroke. *Journal of Neurology, Neurosurgery and Psychiatry, 73*, 160–166. http://dx.doi.org/10.1136/jnnp.73.2.160

Baccarini, M., Martel, M., Cardinali, L., Sillan, O., Farnè, A., & Roy, A. C. (2014). Tool use imagery triggers tool incorporation in the body schema. *Frontiers in Psychology, 5*, 492. http://dx.doi.org/10.3389/fpsyg.2014.00492

Bak, T. H., & Hodges, J. R. (2004). The effects of motor neurone disease on language: Further evidence. *Brain and Language, 89*, 354–361. http://dx.doi.org/10.1016/S0093-934X(03)00357-2

Balcetis, E., & Dunning, D. (2010). Wishful seeing: More desired objects are seen as closer. *Psychological Science, 21*, 147–152. http://dx.doi.org/10.1177/0956797609356283

Bardolph, M., & Coulson, S. (2014). How vertical hand movements impact brain activity elicited by literally and metaphorically related words: An ERP study of embodied metaphor. *Frontiers in Human Neuroscience, 8*, 1031. http://dx.doi.org/10.3389/fnhum.2014.01031

Baron-Cohen, S., Ring, H. A., Bullmore, E. T., Wheelwright, S., Ashwin, C., & Williams, S. C. R. (2000). The amygdala theory of autism. *Neuroscience and Biobehavioral Reviews, 24*, 355–364. http://dx.doi.org/10.1016/S0149-7634(00)00011-7

Baron-Cohen, S., Ring, H. A., Wheelwright, S., Bullmore, E. T., Brammer, M. J., Simmons, A., & Williams, S. C. R. (1999). Social intelligence in the normal and autistic brain: An fMRI study. *European Journal of Neuroscience, 11*, 1891–1898. http://dx.doi.org/10.1046/j.1460-9568.1999.00621.x

Barrett, L. F. (2006a). Are emotions natural kinds? *Perspectives on Psychological Science,* *1,* 28–58. http://dx.doi.org/10.1111/j.1745-6916.2006.00003.x

Barrett, L. F. (2006b). Solving the emotion paradox: Categorization and the experience of emotion. *Personality and Social Psychology Review, 10,* 20–46. http://dx.doi.org/10.1207/s15327957pspr1001_2

Barsalou, L. W. (1999). Perceptual symbol systems. *Behavioral and Brain Sciences, 22,* 577–609.

Barsalou, L. W. (2003). Situated simulation in the human conceptual system. *Language and Cognitive Processes, 18,* 513–562. http://dx.doi.org/10.1080/01690960344000026

Barsalou, L. W. (2008a). Cognitive and neural contributions to understanding the conceptual system. *Current Directions in Psychological Science, 17,* 91–95. http://dx.doi.org/10.1111/j.1467-8721.2008.00555.x

Barsalou, L. W. (2008b). Grounded cognition. *Annual Review of Psychology, 59,* 617–645. http://dx.doi.org/10.1146/annurev.psych.59.103006.093639

Barsalou, L. W. (2016). On staying grounded and avoiding quixotic dead ends. *Psychonomic Bulletin & Review, 23,* 1122–1142. http://dx.doi.org/10.3758/s13423-016-1028-3

Barsalou, L. W., Santos, A., Simmons, W. K., & Wilson, C. D. (2008). Language and simulation in conceptual processing. In M. De Vega, A. M. Glenberg, & A. C. Graesser (Eds.), *Symbols and embodiment: Debates on meaning and cognition* (pp. 245–284). Oxford, England: Oxford University Press. http://dx.doi.org/10.1093/acprof:oso/9780199217274.003.0013

Barsalou, L. W., & Wiemer-Hastings, K. (2005). Situating abstract concepts. In D. Pecher & R. Zwaan (Eds.), *Grounding cognition: The role of perception and action in memory, language, and thinking* (pp. 129–163). Cambridge, England: Cambridge University Press. http://dx.doi.org/10.1017/CBO9780511499968.007

Basso, G., Nichelli, P., Frassinetti, F., & di Pellegrino, G. (1996). Time perception in a neglected space. *Neuroreport, 7,* 2111–2114. http://dx.doi.org/10.1097/00001756-199609020-00009

Basso Moro, S., Dell'Acqua, R., & Cutini, S. (2018). The SNARC effect is not a unitary phenomenon. *Psychonomic Bulletin & Review, 25,* 688–695. http://dx.doi.org/10.3758/s13423-017-1408-3

Baumeister, J. C., Rumiati, R. I., & Foroni, F. (2015). When the mask falls: The role of facial motor resonance in memory for emotional language. *Acta Psychologica, 155,* 29–36. http://dx.doi.org/10.1016/j.actpsy.2014.11.012

Beer, R. D. (2003). The dynamics of active categorical perception in an evolved model agent. *Adaptive Behavior, 11,* 209–243. http://dx.doi.org/10.1177/1059712303114001

Beis, J. M., Keller, C., Morin, N., Bartolomeo, P., Bernati, T., Chokron, S., . . . the French Collaborative Study Group on Assessment of Unilateral Neglect (GEREN/GRECO). (2004). Right spatial neglect after left hemisphere stroke: Qualitative and quantitative study. *Neurology, 63,* 1600–1605. http://dx.doi.org/10.1212/01.WNL.0000142967.60579.32

Bhalla, M., & Proffitt, D. R. (1999). Visual-motor recalibration in geographical slant perception. *Journal of Experimental Psychology: Human Perception and Performance, 25,* 1076–1096. http://dx.doi.org/10.1037/0096-1523.25.4.1076

Bisiach, E., & Luzzatti, C. (1978). Unilateral neglect of representational space. *Cortex, 14,* 129–133. http://dx.doi.org/10.1016/S0010-9452(78)80016-1

Bloesch, E. K., Davoli, C. C., Roth, N., Brockmole, J. R., & Abrams, R. A. (2012). Watch this! Observed tool use affects perceived distance. *Psychonomic Bulletin & Review, 19*, 177–183. http://dx.doi.org/10.3758/s13423-011-0200-z

Bodin, T., & Martinsen, E. W. (2004). Mood and self-efficacy during acute exercise in clinical depression: A randomized, controlled study. *Journal of Sport & Exercise Psychology, 26*, 623–633. http://dx.doi.org/10.1123/jsep.26.4.623

Bohannon, J. (2014). Replication effort provokes praise—and 'bullying' charges. *Science, 344*, 788–789. http://dx.doi.org/10.1126/science.344.6186.788

Booth, A., Shelley, G., Mazur, A., Tharp, G., & Kittok, R. (1989). Testosterone, and winning and losing in human competition. *Hormones and Behavior, 23*, 556–571. http://dx.doi.org/10.1016/0018-506X(89)90042-1

Boroditsky, L. (2000). Metaphoric structuring: Understanding time through spatial metaphors. *Cognition, 75*, 1–28. http://dx.doi.org/10.1016/S0010-0277(99)00073-6

Boroditsky, L. (2011). How languages construct time. In S. Dehaene & E. Brannon (Eds.), *Space, time and number in the brain* (pp. 333–341). Amsterdam, the Netherlands: Elsevier. http://dx.doi.org/10.1016/B978-0-12-385948-8.00020-7

Boroditsky, L., & Ramscar, M. (2002). The roles of body and mind in abstract thought. *Psychological Science, 13*, 185–189. http://dx.doi.org/10.1111/1467-9280.00434

Bottini, R., Bucur, M., & Crepaldi, D. (2016). The nature of semantic priming by subliminal spatial words: Embodied or disembodied? *Journal of Experimental Psychology: General, 145*, 1160–1176. http://dx.doi.org/10.1037/xge0000197

Bottini, R., Crepaldi, D., Casasanto, D., Crollen, V., & Collignon, O. (2015). Space and time in the sighted and blind. *Cognition, 141*, 67–72. http://dx.doi.org/10.1016/j.cognition.2015.04.004

Bower, G. H. (1981). Mood and memory. *American Psychologist, 36*, 129–148. http://dx.doi.org/10.1037/0003-066X.36.2.129

Bowlby, J. (1977). The making and breaking of affectional bonds: I. Aetiology and psychopathology in the light of attachment theory. An expanded version of the Fiftieth Maudsley Lecture, delivered before the Royal College of Psychiatrists, 19 November 1976. *The British Journal of Psychiatry, 130*, 201–210. http://dx.doi.org/10.1192/bjp.130.3.201

Brainerd, C. J., & Reyna, V. F. (2018). Replication, registration, and scientific creativity. *Perspectives on Psychological Science, 13*, 428–432. http://dx.doi.org/10.1177/1745691617739421

Brooks, R. A. (1991a). Intelligence without representation. *Artificial Intelligence, 47*, 139–160. http://dx.doi.org/10.1016/0004-3702(91)90053-M

Brooks, R. A. (1991b). New approaches to robotics. *Science, 253*, 1227–1232. http://dx.doi.org/10.1126/science.253.5025.1227

Brookshire, G., & Casasanto, D. (2012). Motivation and motor control: Hemispheric specialization for approach motivation reverses with handedness. *PLoS ONE, 7*(4), e36036. http://dx.doi.org/10.1371/journal.pone.0036036

Bub, D. N., & Masson, M. E. J. (2010). On the nature of hand-action representations evoked during written sentence comprehension. *Cognition, 116*, 394–408. http://dx.doi.org/10.1016/j.cognition.2010.06.001

Bub, D. N., & Masson, M. E. J. (2012). On the dynamics of action representations evoked by names of manipulable objects. *Journal of Experimental Psychology: General, 141,* 502–517. http://dx.doi.org/10.1037/a0026748

Buccino, G., Binkofski, F., & Riggio, L. (2004). The mirror neuron system and action recognition. *Brain and Language, 89,* 370–376. http://dx.doi.org/10.1016/S0093-934X(03)00356-0

Bueti, D., & Walsh, V. (2009). The parietal cortex and the representation of time, space, number and other magnitudes. *Philosophical Transactions of the Royal Society of London. Series B, Biological Sciences, 364,* 1831–1840. http://dx.doi.org/10.1098/rstb.2009.0028

Cacioppo, J. T., Priester, J. R., & Berntson, G. G. (1993). Rudimentary determinants of attitudes. II: Arm flexion and extension have differential effects on attitudes. *Journal of Personality and Social Psychology, 65,* 5–17. http://dx.doi.org/10.1037/0022-3514.65.1.5

Calder, A. J., Keane, J., Manes, F., Antoun, N., & Young, A. W. (2000). Impaired recognition and experience of disgust following brain injury. *Nature Neuroscience, 3,* 1077–1078. http://dx.doi.org/10.1038/80586

Campos, J. J., Anderson, D. I., Barbu-Roth, M. A., Hubbard, E. M., Hertenstein, M. J., & Witherington, D. (2000). Travel broadens the mind. *Infancy, 1,* 149–219. http://dx.doi.org/10.1207/S15327078IN0102_1

Campos, J. J., Anderson, D. I., & Telzrow, R. (2009). Locomotor experience influences the spatial cognitive development of infants with spina bifida. *Zeitschrift für Entwicklungspsychologie und Pädagogische Psychologie, 41,* 181–188. http://dx.doi.org/10.1026/0049-8637.41.4.181

Campos, J. J., Bertenthal, B. I., & Kermoian, R. (1992). Early experience and emotional development: The emergence of wariness of heights. *Psychological Science, 3,* 61–64. http://dx.doi.org/10.1111/j.1467-9280.1992.tb00259.x

Carney, D. R., Cuddy, A. J. C., & Yap, A. J. (2010). Power posing: Brief nonverbal displays affect neuroendocrine levels and risk tolerance. *Psychological Science, 21,* 1363–1368. http://dx.doi.org/10.1177/0956797610383437

Carney, D. R., Cuddy, A. J. C., & Yap, A. J. (2015). Review and summary of research on the embodied effects of expansive (vs. contractive) nonverbal displays. *Psychological Science, 26,* 657–663. http://dx.doi.org/10.1177/0956797614566855

Carr, L., Iacoboni, M., Dubeau, M. C., Mazziotta, J. C., & Lenzi, G. L. (2003). Neural mechanisms of empathy in humans: A relay from neural systems for imitation to limbic areas. *Proceedings of the National Academy of Sciences, USA, 100,* 5497–5502. http://dx.doi.org/10.1073/pnas.0935845100

Casasanto, D. (2009). Embodiment of abstract concepts: Good and bad in right- and left-handers. *Journal of Experimental Psychology: General, 138,* 351–367. http://dx.doi.org/10.1037/a0015854

Casasanto, D. (2011). Different bodies, different minds: The body specificity of language and thought. *Current Directions in Psychological Science, 20,* 378–383. http://dx.doi.org/10.1177/0963721411422058

Casasanto, D., & Boroditsky, L. (2008). Time in the mind: Using space to think about time. *Cognition, 106,* 579–593. http://dx.doi.org/10.1016/j.cognition.2007.03.004

Casasanto, D., & Chrysikou, E. G. (2011). When left is "right": Motor fluency shapes abstract concepts. *Psychological Science, 22*, 419–422. http://dx.doi.org/10.1177/0956797611401755

Casasanto, D., & Jasmin, K. (2010). Good and bad in the hands of politicians: Spontaneous gestures during positive and negative speech. *PLoS ONE, 5*(7), e11805. http://dx.doi.org/10.1371/journal.pone.0011805

Casasanto, D., Jasmin, K., Brookshire, G., & Gijssels, T. (2014). The QWERTY effect: How typing shapes word meanings and baby names. In P. Bello, M. Guarini, M. McShane, & B. Scassellati (Eds.), *Proceedings of the 36th Annual Conference of the Cognitive Science Society* (pp. 296–301). Austin, TX: Cognitive Science Society. Retrieved from http://escholarship.org/uc/item/2573p1tf

Casasanto, D., & Lupyan, G. (2015). All concepts are ad hoc concepts. In E. Margolis & S. Laurence (Eds.), *The conceptual mind: New directions in the study of concepts* (pp. 543–566). Cambridge, MA: MIT Press.

Cattaneo, L., Fabbri-Destro, M., Boria, S., Pieraccini, C., Monti, A., Cossu, G., & Rizzolatti, G. (2007). Impairment of actions chains in autism and its possible role in intention understanding. *Proceedings of the National Academy of Sciences, USA, 104*, 17825–17830. http://dx.doi.org/10.1073/pnas.0706273104

Chandler, J., Reinhard, D., & Schwarz, N. (2012). To judge a book by its weight you need to know its content: Knowledge moderates the use of embodied cues. *Journal of Experimental Social Psychology, 48*, 948–952. http://dx.doi.org/10.1016/j.jesp.2012.03.003

Chao, L. L., & Martin, A. (2000). Representation of manipulable man-made objects in the dorsal stream. *NeuroImage, 12*, 478–484. http://dx.doi.org/10.1006/nimg.2000.0635

Charpentier, A. (1891). Experimental study of some aspects of weight perception. *Archives de Physiologie Normale et Pathologique, 3*, 122–135.

Chemero, A. (2009). *Radical embodied cognitive science.* Cambridge, MA: The MIT Press.

Chomsky, N. (1980). *Rules and representations.* New York, NY: Columbia University Press.

Clark, A. (1998). Embodied, situated, and distributed cognition. In W. Bechtel & G. Graham (Eds.), *A companion to cognitive science* (pp. 506–517). Malden, MA: Blackwell.

Clark, A. (1999). An embodied cognitive science? *Trends in Cognitive Sciences, 3*, 345–351. http://dx.doi.org/10.1016/S1364-6613(99)01361-3

Clark, A. (2008). Embodiment and explanation. In P. Calvo & A. Gomila (Eds.), *Handbook of cognitive science: An embodied approach* (pp. 41–58). Amsterdam, the Netherlands: Elsevier. http://dx.doi.org/10.1016/B978-0-08-046616-3.00003-7

Clearfield, M. W., Diedrich, F. J., Smith, L. B., & Thelen, E. (2006). Young infants reach correctly in A-not-B tasks: On the development of stability and perseveration. *Infant Behavior and Development, 29*, 435–444. http://dx.doi.org/10.1016/j.infbeh.2006.03.001

Cohen, D. (2003). The American national conversation about (everything but) shame. *Social Research, 70*, 1075–1108.

Cole, S., Balcetis, E., & Dunning, D. (2013). Affective signals of threat increase perceived proximity. *Psychological Science, 24*, 34–40. http://dx.doi.org/10.1177/0956797612446953

Collins, A. M., & Loftus, E. F. (1975). A spreading-activation theory of semantic process-ing. *Psychological Review, 82,* 407–428. http://dx.doi.org/10.1037/0033-295X.82.6.407

Cook, J. (2016). From movement kinematics to social cognition: The case of autism. *Philosophical Transactions of the Royal Society of London. Series B, Biological Sciences, 371*(1693). http://dx.doi.org/10.1098/rstb.2015.0372

Cook, J. L., & Bird, G. (2012). Atypical social modulation of imitation in autism spectrum conditions. *Journal of Autism and Developmental Disorders, 42,* 1045–1051. http://dx.doi.org/10.1007/s10803-011-1341-7

Cracco, E., Bardi, L., Desmet, C., Genschow, O., Rigoni, D., De Coster, L., . . . Brass, M. (2018). Automatic imitation: A meta-analysis. *Psychological Bulletin, 144,* 453–500. http://dx.doi.org/10.1037/bul0000143

Cree, G. S., & McRae, K. (2003). Analyzing the factors underlying the structure and computation of the meaning of *chipmunk, cherry, chisel, cheese,* and *cello* (and many other such concrete nouns). *Journal of Experimental Psychology: General, 132,* 163–201. http://dx.doi.org/10.1037/0096-3445.132.2.163

Crollen, V., Dormal, G., Seron, X., Lepore, F., & Collignon, O. (2013). Embodied numbers: The role of vision in the development of number–space interactions. *Cortex, 49,* 276–283. http://dx.doi.org/10.1016/j.cortex.2011.11.006

Cuddy, A. J. C., Schultz, S. J., & Fosse, N. E. (2018). *P*-curving a more comprehensive body of research on postural feedback reveals clear evidential value for power-posing effects: Reply to Simmons and Simonsohn (2017). *Psychological Science, 29,* 656–666. http://dx.doi.org/10.1177/0956797617746749

Cutini, S., Scarpa, F., Scatturin, P., Dell'Acqua, R., & Zorzi, M. (2014). Number–space interactions in the human parietal cortex: Enlightening the SNARC effect with functional near-infrared spectroscopy. *Cerebral Cortex, 24,* 444–451. http://dx.doi.org/10.1093/cercor/bhs321

Dahl, A., Campos, J. J., Anderson, D. I., Uchiyama, I., Witherington, D. C., Ueno, M., . . . Barbu-Roth, M. (2013). The epigenesis of wariness of heights. *Psychological Science, 24,* 1361–1367. http://dx.doi.org/10.1177/0956797613476047

Davidson, R. J. (1992). Anterior cerebral asymmetry and the nature of emotion. *Brain and Cognition, 20,* 125–151. http://dx.doi.org/10.1016/0278-2626(92)90065-T

de Groot, J. H. B., Smeets, M. A. M., Rowson, M. J., Bulsing, P. J., Blonk, C. G., Wilkinson, J. E., & Semin, G. R. (2015). A sniff of happiness. *Psychological Science, 26,* 684–700. http://dx.doi.org/10.1177/0956797614566318

Dehaene, S., Bossini, S., & Giraux, P. (1993). The mental representation of parity and number magnitude. *Journal of Experimental Psychology: General, 122,* 371–396. http://dx.doi.org/10.1037/0096-3445.122.3.371

de Hevia, M. D., Girelli, L., Addabbo, M., & Macchi Cassia, V. (2014). Human infants' preference for left-to-right oriented increasing numerical sequences. *PLoS ONE, 9,* e96412. http://dx.doi.org/10.1371/journal.pone.0096412

de la Fuente, J., Santiago, J., Román, A., Dumitrache, C., & Casasanto, D. (2014). When you think about it, your past is in front of you: How culture shapes spatial conceptions of time. *Psychological Science, 25,* 1682–1690. http://dx.doi.org/10.1177/0956797614534695

DeLoache, J. S., Uttal, D. H., & Rosengren, K. S. (2004). Scale errors offer evidence for a perception-action dissociation early in life. *Science, 304,* 1027–1029. http://dx.doi.org/10.1126/science.1093567

Deschrijver, E., Wiersema, J. R., & Brass, M. (2017). Action-based touch observation in adults with high functioning autism: Can compromised self–other distinction abilities link social and sensory everyday problems? *Social Cognitive and Affective Neuroscience, 12,* 273–282.

DeSutter, D., & Stieff, M. (2017). Teaching students to think spatially through embodied actions: Design principles for learning environments in science, technology, engineering, and mathematics. *Cognitive Research: Principles and Implications, 2,* 22–42. http://dx.doi.org/10.1186/s41235-016-0039-y

de Vega, M., Glenberg, A. M., & Graesser, A. C. (Eds.). (2008). *Symbols and embodiment: Debates on meaning and cognition.* Oxford, England: Oxford University Press. http://dx.doi.org/10.1093/acprof:oso/9780199217274.001.0001

Diamond, A. (1990). The development and neural bases of memory functions as indexed by the AB and delayed response tasks in human infants and infant monkeys. *Annals of the New York Academy of Sciences, 608,* 267–317. http://dx.doi.org/10.1111/j.1749-6632.1990.tb48900.x

Di Cesare, G., Di Dio, C., Rochat, M. J., Sinigaglia, C., Bruschweiler-Stern, N., Stern, D. N., & Rizzolatti, G. (2014). The neural correlates of 'vitality form' recognition: An fMRI study: This work is dedicated to Daniel Stern, whose immeasurable contribution to science has inspired our research. *Social Cognitive and Affective Neuroscience, 9,* 951–960. http://dx.doi.org/10.1093/scan/nst068

Di Cesare, G., Sparaci, L., Pelosi, A., Mazzone, L., Giovagnoli, G., Menghini, D., . . . Vicari, S. (2017). Differences in action style recognition in children with autism spectrum disorders. *Frontiers in Psychology, 8,* 1456. http://dx.doi.org/10.3389/fpsyg.2017.01456

Di Cesare, G., Valente, G., Di Dio, C., Ruffaldi, E., Bergamasco, M., Goebel, R., & Rizzolatti, G. (2016). Vitality forms processing in the insula during action observation: A multivoxel pattern analysis. *Frontiers in Human Neuroscience, 10,* 267. http://dx.doi.org/10.3389/fnhum.2016.00267

Dimberg, U., Thunberg, M., & Elmehed, K. (2000). Unconscious facial reactions to emotional facial expressions. *Psychological Science, 11,* 86–89. http://dx.doi.org/10.1111/1467-9280.00221

Ding, X., Feng, N., Cheng, X., Liu, H., & Fan, Z. (2015). Are past and future symmetric in mental time line? *Frontiers in Psychology, 6,* 208. http://dx.doi.org/10.3389/fpsyg.2015.00208

di Pellegrino, G., Fadiga, L., Fogassi, L., Gallese, V., & Rizzolatti, G. (1992). Understanding motor events: A neurophysiological study. *Experimental Brain Research, 91,* 176–180. http://dx.doi.org/10.1007/BF00230027

Dove, G. (2009). Beyond perceptual symbols: A call for representational pluralism. *Cognition, 110,* 412–431. http://dx.doi.org/10.1016/j.cognition.2008.11.016

Dove, G. (2016). Three symbol ungrounding problems: Abstract concepts and the future of embodied cognition. *Psychonomic Bulletin & Review, 23,* 1109–1121. http://dx.doi.org/10.3758/s13423-015-0825-4

Duclos, S. E., Laird, J. D., Schneider, E., Sexter, M., Stern, L., & Van Lighten, O. (1989). Emotion-specific effects of facial expressions and postures on emotional experience. *Journal of Personality and Social Psychology, 57*, 100–108. http://dx.doi.org/10.1037/0022-3514.57.1.100

Durgin, F. H., Baird, J. A., Greenburg, M., Russell, R., Shaughnessy, K., & Waymouth, S. (2009). Who is being deceived? The experimental demands of wearing a backpack. *Psychonomic Bulletin & Review, 16*, 964–969. http://dx.doi.org/10.3758/PBR.16.5.964

Durgin, F. H., Klein, B., Spiegel, A., Strawser, C. J., & Williams, M. (2012). The social psychology of perception experiments: Hills, backpacks, glucose, and the problem of generalizability. *Journal of Experimental Psychology: Human Perception and Performance, 38*, 1582–1595. http://dx.doi.org/10.1037/a0027805

Ebersole, C. R., Atherton, O. E., Belanger, A. L., Skulborstad, H. M., Allen, J. M., Banks, J. B., . . . Nosek, B. A. (2016). Many Labs 3: Evaluating participant pool quality across the academic semester via replication. *Journal of Experimental Social Psychology, 67*, 68–82. http://dx.doi.org/10.1016/j.jesp.2015.10.012

Eerland, A., Guadalupe, T. M., & Zwaan, R. A. (2011). Leaning to the left makes the Eiffel Tower seem smaller: Posture-modulated estimation. *Psychological Science, 22*, 1511–1514. http://dx.doi.org/10.1177/0956797611420731

Eich, J. M. (1985). Levels of processing, encoding specificity, elaboration, and CHARM. *Psychological Review, 92*, 1–38. http://dx.doi.org/10.1037/0033-295X.92.1.1

Eikmeier, V., Schröter, H., Maienborn, C., Alex-Ruf, S., & Ulrich, R. (2013). Dimensional overlap between time and space. *Psychonomic Bulletin & Review, 20*, 1120–1125. http://dx.doi.org/10.3758/s13423-013-0431-2

Engelkamp, J., Zimmer, H. D., Mohr, G., & Sellen, O. (1994). Memory of self-performed tasks: Self-performing during recognition. *Memory & Cognition, 22*, 34–39. http://dx.doi.org/10.3758/BF03202759

Ent, M. R., & Baumeister, R. F. (2014). Embodied free will beliefs: Some effects of physical states on metaphysical opinions. *Consciousness and Cognition, 27*, 147–154. http://dx.doi.org/10.1016/j.concog.2014.05.001

Ernst, M. O., & Banks, M. S. (2002). Humans integrate visual and haptic information in a statistically optimal fashion. *Nature, 415*, 429–433. http://dx.doi.org/10.1038/415429a

Eves, F. F. (2014). Is there any Proffitt in stair climbing? A headcount of studies testing for demographic differences in choice of stairs. *Psychonomic Bulletin & Review, 21*, 71–77. http://dx.doi.org/10.3758/s13423-013-0463-7

Eves, F. F., Thorpe, S. K., Lewis, A., & Taylor-Covill, G. A. (2014). Does perceived steepness deter stair climbing when an alternative is available? *Psychonomic Bulletin & Review, 21*, 637–644. http://dx.doi.org/10.3758/s13423-013-0535-8

Fajen, B. R. (2005). The scaling of information to action in visually guided braking. *Journal of Experimental Psychology: Human Perception and Performance, 31*, 1107–1123. http://dx.doi.org/10.1037/0096-1523.31.5.1107

Feingold, A. (1994). Gender differences in personality: A meta-analysis. *Psychological Bulletin, 116*, 429–456. http://dx.doi.org/10.1037/0033-2909.116.3.429

Fernandino, L., Conant, L. L., Binder, J. R., Blindauer, K., Hiner, B., Spangler, K., & Desai, R. H. (2013). Where is the action? Action sentence processing in Parkinson's disease. *Neuropsychologia, 51*, 1510–1517. http://dx.doi.org/10.1016/j.neuropsychologia.2013.04.008

Fincher-Kiefer, R. (2001). Perceptual components of situation models. *Memory & Cognition, 29*, 336–343. http://dx.doi.org/10.3758/BF03194928

Fincher-Kiefer, R., & D'Agostino, R. (2004). The role of visuospatial resources in generating predictive and bridging inferences. *Discourse Processes, 37*, 205–224. http://dx.doi.org/10.1207/s15326950dp3703_2

Finzi, E., & Rosenthal, N. E. (2014). Treatment of depression with onabotulinum-toxinA: A randomized, double-blind, placebo controlled trial. *Journal of Psychiatric Research, 52*, 1–6. http://dx.doi.org/10.1016/j.jpsychires.2013.11.006

Firestone, C. (2013). How "paternalistic" is spatial perception? Why wearing a heavy backpack doesn't—and *couldn't*—make hills look steeper. *Perspectives on Psychological Science, 8*, 455–473. http://dx.doi.org/10.1177/1745691613489835

Firestone, C., & Scholl, B. J. (2017). Seeing and thinking in studies of embodied "perception": How (not) to integrate vision science and social psychology. *Perspectives on Psychological Science, 12*, 341–343. http://dx.doi.org/10.1177/1745691616679944

Fischer, M. H., & Brugger, P. (2011). When digits help digits: Spatial–numerical associations point to finger counting as prime example of embodied cognition. *Frontiers in Psychology, 2*, 260. http://dx.doi.org/10.3389/fpsyg.2011.00260

Fodor, J. A. (1983). *The modularity of mind*. Cambridge, MA: MIT Press.

Fodor, J. A., & Pylyshyn, Z. W. (1988). Connectionism and cognitive architecture: A critical analysis. *Cognition, 28*, 3–71. http://dx.doi.org/10.1016/0010-0277(88)90031-5

Forbes, P. A. G., Wang, Y., & de C. Hamilton, A. F. (2017). STORMy interactions: Gaze and the modulation of mimicry in adults on the autism spectrum. *Psychonomic Bulletin & Review, 24*, 529–535. http://dx.doi.org/10.3758/s13423-016-1136-0

Forest, A. L., Kille, D. R., Wood, J. V., & Stehouwer, L. R. (2015). Turbulent times, rocky relationships: Relational consequences of experiencing physical instability. *Psychological Science, 26*, 1261–1271. http://dx.doi.org/10.1177/0956797615586402

Frith, C. D., & Frith, U. (2006). The neural basis of mentalizing. *Neuron, 50*, 531–534. http://dx.doi.org/10.1016/j.neuron.2006.05.001

Fuhrman, O., & Boroditsky, L. (2010). Cross-cultural differences in mental representations of time: Evidence from an implicit nonlinguistic task. *Cognitive Science, 34*, 1430–1451. http://dx.doi.org/10.1111/j.1551-6709.2010.01105.x

Gainotti, G. (2006). Anatomical functional and cognitive determinants of semantic memory disorders. *Neuroscience and Biobehavioral Reviews, 30*, 577–594. http://dx.doi.org/10.1016/j.neubiorev.2005.11.001

Gallagher, S. (2005). *How the body shapes the mind*. New York, NY: Oxford University Press. http://dx.doi.org/10.1093/0199271941.001.0001

Gallese, V. (2003). The manifold nature of interpersonal relations: The quest for a common mechanism. *Philosophical Transactions of the Royal Society of London. Series B, Biological Sciences, 358*, 517–528. http://dx.doi.org/10.1098/rstb.2002.1234

Gallese, V. (2005). Embodied simulation: From neurons to phenomenal experience. *Phenomenology and the Cognitive Sciences, 4,* 23–48. http://dx.doi.org/10.1007/s11097-005-4737-z

Gallese, V., Keysers, C., & Rizzolatti, G. (2004). A unifying view of the basis of social cognition. *Trends in Cognitive Sciences, 8,* 396–403. http://dx.doi.org/10.1016/j.tics.2004.07.002

Gallese, V., & Lakoff, G. (2005). The Brain's concepts: The role of the sensory-motor system in conceptual knowledge. *Cognitive Neuropsychology, 22,* 455–479. http://dx.doi.org/10.1080/02643290442000310

Gallese, V., & Sinigaglia, C. (2011). What is so special about embodied simulation? *Trends in Cognitive Sciences, 15,* 512–519. http://dx.doi.org/10.1016/j.tics.2011.09.003

Gentsch, A., Weber, A., Synofzik, M., Vosgerau, G., & Schütz-Bosbach, S. (2016). Towards a common framework of grounded action cognition: Relating motor control, perception and cognition. *Cognition, 146,* 81–89. http://dx.doi.org/10.1016/j.cognition.2015.09.010

Gibbs, R. W. (1994). *The poetics of mind.* Cambridge, England: Cambridge University Press.

Gibbs, R. W., Jr. (2011). Evaluating conceptual metaphor theory. *Discourse Processes, 48,* 529–562. http://dx.doi.org/10.1080/0163853X.2011.606103

Gibson, E. J., & Walk, R. D. (1960). The "visual cliff." *Scientific American, 202,* 64–71. http://dx.doi.org/10.1038/scientificamerican0460-64

Gibson, J. J. (1977). The theory of affordances. In R. Shaw & J. Bransford (Eds.), *Perceiving, acting, and knowing: Toward an ecological psychology* (pp. 67–82). Hillsdale, NJ: Erlbaum.

Gibson, J. J. (1979). *The ecological approach to visual perception.* Boston, MA: Houghton-Mifflin.

Glenberg, A. M. (1997). What memory is for. *Behavioral and Brain Sciences, 20,* 1–19.

Glenberg, A. M. (2010). Embodiment as a unifying perspective for psychology. *WIREs: Cognitive Science, 1,* 586–596. http://dx.doi.org/10.1002/wcs.55

Glenberg, A. M. (2015). Few believe the world is flat: How embodiment is changing the scientific understanding of cognition. *Canadian Journal of Experimental Psychology, 69,* 165–171. http://dx.doi.org/10.1037/cep0000056

Glenberg, A. M., & Gallese, V. (2012). Action-based language: A theory of language acquisition, comprehension, and production. *Cortex, 48,* 905–922. http://dx.doi.org/10.1016/j.cortex.2011.04.010

Glenberg, A. M., Goldberg, A. B., & Zhu, X. (2011). Improving early reading comprehension using embodied CAI. *Instructional Science, 39,* 27–39. http://dx.doi.org/10.1007/s11251-009-9096-7

Glenberg, A. M., Gutierrez, T., Levin, J. R., Japuntich, S., & Kaschak, M. P. (2004). Activity and imagined activity can enhance young children's reading comprehension. *Journal of Educational Psychology, 96,* 424–436. http://dx.doi.org/10.1037/0022-0663.96.3.424

Glenberg, A. M., & Hayes, J. (2016). Contribution of embodiment to solving the riddle of infantile amnesia. *Frontiers in Psychology, 7,* 10. http://dx.doi.org/10.3389/fpsyg.2016.00010

Glenberg, A. M., & Kaschak, M. P. (2002). Grounding language in action. *Psychonomic Bulletin & Review, 9,* 558–565. http://dx.doi.org/10.3758/BF03196313

Glenberg, A. M., & Robertson, D. A. (1999). Indexical understanding of instructions. *Discourse Processes, 28,* 1–26. http://dx.doi.org/10.1080/01638539909545067

Glenberg, A. M., & Robertson, D. A. (2000). Symbol grounding and meaning: A comparison of high-dimensional and embodied theories of meaning. *Journal of Memory and Language, 43,* 379–401. http://dx.doi.org/10.1006/jmla.2000.2714

Glenberg, A. M., Sato, M., Cattaneo, L., Riggio, L., Palumbo, D., & Buccino, G. (2008). Processing abstract language modulates motor system activity. *Quarterly Journal of Experimental Psychology, 61,* 905–919. http://dx.doi.org/10.1080/17470210701625550

Glenberg, A. M., Witt, J. K., & Metcalfe, J. (2013). From the revolution to embodiment: 25 years of cognitive psychology. *Perspectives on Psychological Science, 8,* 573–585. http://dx.doi.org/10.1177/1745691613498098

Goldinger, S. D., Papesh, M. H., Barnhart, A. S., Hansen, W. A., & Hout, M. C. (2016). The poverty of embodied cognition. *Psychonomic Bulletin & Review, 23,* 959–978. http://dx.doi.org/10.3758/s13423-015-0860-1

González, J., Barros-Loscertales, A., Pulvermüller, F., Meseguer, V., Sanjuán, A., Belloch, V., & Ávila, C. (2006). Reading *cinnamon* activates olfactory brain regions. *NeuroImage, 32,* 906–912. http://dx.doi.org/10.1016/j.neuroimage.2006.03.037

Goodale, M. A., & Milner, A. D. (1992). Separate visual pathways for perception and action. *Trends in Neurosciences, 15,* 20–25. http://dx.doi.org/10.1016/0166-2236(92)90344-8

Gottwald, J. M., Achermann, S., Marciszko, C., Lindskog, M., & Gredebäck, G. (2016). An embodied account of early executive-function development: Prospective motor control in infancy is related to inhibition and working memory. *Psychological Science, 27,* 1600–1610. http://dx.doi.org/10.1177/0956797616667447

Grossman, M., Anderson, C., Khan, A., Avants, B., Elman, L., & McCluskey, L. (2008). Impaired action knowledge in amyotrophic lateral sclerosis. *Neurology, 71,* 1396–1401. http://dx.doi.org/10.1212/01.wnl.0000319701.50168.8c

Haith, M. M., & Campos, J. J. (1977). Human infancy. *Annual Review of Psychology, 28,* 251–293. http://dx.doi.org/10.1146/annurev.ps.28.020177.001343

Hansen, T., Olkkonen, M., Walter, S., & Gegenfurtner, K. R. (2006). Memory modulates color appearance. *Nature Neuroscience, 9,* 1367–1368. http://dx.doi.org/10.1038/nn1794

Harlow, H. (1958). The nature of love. *American Psychologist, 13,* 673–685. http://dx.doi.org/10.1037/h0047884

Harnad, S. (1990). The symbol grounding problem. *Physica D: Nonlinear Phenomena, 42,* 335–346. http://dx.doi.org/10.1016/0167-2789(90)90087-6

Hart, J., Jr., & Gordon, B. (1990). Delineation of single-word semantic comprehension deficits in aphasia, with anatomical correlation. *Annals of Neurology, 27,* 226–231. http://dx.doi.org/10.1002/ana.410270303

Hauk, O., Johnsrude, I., & Pulvermüller, F. (2004). Somatotopic representation of action words in human motor and premotor cortex. *Neuron, 41,* 301–307. http://dx.doi.org/10.1016/S0896-6273(03)00838-9

Havas, D. A., Glenberg, A. M., Gutowski, K. A., Lucarelli, M. J., & Davidson, R. J. (2010). Cosmetic use of botulinum toxin-a affects processing of emotional language. *Psychological Science, 21*, 895–900. http://dx.doi.org/10.1177/0956797610374742

Havas, D. A., Glenberg, A. M., & Rinck, M. (2007). Emotion simulation during language comprehension. *Psychonomic Bulletin & Review, 14*, 436–441. http://dx.doi.org/10.3758/BF03194085

Held, R., & Hein, A. (1963). Movement-induced stimulation in the development of visually guided behavior. *Journal of Comparative and Physiological Psychology, 56*, 872–876. http://dx.doi.org/10.1037/h0040546

Hellmann, J. H., Echterhoff, G., & Thoben, D. F. (2013). Metaphor in embodied cognition is more than just combining two related concepts: A comment on Wilson and Golonka (2013). *Frontiers in Psychology, 4*, 201. http://dx.doi.org/10.3389/fpsyg.2013.00201

Hellmann, J. H., Thoben, D. F., & Echterhoff, G. (2013). The sweet taste of revenge: Gustatory experience induces metaphor-consistent judgments of a harmful act. *Social Cognition, 31*, 531–542. http://dx.doi.org/10.1521/soco.2013.31.5.531

Hendricks, R. K., & Boroditsky, L. (2015). Constructing mental time without visual experience. *Trends in Cognitive Sciences, 19*, 429–430. http://dx.doi.org/10.1016/j.tics.2015.06.011

Hess, U., & Fischer, A. (2014). Emotional mimicry: Why and when we mimic emotions. *Social and Personality Psychology Compass, 8*, 45–57. http://dx.doi.org/10.1111/spc3.12083

Hobson, R. P., & Lee, A. (1998). Hello and goodbye: A study of social engagement in autism. *Journal of Autism and Developmental Disorders, 28*, 117–127. http://dx.doi.org/10.1023/A:1026088531558

Hoeben Mannaert, L. N., Dijkstra, K., & Zwaan, R. A. (2017). Is color an integral part of a rich mental simulation? *Memory & Cognition, 45*, 974–982. http://dx.doi.org/10.3758/s13421-017-0708-1

Hoffmann, D., Hornung, C., Martin, R., & Schiltz, C. (2013). Developing number–space associations: SNARC effects using a color discrimination task in 5-year-olds. *Journal of Experimental Child Psychology, 116*, 775–791. http://dx.doi.org/10.1016/j.jecp.2013.07.013

Huang, L., Galinsky, A. D., Gruenfeld, D. H., & Guillory, L. E. (2011). Powerful postures versus powerful roles: Which is the proximate correlate of thought and behavior? *Psychological Science, 22*, 95–102. http://dx.doi.org/10.1177/0956797610391912

Hubbard, E. M., Piazza, M., Pinel, P., & Dehaene, S. (2005). Interactions between number and space in parietal cortex. *Nature Reviews Neuroscience, 6*, 435–448. http://dx.doi.org/10.1038/nrn1684

Humphreys, G. W., & Forde, E. M. E. (2001). Hierarchies, similarity, and interactivity in object recognition: "Category-specific" neuropsychological deficits. *Behavioral and Brain Sciences, 24*, 453–476.

Hwang, H. C., & Matsumoto, D. (2014). Dominance threat display for victory and achievement in competition context. *Motivation and Emotion, 38*, 206–214. http://dx.doi.org/10.1007/s11031-013-9390-1

Iacoboni, M. (2009). Imitation, empathy, and mirror neurons. *Annual Review of Psychology, 60*, 653–670. http://dx.doi.org/10.1146/annurev.psych.60.110707.163604

Iacoboni, M., Molnar-Szakacs, I., Gallese, V., Buccino, G., Mazziotta, J. C., & Rizzolatti, G. (2005). Grasping the intentions of others with one's own mirror neuron system. *PLoS Biology, 3*(3), e79. http://dx.doi.org/10.1371/journal.pbio.0030079

Ijzerman, H., & Cohen, D. (2011). Grounding cultural syndromes: Body comportment and values in honor and dignity cultures. *European Journal of Social Psychology, 41*, 456–467. http://dx.doi.org/10.1002/ejsp.806

International Telecommunication Union. (2001). *ITU-T Recommendation E.161: Arrangement of digits, letters and symbols on telephones and other devices that can be used for gaining access to a telephone network.* Geneva, Switzerland: Author.

Iriki, A., Tanaka, M., & Iwamura, Y. (1996). Coding of modified body schema during tool use by macaque postcentral neurones. *NeuroReport, 7*, 2325–2330. http://dx.doi.org/10.1097/00001756-199610020-00010

Irving, L. T. (2015). Teaching statistics using dance and movement. *Frontiers in Psychology, 6*, 50. http://dx.doi.org/10.3389/fpsyg.2015.00050

Ishikawa, T., Fujiwara, H., Imai, O., & Okabe, A. (2008). Wayfinding with a GPS-based mobile navigation system: A comparison with maps and direct experience. *Journal of Environmental Psychology, 28*, 74–82. http://dx.doi.org/10.1016/j.jenvp.2007.09.002

Jack, R. E., Garrod, O. G. B., Yu, H., Caldara, R., & Schyns, P. G. (2012). Facial expressions of emotion are not culturally universal. *Proceedings of the National Academy of Sciences, USA, 109*, 7241–7244. http://dx.doi.org/10.1073/pnas.1200155109

Jacoby, L. L., & Hayman, C. A. G. (1987). Specific visual transfer in word identification. *Journal of Experimental Psychology: Learning, Memory, and Cognition, 13*, 456–463. http://dx.doi.org/10.1037/0278-7393.13.3.456

Jamrozik, A., McQuire, M., Cardillo, E. R., & Chatterjee, A. (2016). Metaphor: Bridging embodiment to abstraction. *Psychonomic Bulletin & Review, 23*, 1080–1089. http://dx.doi.org/10.3758/s13423-015-0861-0

Jasmin, K., & Casasanto, D. (2012). The QWERTY effect: How typing shapes the meanings of words. *Psychonomic Bulletin & Review, 19*, 499–504. http://dx.doi.org/10.3758/s13423-012-0229-7

Johnson, D. J., Wortman, J., Cheung, F., Hein, M., Lucas, R. E., Donnellan, M. B., . . . Narr, R. K. (2016). The effects of disgust on moral judgments: Testing moderators. *Social Psychological & Personality Science, 7*, 640–647. http://dx.doi.org/10.1177/1948550616654211

Jones, E. E., & Harris, V. A. (1967). The attribution of attitudes. *Journal of Experimental Social Psychology, 3*, 1–24. http://dx.doi.org/10.1016/0022-1031(67)90034-0

Jostmann, N. B., Lakens, D., & Schubert, T. W. (2009). Weight as an embodiment of importance. *Psychological Science, 20*, 1169–1174. http://dx.doi.org/10.1111/j.1467-9280.2009.02426.x

Kaschak, M. P., Connor, C. M., & Dombek, J. L. (2017). Enacted reading comprehension: Using bodily movement to aid the comprehension of abstract text content. *PLoS ONE, 12*(1), e0169711. http://dx.doi.org/10.1371/journal.pone.0169711

Kaschak, M. P., Madden, C. J., Therriault, D. J., Yaxley, R. H., Aveyard, M., Blanchard, A. A., & Zwaan, R. A. (2005). Perception of motion affects language processing. *Cognition, 94*, B79–B89. http://dx.doi.org/10.1016/j.cognition.2004.06.005

Kaschak, M. P., Zwaan, R. A., Aveyard, M., & Yaxley, R. H. (2006). Perception of auditory motion affects language processing. *Cognitive Science, 30,* 733–744. http://dx.doi.org/10.1207/s15516709cog0000_54

Kaufman, L. (1974). *Sight and mind: An introduction to visual perception.* New York, NY: Oxford University Press.

Kermoian, R., & Campos, J. J. (1988). Locomotor experience: A facilitator of spatial cognitive development. *Child Development, 59,* 908–917. http://dx.doi.org/10.2307/1130258

Keus, I. M., & Schwarz, W. (2005). Searching for the functional locus of the SNARC effect: Evidence for a response-related origin. *Memory & Cognition, 33,* 681–695. http://dx.doi.org/10.3758/BF03195335

Kille, D. R., Forest, A. L., & Wood, J. V. (2013). Tall, dark, and stable: Embodiment motivates mate selection preferences. *Psychological Science, 24,* 112–114. http://dx.doi.org/10.1177/0956797612457392

Kintsch, W. (1998). *Comprehension: A paradigm for cognition.* New York, NY: Cambridge University Press.

Korb, S., With, S., Niedenthal, P., Kaiser, S., & Grandjean, D. (2014). The perception and mimicry of facial movements predict judgments of smile authenticity. *PLoS ONE, 9*(6), e99194. http://dx.doi.org/10.1371/journal.pone.0099194

Kousta, S. T., Vigliocco, G., Vinson, D. P., Andrews, M., & Del Campo, E. (2011). The representation of abstract words: Why emotion matters. *Journal of Experimental Psychology: General, 140,* 14–34. http://dx.doi.org/10.1037/a0021446

Kövecses, Z. (2003). Language, figurative thought, and cross-cultural comparison. *Metaphor and Symbol, 18,* 311–320. http://dx.doi.org/10.1207/S15327868MS1804_6

Kövecses, Z. (2010). *Metaphor: A practical introduction.* New York, NY: Oxford University Press.

Krumhuber, E. G., Likowski, K. U., & Weyers, P. (2014). Facial mimicry of spontaneous and deliberate Duchenne and Non-Duchenne smiles. *Journal of Nonverbal Behavior, 38,* 1–11. http://dx.doi.org/10.1007/s10919-013-0167-8

Lai, V. T., & Desai, R. H. (2016). The grounding of temporal metaphors. *Cortex, 76,* 43–50. http://dx.doi.org/10.1016/j.cortex.2015.12.007

Lakoff, G. (1993). The contemporary theory of metaphor. In A. Ortoney (Ed.), *Metaphor and thought* (pp. 202–251). Cambridge, England: Cambridge University Press. http://dx.doi.org/10.1017/CBO9781139173865.013

Lakoff, G. (2014). Mapping the brain's metaphor circuitry: Metaphorical thought in everyday reason. *Frontiers in Human Neuroscience, 8,* 958. http://dx.doi.org/10.3389/fnhum.2014.00958

Lakoff, G., & Johnson, M. (1980). *Metaphors we live by.* Chicago, IL: University of Chicago Press.

Lakoff, G., & Johnson, M. (1999). *Philosophy in the flesh.* New York, NY: Basic Books.

Lambie, J. A., & Marcel, A. J. (2002). Consciousness and the varieties of emotion experience: A theoretical framework. *Psychological Review, 109,* 219–259. http://dx.doi.org/10.1037/0033-295X.109.2.219

Landau, M. J., Meier, B. P., & Keefer, L. A. (2010). A metaphor-enriched social cognition. *Psychological Bulletin, 136,* 1045–1067. http://dx.doi.org/10.1037/a0020970

Landau, M. J., Robinson, M. D., & Meier, B. P. (Eds.). (2014). *The power of metaphor: Examining its influence on social life.* Washington, DC: American Psychological Association. http://dx.doi.org/10.1037/14278-000

Lebois, L. A. M., Wilson-Mendenhall, C. D., & Barsalou, L. W. (2015). Are automatic conceptual cores the gold standard of semantic processing? The context-dependence of spatial meaning in grounded congruency effects. *Cognitive Science, 39,* 1764–1801. http://dx.doi.org/10.1111/cogs.12174

Lee, S. W. S., & Schwarz, N. (2010). Dirty hands and dirty mouths: Embodiment of the moral-purity metaphor is specific to the motor modality involved in moral transgression. *Psychological Science, 21,* 1423–1425. http://dx.doi.org/10.1177/0956797610382788

Lee, T. W., Dolan, R. J., & Critchley, H. D. (2008). Controlling emotional expression: Behavioral and neural correlates of nonimitative emotional responses. *Cerebral Cortex, 18,* 104–113. http://dx.doi.org/10.1093/cercor/bhm035

Leshed, G., Velden, T., Rieger, O., Kot, B., & Sengers, P. (2008). In-car GPS navigation: Engagement with and disengagement from the environment. *Proceedings of the SIGCHI Conference on Human Factors in Computing Systems 2008* (pp. 1675–1684). New York, NY: ACM. http://dx.doi.org/10.1145/1357054.1357316

Liew, S. L., Han, S., & Aziz-Zadeh, L. (2011). Familiarity modulates mirror neuron and mentalizing regions during intention understanding. *Human Brain Mapping, 32,* 1986–1997. http://dx.doi.org/10.1002/hbm.21164

Lindeman, L. M., & Abramson, L. Y. (2008). The mental simulation of motor incapacity in depression. *Journal of Cognitive Psychotherapy, 22,* 228–249. http://dx.doi.org/10.1891/0889-8391.22.3.228

Linkenauger, S. A., Mohler, B. J., & Proffitt, D. R. (2011). Body-based perceptual rescaling revealed through the size—weight illusion. *Perception, 40,* 1251–1253. http://dx.doi.org/10.1068/p7049

Linkenauger, S. A., Ramenzoni, V., & Proffitt, D. R. (2010). Illusory shrinkage and growth: Body-based rescaling affects the perception of size. *Psychological Science, 21,* 1318–1325. http://dx.doi.org/10.1177/0956797610380700

Linkenauger, S. A., Witt, J. K., & Proffitt, D. R. (2011). Taking a hands-on approach: Apparent grasping ability scales the perception of object size. *Journal of Experimental Psychology: Human Perception and Performance, 37,* 1432–1441. http://dx.doi.org/10.1037/a0024248

Linkenauger, S. A., Witt, J. K., Stefanucci, J. K., Bakdash, J. Z., & Proffitt, D. R. (2009). The effects of handedness and reachability on perceived distance. *Journal of Experimental Psychology: Human Perception and Performance, 35,* 1649–1660. http://dx.doi.org/10.1037/a0016875

Loue, S. (2008). *The transformative power of metaphor in therapy.* New York, NY: Springer.

Louwerse, M. M. (2011). Symbol interdependency in symbolic and embodied cognition. *Topics in Cognitive Science, 3,* 273–302. http://dx.doi.org/10.1111/j.1756-8765.2010.01106.x

Louwerse, M. M., & Jeuniaux, P. (2008). Language comprehension is both embodied and symbolic. In A. M. Glenberg, A. C. Graesser, & M. de Vega (Eds.), *Symbols and embodiment: Debates on meaning and cognition* (pp. 309–326). Oxford, England: Oxford University Press. http://dx.doi.org/10.1093/acprof:oso/9780199217274.003.0015

Lozada, M., & Carro, N. (2016). Embodied action improves cognition in children: Evidence from a study based on Piagetian conservation tasks. *Frontiers in Psychology, 7*, 393. http://dx.doi.org/10.3389/fpsyg.2016.00393

Luttrell, A., Petty, R. E., & Xu, M. (2017). Replicating and fixing failed replications: The case of need for cognition and argument quality. *Journal of Experimental Social Psychology, 69*, 178–183. http://dx.doi.org/10.1016/j.jesp.2016.09.006

Mahon, B. Z. (2015). The burden of embodied cognition. *Canadian Journal of Experimental Psychology, 69*, 172–178. http://dx.doi.org/10.1037/cep0000060

Mahon, B. Z., & Caramazza, A. (2008). A critical look at the embodied cognition hypothesis and a new proposal for grounding conceptual content. *Journal of Physiology–Paris, 102*, 59–70. http://dx.doi.org/10.1016/j.jphysparis.2008.03.004

Martin, A. (2007). The representation of object concepts in the brain. *Annual Review of Psychology, 58*, 25–45. http://dx.doi.org/10.1146/annurev.psych.57.102904.190143

Masson, M., Bub, D., & Warren, C. (2008). Kicking calculators: Contributions of embodied representations to sentence comprehension. *Journal of Memory and Language, 59*, 256–265. http://dx.doi.org/10.1016/j.jml.2008.05.003

Masson, M. E. J., & Loftus, G. R. (2003). Using confidence intervals for graphically based data interpretation. *Canadian Journal of Experimental Psychology, 57*, 203–220. http://dx.doi.org/10.1037/h0087426

Mathôt, S., Grainger, J., & Strijkers, K. (2017). Pupillary responses to words that convey a sense of brightness or darkness. *Psychological Science, 28*, 1116–1124. http://dx.doi.org/10.1177/0956797617702699

Matsumoto, D., & Hwang, H. C. (2013). Cultural similarities and differences in emblematic gestures. *Journal of Nonverbal Behavior, 37*, 1–27. http://dx.doi.org/10.1007/s10919-012-0143-8

McCarthy, J., Minsky, M., Rochester, N., & Shannon, C. E. (2006). A proposal for the Dartmouth Summer Research Project on artificial intelligence. *AI Magazine, 27*, 12–14.

McClelland, J. L., & Elman, J. L. (1986). The TRACE model of speech perception. *Cognitive Psychology, 18*, 1–86. http://dx.doi.org/10.1016/0010-0285(86)90015-0

McClelland, J. L., & Rogers, T. T. (2003). The parallel distributed processing approach to semantic cognition. *Nature Reviews Neuroscience, 4*, 310–322. http://dx.doi.org/10.1038/nrn1076

McMullen, L. M. (2008). Putting it in context: Metaphor and psychotherapy. In R. W. Gibbs (Ed.), *The Cambridge handbook of metaphor and thought* (pp. 397–411). New York, NY: Cambridge University Press. http://dx.doi.org/10.1017/CBO9780511816802.024

Meier, B. P., Hauser, D. J., Robinson, M. D., Friesen, C. K., & Schjeldahl, K. (2007). What's "up" with God? Vertical space as a representation of the divine. *Journal of Personality and Social Psychology, 93*, 699–710. http://dx.doi.org/10.1037/0022-3514.93.5.699

Meier, B. P., & Robinson, M. D. (2004). Why the sunny side is up: Association between affect and vertical position. *Psychological Science, 15*, 243–247. http://dx.doi.org/10.1111/j.0956-7976.2004.00659.x

Meier, B. P., & Robinson, M. D. (2005). The metaphorical representation of affect. *Metaphor and Symbol, 20*, 239–257. http://dx.doi.org/10.1207/s15327868ms2004_1

Meteyard, L., Bahrami, B., & Vigliocco, G. (2007). Motion detection and motion verbs: Language affects low-level visual perception. *Psychological Science, 18*, 1007–1013. http://dx.doi.org/10.1111/j.1467-9280.2007.02016.x

Meyer-Lindenberg, A. (2008). Trust me on this. *Science, 321*, 778–780. http://dx.doi.org/10.1126/science.1162908

Miles, L. K., Nind, L. K., & Macrae, C. N. (2010). Moving through time. *Psychological Science, 21*, 222–223. http://dx.doi.org/10.1177/0956797609359333

Miller, G. A. (1956). The magical number seven plus or minus two: Some limits on our capacity for processing information. *Psychological Review, 63*, 81–97. http://dx.doi.org/10.1037/h0043158

Miller, L. E., Longo, M. R., & Saygin, A. P. (2017). Visual illusion of tool use recalibrates tactile perception. *Cognition, 162*, 32–40. http://dx.doi.org/10.1016/j.cognition.2017.01.022

Milner, A. D., & Goodale, M. A. (2008). Two visual systems re-viewed. *Neuropsychologia, 46*, 774–785. http://dx.doi.org/10.1016/j.neuropsychologia.2007.10.005

Monroe, A. E., & Malle, B. F. (2010). From uncaused will to conscious choice: The need to study, not speculate about people's folk concept of free will. *Review of Philosophy and Psychology, 1*, 211–224. http://dx.doi.org/10.1007/s13164-009-0010-7

Murdock, B. B., Jr. (1982). A theory for the storage and retrieval of item and associative information. *Psychological Review, 89*, 609–626. http://dx.doi.org/10.1037/0033-295X.89.6.609

Myers, J. L., & O'Brien, E. J. (1998). Accessing the discourse representation during reading. *Discourse Processes, 26*, 131–157. http://dx.doi.org/10.1080/01638539809545042

Newell, A., & Simon, H. A. (1972). *Human problem solving*. Englewood Cliffs, NJ: Prentice Hall.

Newell, A., & Simon, H. A. (1976). Computer science as empirical inquiry: Symbols and search. *Communications of the ACM, 19*, 113–126. http://dx.doi.org/10.1145/360018.360022

Niedenthal, P. M. (2007). Embodying emotion. *Science, 316*(5827), 1002–1005. http://dx.doi.org/10.1126/science.1136930

Niedenthal, P. M., Augustinova, M., Rychlowska, M., Droit-Volet, S., Zinner, L., Knafo, A., & Brauer, M. (2012). Negative relations between pacifier use and emotional competence. *Basic and Applied Social Psychology, 34*, 387–394. http://dx.doi.org/10.1080/01973533.2012.712019

Niedenthal, P. M., Barsalou, L. W., Winkielman, P., Krauth-Gruber, S., & Ric, F. (2005). Embodiment in attitudes, social perception, and emotion. *Personality and Social Psychology Review, 9*, 184–211. http://dx.doi.org/10.1207/s15327957pspr0903_1

Niedenthal, P. M., Wood, A., & Rychlowska, M. (2014). Embodied emotion concepts. In L. Shapiro (Ed.), *The Routledge handbook of embodied cognition* (pp. 240–249). Oxford, England: Routledge Philosophy.

Nijhof, A. D., & Willems, R. M. (2015). Simulating fiction: Individual differences in literature comprehension revealed with fMRI. *PLoS ONE, 10*(2), e0116492. http://dx.doi.org/10.1371/journal.pone.0116492

Noah, T., Schul, Y., & Mayo, R. (2018). When both the original study and its failed replication are correct: Feeling observed eliminates the facial-feedback effect. *Journal of Personality and Social Psychology, 114*, 657–664. http://dx.doi.org/10.1037/pspa0000121

Oudgenoeg-Paz, O., & Rivière, J. (2014). Self-locomotion and spatial language and spatial cognition: Insights from typical and atypical development. *Frontiers in Psychology, 5*, 521. http://dx.doi.org/10.3389/fpsyg.2014.00521

Papesh, M. H. (2015). Just out of reach: On the reliability of the action-sentence compatibility effect. *Journal of Experimental Psychology: General, 144*, e116–e141. http://dx.doi.org/10.1037/xge0000125

Pecher, D., Zeelenberg, R., & Barsalou, L. W. (2003). Verifying different-modality properties for concepts produces switching costs. *Psychological Science, 14*, 119–124. http://dx.doi.org/10.1111/1467-9280.t01-1-01429

Petroni, A., Baguear, F., & Della-Maggiore, V. (2010). Motor resonance may originate from sensorimotor experience. *Journal of Neurophysiology, 104*, 1867–1871. http://dx.doi.org/10.1152/jn.00386.2010

Petrova, A., Navarrete, E., Suitner, C., Sulpizio, S., Reynolds, M., Job, R., & Peressotti, F. (2018). Spatial congruency effects exist, just not for words: Looking into Estes, Verges, and Barsalou (2008). *Psychological Science, 29*, 1195–1199. http://dx.doi.org/10.1177/0956797617728127

Philbeck, J. W., & Witt, J. K. (2015). Action-specific influences on perception and postperceptual processes: Present controversies and future directions. *Psychological Bulletin, 141*, 1120–1144. http://dx.doi.org/10.1037/a0039738

Piaget, J. (1952). *The origins of intelligence in children*. New York, NY: International Universities Press. http://dx.doi.org/10.1037/11494-000

Piaget, J. (1954). *The construction of reality in the child*. New York, NY: Basic Books. http://dx.doi.org/10.1037/11168-000

Piaget, J., & Inhelder, B. (1969). *The psychology of the child* (H. Weaver, Trans.). New York, NY: Basic Books. (Original work published 1966)

Pitt, B., & Casasanto, D. (2017, April). *Experiential origins of the mental time line and mental number line*. Paper presented at the Midwestern Psychological Association meeting, Chicago, Illinois.

Ponari, M., Norbury, C. F., & Vigliocco, G. (2018). Acquisition of abstract concepts is influenced by emotional valence. *Developmental Science, 21*, e12549. http://dx.doi.org/10.1111/desc.12549

Proctor, R. W., & Cho, Y. S. (2006). Polarity correspondence: A general principle for performance of speeded binary classification tasks. *Psychological Bulletin, 132*, 416–442. http://dx.doi.org/10.1037/0033-2909.132.3.416

Proffitt, D. R. (2006). Embodied perception and the economy of action. *Perspectives on Psychological Science, 1*, 110–122. http://dx.doi.org/10.1111/j.1745-6916.2006.00008.x

Proffitt, D. R. (2013). An embodied approach to perception: By what units are visual perceptions scaled? *Perspectives on Psychological Science, 8*, 474–483. http://dx.doi.org/10.1177/1745691613489837

Proffitt, D. R., Bhalla, M., Gossweiler, R., & Midgett, J. (1995). Perceiving geograph-ical slant. *Psychonomic Bulletin & Review, 2,* 409–428. http://dx.doi.org/10.3758/BF03210980

Proffitt, D. R., & Linkenauger, S. A. (2013). Perception viewed as a phenotypic expression. In W. Prinz, M. Beisert, & A. Herwig (Eds.), *Action science: Foundations of an emerging discipline* (pp. 171–197). Cambridge, MA: MIT Press. http://dx.doi.org/10.7551/mitpress/9780262018555.003.0007

Proffitt, D. R., Stefanucci, J., Banton, T., & Epstein, W. (2003). The role of effort in perceiving distance. *Psychological Science, 14,* 106–112. http://dx.doi.org/10.1111/1467-9280.t01-1-01427

Pulvermüller, F. (2013). How neurons make meaning: Brain mechanisms for embodied and abstract-symbolic semantics. *Trends in Cognitive Sciences, 17,* 458–470. http://dx.doi.org/10.1016/j.tics.2013.06.004

Pulvermüller, F., Hauk, O., Nikulin, V. V., & Ilmoniemi, R. J. (2005). Functional links between motor and language systems. *European Journal of Neuroscience, 21,* 793–797. http://dx.doi.org/10.1111/j.1460-9568.2005.03900.x

Pulvermüller, F., Shtyrov, Y., & Ilmoniemi, R. (2005). Brain signatures of meaning access in action word recognition. *Journal of Cognitive Neuroscience, 17,* 884–892. http://dx.doi.org/10.1162/0898929054021111

Ranehill, E., Dreber, A., Johannesson, M., Leiberg, S., Sul, S., & Weber, R. A. (2015). Assessing the robustness of power posing: No effect on hormones and risk tolerance in a large sample of men and women. *Psychological Science, 26,* 653–656. http://dx.doi.org/10.1177/0956797614553946

Repetto, C., Serino, S., Macedonia, M., & Riva, G. (2016). Virtual reality as an embodied tool to enhance episodic memory in elderly. *Frontiers in Psychology, 7,* 1839. http://dx.doi.org/10.3389/fpsyg.2016.01839

Restle, F. (1970). Speed of adding and comparing numbers. *Journal of Experimental Psychology, 83,* 274–278. http://dx.doi.org/10.1037/h0028573

Riener, C. R., Stefanucci, J. K., Proffitt, D. R., & Clore, G. (2003). An effect of mood on perceiving spatial layout. *Journal of Vision, 3,* 227. http://dx.doi.org/10.1167/3.9.227

Rieser, J. J., Pick, H. L., Jr., Ashmead, D. H., & Garing, A. E. (1995). Calibration of human locomotion and models of perceptual-motor organization. *Journal of Experimental Psychology: Human Perception and Performance, 21,* 480–497. http://dx.doi.org/10.1037/0096-1523.21.3.480

Riggins, T., Blankenship, S. L., Mulligan, E., Rice, K., & Redcay, E. (2015). Devel-opmental differences in relations between episodic memory and hippocampal subregion volume during early childhood. *Child Development, 86,* 1710–1718. http://dx.doi.org/10.1111/cdev.12445

Riskind, J. H., & Gotay, C. C. (1982). Physical posture: Could it have regulatory or feedback effects on motivation and emotion? *Motivation and Emotion, 6,* 273–298. http://dx.doi.org/10.1007/BF00992249

Rivière, J. (2014). Embodiment in children's choice: Linking bodily constraints with decisional dynamics. *Current Directions in Psychological Science, 23,* 408–413. http://dx.doi.org/10.1177/0963721414548214

Rivière, J., & David, E. (2013). Perceptual–motor constraints on decision making: The case of the manual search behavior for hidden objects in toddlers. *Journal of Experimental Child Psychology, 115,* 42–52. http://dx.doi.org/10.1016/j.jecp.2012.11.006

Rivière, J., & Lécuyer, R. (2003). The C-not-B error: A comparative study. *Cognitive Development, 18,* 285–297. http://dx.doi.org/10.1016/S0885-2014(03)00003-0

Rivière, J., & Lécuyer, R. (2008). Effects of arm weight on C-not-B task performance: Implications for the motor inhibitory deficit account of search failures. *Journal of Experimental Child Psychology, 100,* 1–16. http://dx.doi.org/10.1016/j.jecp.2008.01.005

Rizzolatti, G., & Craighero, L. (2004). The mirror-neuron system. *Annual Review of Neuroscience, 27,* 169–192. http://dx.doi.org/10.1146/annurev.neuro.27.070203.144230

Rizzolatti, G., & Sinigaglia, C. (2010). The functional role of the parieto-frontal mirror circuit: Interpretations and misinterpretations. *Nature Reviews Neuroscience, 11,* 264–274. http://dx.doi.org/10.1038/nrn2805

Rosch, E. H. (1973). Natural categories. *Cognitive Psychology, 4,* 328–350. http://dx.doi.org/10.1016/0010-0285(73)90017-0

Russell, J. A. (1991). In defense of a prototype approach to emotion concepts. *Journal of Personality and Social Psychology, 60,* 37–47. http://dx.doi.org/10.1037/0022-3514.60.1.37

Rychlowska, M., Cañadas, E., Wood, A., Krumhuber, E. G., Fischer, A., & Niedenthal, P. M. (2014). Blocking mimicry makes true and false smiles look the same. *PLoS ONE, 9*(3), e90876. http://dx.doi.org/10.1371/journal.pone.0090876

Rychlowska, M., Miyamoto, Y., Matsumoto, D., Hess, U., Gilboa-Schechtman, E., & Kamble, S., . . . Niedenthal, P. M. (2015). Heterogeneity of long-history migration explains cultural differences in reports of emotional expressivity and the functions of smiles. *Proceedings of the National Academy of Sciences, USA, 112,* E2429–2436. http://dx.doi.org/10.1073/pnas.1413661112

Saj, A., Fuhrman, O., Vuilleumier, P., & Boroditsky, L. (2014). Patients with left spatial neglect also neglect the "left side" of time. *Psychological Science, 25,* 207–214. http://dx.doi.org/10.1177/0956797612475222

Santiago, J., Lupáñez, J., Pérez, E., & Funes, M. J. (2007). Time (also) flies from left to right. *Psychonomic Bulletin & Review, 14,* 512–516. http://dx.doi.org/10.3758/BF03194099

Sapolsky, R. M., Alberts, S. C., & Altmann, J. (1997). Hypercortisolism associated with social subordinance or social isolation among wild baboons. *Archives of General Psychiatry, 54,* 1137–1143. http://dx.doi.org/10.1001/archpsyc.1997.01830240097014

Schacter, D. L., Dobbins, I. G., & Schnyer, D. M. (2004). Specificity of priming: A cognitive neuroscience perspective. *Nature Reviews Neuroscience, 5,* 853–862. http://dx.doi.org/10.1038/nrn1534

Schaefer, M., Denke, C., Heinze, H. J., & Rotte, M. (2014). Rough primes and rough conversations: Evidence for a modality-specific basis to mental metaphors. *Social Cognitive and Affective Neuroscience, 9,* 1653–1659. http://dx.doi.org/10.1093/scan/nst163

Schnall, S. (2017). Social and contextual constraints on embodied perception. *Perspectives on Psychological Science, 12*, 325–340. http://dx.doi.org/10.1177/1745691616660199

Schnall, S., Benton, J., & Harvey, S. (2008). With a clean conscience: Cleanliness reduces the severity of moral judgments. *Psychological Science, 19*, 1219–1222. http://dx.doi.org/10.1111/j.1467-9280.2008.02227.x

Schnall, S., Haidt, J., Clore, G. L., & Jordan, A. H. (2008). Disgust as embodied moral judgment. *Personality and Social Psychology Bulletin, 34*, 1096–1109. http://dx.doi.org/10.1177/0146167208317771

Schnall, S., Harber, K. D., Stefanucci, J. K., & Proffitt, D. R. (2008). Social support and the perception of geographical slant. *Journal of Experimental Social Psychology, 44*, 1246–1255. http://dx.doi.org/10.1016/j.jesp.2008.04.011

Schnall, S., Zadra, J. R., & Proffitt, D. R. (2010). Direct evidence for the economy of action: Glucose and the perception of geographical slant. *Perception, 39*, 464–482. http://dx.doi.org/10.1068/p6445

Schneider, I. K., Parzuchowski, M., Wojciszke, B., Schwarz, N., & Koole, S. L. (2015). Weighty data: Importance information influences estimated weight of digital information storage devices. *Frontiers in Psychology, 5*, 1536. Advance online publication. http://dx.doi.org/10.3389/fpsyg.2014.01536

Schneider, I. K., Rutjens, B. T., Jostmann, N. B., & Lakens, D. (2011). Weighty matters: Importance literally feels heavy. *Social Psychological and Personality Science, 2*, 474–478. http://dx.doi.org/10.1177/1948550610397895

Schubert, T. W. (2004). The power in your hand: Gender differences in bodily feedback from making a fist. *Personality and Social Psychology Bulletin, 30*, 757–769. http://dx.doi.org/10.1177/0146167204263780

Schubert, T. W. (2005). Your highness: Vertical positions as perceptual symbols of power. *Journal of Personality and Social Psychology, 89*, 1–21. http://dx.doi.org/10.1037/0022-3514.89.1.1

Searle, J. R. (1980). Minds, brains, and programs. *Behavioral and Brain Sciences, 3*, 417–424. http://dx.doi.org/10.1017/S0140525X00005756

Sedgwick, H. (1986). Space perception. In K. L. Boff, L. Kaufman, & J. P. Thomas (Eds.), *Handbook of perception and human performance: Vol. 1. Sensory processes and perception* (pp. 1–57). New York, NY: Wiley.

Shapiro, L. (2011). *Embodied cognition*. New York, NY: Routledge.

Shapiro, L. (Ed.). (2014). *The Routledge handbook of embodied cognition*. New York, NY: Routledge. http://dx.doi.org/10.4324/9781315775845

Simmons, J. P., & Simonsohn, U. (2017). Power posing: *P*-curving the evidence. *Psychological Science, 28*, 687–693. http://dx.doi.org/10.1177/0956797616658563

Simmons, W. K., Martin, A., & Barsalou, L. W. (2005). Pictures of appetizing foods activate gustatory cortices for taste and reward. *Cerebral Cortex, 15*, 1602–1608. http://dx.doi.org/10.1093/cercor/bhi038

Simmons, W. K., Ramjee, V., Beauchamp, M. S., McRae, K., Martin, A., & Barsalou, L. W. (2007). A common neural substrate for perceiving and knowing about color. *Neuropsychologia, 45*, 2802–2810. http://dx.doi.org/10.1016/j.neuropsychologia.2007.05.002

Slepian, M. L., Rule, N. O., & Ambady, N. (2012). Proprioception and person perception: Politicians and professors. *Personality and Social Psychology Bulletin, 38,* 1621–1628. http://dx.doi.org/10.1177/0146167212457786

Slepian, M. L., Weisbuch, M., Rule, N. O., & Ambady, N. (2011). Tough and tender: Embodied categorization of gender. *Psychological Science, 22,* 26–28. http://dx.doi.org/10.1177/0956797610390388

Slotnick, S. D., & Schacter, D. L. (2004). A sensory signature that distinguishes true from false memories. *Nature Neuroscience, 7,* 664–672. http://dx.doi.org/10.1038/nn1252

Smith, E. E., Shoben, E. J., & Rips, L. J. (1974). Structure and process in semantic memory: A featural model for semantic decisions. *Psychological Review, 81,* 214–241. http://dx.doi.org/10.1037/h0036351

Soliman, T., Gibson, A., & Glenberg, A. M. (2013). Sensory motor mechanisms unify psychology: The embodiment of culture. *Frontiers in Psychology, 4,* 885. http://dx.doi.org/10.3389/fpsyg.2013.00885

Solomon, K. O., & Barsalou, L. W. (2004). Perceptual simulation in property verification. *Memory & Cognition, 32,* 244–259. http://dx.doi.org/10.3758/BF03196856

Speer, N. K., Reynolds, J. R., Swallow, K. M., & Zacks, J. M. (2009). Reading stories activates neural representations of visual and motor experiences. *Psychological Science, 20,* 989–999. http://dx.doi.org/10.1111/j.1467-9280.2009.02397.x

Spence, C., Nicholls, M. E. R., & Driver, J. (2001). The cost of expecting events in the wrong sensory modality. *Perception & Psychophysics, 63,* 330–336. http://dx.doi.org/10.3758/BF03194473

Stanfield, R. A., & Zwaan, R. A. (2001). The effect of implied orientation derived from verbal context on picture recognition. *Psychological Science, 12,* 153–156. http://dx.doi.org/10.1111/1467-9280.00326

Stern, D. N. (2010). *Forms of vitality: Exploring dynamic experience in psychology, arts, psychotherapy, and development.* Oxford, England: Oxford University Press.

Stevens, J. A., Fonlupt, P., Shiffrar, M., & Decety, J. (2000). New aspects of motion perception: Selective neural encoding of apparent human movements. *NeuroReport, 11,* 109–115. http://dx.doi.org/10.1097/00001756-200001170-00022

Strack, F., Martin, L. L., & Stepper, S. (1988). Inhibiting and facilitating conditions of the human smile: A nonobtrusive test of the facial feedback hypothesis. *Journal of Personality and Social Psychology, 54,* 768–777. http://dx.doi.org/10.1037/0022-3514.54.5.768

Tamietto, M., Castelli, L., Vighetti, S., Perozzo, P., Geminiani, G., Weiskrantz, L., & de Gelder, B. (2009). Unseen facial and bodily expressions trigger fast emotional reactions. *Proceedings of the National Academy of Sciences, USA, 106,* 17661–17666. http://dx.doi.org/10.1073/pnas.0908994106

Taylor, L. J., Lev-Ari, S., & Zwaan, R. A. (2008). Inferences about action engage action systems. *Brain and Language, 107,* 62–67. http://dx.doi.org/10.1016/j.bandl.2007.08.004

Taylor, L. J., & Zwaan, R. A. (2009). Action in cognition: The case of language. *Language and Cognition, 1,* 45–58. http://dx.doi.org/10.1515/LANGCOG.2009.003

Tettamanti, M., Buccino, G., Saccuman, M. C., Gallese, V., Danna, M., Scifo, P., . . . Perani, D. (2005). Listening to action-related sentences activates fronto-parietal motor circuits. *Journal of Cognitive Neuroscience, 17,* 273–281. http://dx.doi.org/10.1162/0898929053124965

Teufel, C., & Nanay, B. (2017). How to (and how not to) think about top-down influences on visual perception. *Consciousness and Cognition, 47,* 17–25. http://dx.doi.org/10.1016/j.concog.2016.05.008

Thelen, E., & Smith, L. B. (1994). *A dynamic systems approach to development of cognition and action.* Cambridge, MA: MIT Press.

Thibodeau, P. H., Crow, L., & Flusberg, S. J. (2017). The metaphor police: A case study of the role of metaphor in explanation. *Psychonomic Bulletin & Review, 24,* 1375–1386. http://dx.doi.org/10.3758/s13423-016-1192-5

Thomas, A. G., Dennis, A., Bandettini, P. A., & Johansen-Berg, H. (2012). The effects of aerobic activity on brain structure. *Frontiers in Psychology, 3,* 86. http://dx.doi.org/10.3389/fpsyg.2012.00086

Topolinski, S. (2011). I 5683 you: Dialing phone numbers on cell phones activates key-concordant concepts. *Psychological Science, 22,* 355–360. http://dx.doi.org/10.1177/0956797610397668

Tracy, J. L., & Matsumoto, D. (2008). The spontaneous expression of pride and shame: Evidence for biologically innate nonverbal displays. *Proceedings of the National Academy of Sciences, USA, 105,* 11655–11660. http://dx.doi.org/10.1073/pnas.0802686105

Tran, C., Smith, B., & Buschkuehl, M. (2017). Support of mathematical thinking through embodied cognition: Nondigital and digital approaches. *Cognitive Research: Principles and Implications, 2,* 16–34. http://dx.doi.org/10.1186/s41235-017-0053-8

Tulving, E., & Thomson, D. M. (1973). Encoding specificity and retrieval processes in episodic memory. *Psychological Review, 80,* 352–373. http://dx.doi.org/10.1037/h0020071

Uleman, J. S. (1987). Consciousness and control: The case of spontaneous trait inferences. *Personality and Social Psychology Bulletin, 13,* 337–354. http://dx.doi.org/10.1177/0146167287133004

van Dam, W. O., Speed, L. J., Lai, V. T., Vigliocco, G., & Desai, R. H. (2017). Effects of motion speed in action representations. *Brain and Language, 168,* 47–56. http://dx.doi.org/10.1016/j.bandl.2017.01.003

van Dantzig, S., Pecher, D., Zeelenberg, R., & Barsalou, L. W. (2008). Perceptual processing affects conceptual processing. *Cognitive Science, 32,* 579–590. http://dx.doi.org/10.1080/03640210802035365

van Dantzig, S., Zeelenberg, R., & Pecher, D. (2009). Unconstraining theories of embodied cognition. *Journal of Experimental Social Psychology, 45,* 345–351. http://dx.doi.org/10.1016/j.jesp.2008.11.001

Van Overwalle, F., & Baetens, K. (2009). Understanding others' actions and goals by mirror and mentalizing systems: A meta-analysis. *NeuroImage, 48,* 564–584. http://dx.doi.org/10.1016/j.neuroimage.2009.06.009

Varela, F. J., Thompson, E., & Rosch, E. (1991). *The embodied mind: Cognitive science and human experience.* Cambridge, MA: MIT Press.

Vigliocco, G., Kousta, S. T., Della Rosa, P. A., Vinson, D. P., Tettamanti, M., Devlin, J. T., & Cappa, S. F. (2014). The neural representation of abstract words: The role of emotion. *Cerebral Cortex, 24*, 1767–1777. http://dx.doi.org/10.1093/cercor/bht025

Warren, R. M. (1970). Perceptual restoration of missing speech sounds. *Science, 167*, 392–393. http://dx.doi.org/10.1126/science.167.3917.392

Weger, U. W., & Pratt, J. (2008). Time flies like an arrow: Space–time compatibility effects suggest the use of a mental timeline. *Psychonomic Bulletin & Review, 15*, 426–430. http://dx.doi.org/10.3758/PBR.15.2.426

Weisberg, S. M., & Newcombe, N. S. (2016). How do (some) people make a cognitive map? Routes, places, and working memory. *Journal of Experimental Psychology: Learning, Memory, and Cognition, 42*, 768–785. http://dx.doi.org/10.1037/xlm0000200

Wells, G. L., & Petty, R. E. (1980). The effects of overt head movements on persuasion: Compatibility and incompatibility of responses. *Basic and Applied Social Psychology, 1*, 219–230. http://dx.doi.org/10.1207/s15324834basp0103_2

Wesp, R., Cichello, P., Gracia, E. B., & Davis, K. (2004). Observing and engaging in purposeful actions with objects influences estimates of their size. *Perception & Psychophysics, 66*, 1261–1267. http://dx.doi.org/10.3758/BF03194996

Wheeler, M. E., Petersen, S. E., & Buckner, R. L. (2000). Memory's echo: Vivid remembering reactivates sensory-specific cortex. *Proceedings of the National Academy of Sciences, USA, 97*, 11125–11129. http://dx.doi.org/10.1073/pnas.97.20.11125

Willems, R. M., & Casasanto, D. (2011). Flexibility in embodied language understanding. *Frontiers in Psychology, 2*, 116. http://dx.doi.org/10.3389/fpsyg.2011.00116

Willems, R. M., Hagoort, P., & Casasanto, D. (2010). Body-specific representations of action verbs: Neural evidence from right- and left-handers. *Psychological Science, 21*, 67–74. http://dx.doi.org/10.1177/0956797609354072

Willems, R. M., Labruna, L., D'Esposito, M., Ivry, R., & Casasanto, D. (2011). A functional role for the motor system in language understanding: Evidence from theta-burst transcranial magnetic stimulation. *Psychological Science, 22*, 849–854. http://dx.doi.org/10.1177/0956797611412387

Willems, R. M., Toni, I., Hagoort, P., & Casasanto, D. (2009). Body-specific motor imagery of hand actions: Neural evidence from right- and left-handers. *Frontiers in Human Neuroscience, 3*, 39. http://dx.doi.org/10.3389/neuro.09.039.2009

Williams, L. E., & Bargh, J. A. (2008). Experiencing physical warmth promotes interpersonal warmth. *Science, 322*, 606–607. http://dx.doi.org/10.1126/science.1162548

Williams, L. E., Huang, J. Y., & Bargh, J. A. (2009). The scaffolded mind: Higher mental processes are grounded in early experience of the physical world. *European Journal of Social Psychology, 39*, 1257–1267. http://dx.doi.org/10.1002/ejsp.665

Wilson, A. D., & Golonka, S. (2013). Embodied cognition is not what you think it is. *Frontiers in Psychology, 4*, 58. http://dx.doi.org/10.3389/fpsyg.2013.00058

Wilson, M. (2002). Six views of embodied cognition. *Psychonomic Bulletin & Review, 9*, 625–636. http://dx.doi.org/10.3758/BF03196322

Winter, S. S., Mehlman, M. L., Clark, B. J., & Taube, J. S. (2015). Passive transport disrupts grid signals in the parhippocampal cortex. *Current Biology, 25*, 2493–2502. http://dx.doi.org/10.1016/j.cub.2015.08.034

Witt, J. K. (2011). Action's effect on perception. *Current Directions in Psychological Science, 20*, 201–206. http://dx.doi.org/10.1177/0963721411408770

Witt, J. K. (2015). Awareness is not a necessary characteristic of a perceptual effect: Commentary on Firestone (2013). *Perspectives on Psychological Science, 10*, 865–872. http://dx.doi.org/10.1177/1745691615598525

Witt, J. K., & Dorsch, T. E. (2009). Kicking to bigger uprights: Field goal kicking performance influences perceived size. *Perception, 38*, 1328–1340. http://dx.doi.org/10.1068/p6325

Witt, J. K., Linkenauger, S. A., Bakdash, J. Z., Augustyn, J. S., Cook, A., & Proffitt, D. R. (2009). The long road of pain: Chronic pain increases perceived distance. *Experimental Brain Research, 192*, 145–148. http://dx.doi.org/10.1007/s00221-008-1594-3

Witt, J. K., Linkenauger, S. A., Bakdash, J. Z., & Proffitt, D. R. (2008). Putting to a bigger hole: Golf performance relates to perceived size. *Psychonomic Bulletin & Review, 15*, 581–585. http://dx.doi.org/10.3758/PBR.15.3.581

Witt, J. K., Linkenauger, S. A., & Proffitt, D. R. (2012). Get me out of this slump! Visual illusions improve sports performance. *Psychological Science, 23*, 397–399. http://dx.doi.org/10.1177/0956797611428810

Witt, J. K., & Proffitt, D. R. (2005). See the ball, hit the ball: Apparent ball size is correlated with batting average. *Psychological Science, 16*, 937–938. http://dx.doi.org/10.1111/j.1467-9280.2005.01640.x

Witt, J. K., & Proffitt, D. R. (2008). Action-specific influences on distance perception: A role for motor simulation. *Journal of Experimental Psychology: Human Perception and Performance, 34*, 1479–1492. http://dx.doi.org/10.1037/a0010781

Witt, J. K., Proffitt, D. R., & Epstein, W. (2004). Perceiving distance: A role of effort and intent. *Perception, 33*, 577–590. http://dx.doi.org/10.1068/p5090

Witt, J. K., Proffitt, D. R., & Epstein, W. (2005). Tool use affects perceived distance, but only when you intend to use it. *Journal of Experimental Psychology: Human Perception and Performance, 31*, 880–888. http://dx.doi.org/10.1037/0096-1523.31.5.880

Witt, J. K., South, S. C., & Sugovic, M. (2014). A perceiver's own abilities influence perception, even when observing others. *Psychonomic Bulletin & Review, 21*, 384–389. http://dx.doi.org/10.3758/s13423-013-0505-1

Witt, J. K., & Sugovic, M. (2012). Does ease to block a ball affect perceived ball speed? Examination of alternative hypotheses. *Journal of Experimental Psychology: Human Perception and Performance, 38*, 1202–1214. http://dx.doi.org/10.1037/a0026512

Witt, J. K., Sugovic, M., & Taylor, J. E. T. (2012). Action-specific effects in a social context: Others' abilities influence perceived speed. *Journal of Experimental Psychology: Human Perception and Performance, 38*, 715–725. http://dx.doi.org/10.1037/a0026261

Witt, J. K., Tenhundfeld, N. L., & Tymoski, M. J. (2017). Is there a chastity belt on perception? *Psychological Science.* Advance online publication.

Wood, A., Lupyan, G., Sherrin, S., & Niedenthal, P. (2016). Altering sensorimotor feedback disrupts visual discrimination of facial expressions. *Psychonomic Bulletin & Review, 23*, 1150–1156. http://dx.doi.org/10.3758/s13423-015-0974-5

Wood, A., Rychlowska, M., Korb, S., & Niedenthal, P. (2016). Fashioning the face: Sensorimotor simulation contributes to facial expression recognition. *Trends in Cognitive Sciences, 20*, 227–240. http://dx.doi.org/10.1016/j.tics.2015.12.010

Wood, A., Rychlowska, M., & Niedenthal, P. M. (2016). Heterogeneity of long-history migration predicts emotion recognition accuracy. *Emotion, 16,* 413–420. http://dx.doi.org/10.1037/emo0000137

Wood, G., Vine, S. J., & Wilson, M. R. (2013). The impact of visual illusions on perception, action planning, and motor performance. *Attention, Perception, & Psychophysics, 75,* 830–834. http://dx.doi.org/10.3758/s13414-013-0489-y

Woods, A. J., Philbeck, J. W., & Danoff, J. V. (2009). The various perceptions of distance: An alternative view of how effort affects distance judgments. *Journal of Experimental Psychology: Human Perception and Performance, 35,* 1104–1117. http://dx.doi.org/10.1037/a0013622

Wraga, M. (1999). The role of eye height in perceiving affordances and object dimensions. *Perception & Psychophysics, 61,* 490–507. http://dx.doi.org/10.3758/BF03211968

Yang, S. J., Gallo, D. A., & Beilock, S. L. (2009). Embodied memory judgments: A case of motor fluency. *Journal of Experimental Psychology: Learning, Memory, and Cognition, 35,* 1359–1365. http://dx.doi.org/10.1037/a0016547

Yap, A. J., Wazlawek, A. S., Lucas, B. J., Cuddy, A. J. C., & Carney, D. R. (2013). The ergonomics of dishonesty: The effect of incidental posture on stealing, cheating, and traffic violations. *Psychological Science, 24,* 2281–2289. http://dx.doi.org/10.1177/0956797613492425

Yee, E., Chrysikou, E. G., Hoffman, E., & Thompson-Schill, S. L. (2013). Manual experience shapes object representations. *Psychological Science, 24,* 909–919. http://dx.doi.org/10.1177/0956797612464658

Yu, N. (2003). Chinese metaphors of thinking. *Cognitive Linguistics, 14,* 141–165. http://dx.doi.org/10.1515/cogl.2003.006

Yu, N. (2008). *The Chinese heart in a cognitive perspective: Culture, body, and language.* Berlin, Germany: Mouton.

Zadra, J. R., Schnall, S., Weltman, A. L., & Proffitt, D. R. (2010). Direct physiological evidence for an economy of action: Bioenergetics and the perception of spatial layout. *Journal of Vision, 10,* 54. http://dx.doi.org/10.1167/10.7.54

Zadra, J. R., Weltman, A. L., & Proffitt, D. R. (2016). Walkable distances are bioenergetically scaled. *Journal of Experimental Psychology: Human Perception and Performance, 42,* 39–51. http://dx.doi.org/10.1037/xhp0000107

Zanolie, K., van Dantzig, S., Boot, I., Wijnen, J., Schubert, T. W., Giessner, S. R., & Pecher, D. (2012). Mighty metaphors: Behavioral and ERP evidence that power shifts attention on a vertical dimension. *Brain and Cognition, 78,* 50–58. http://dx.doi.org/10.1016/j.bandc.2011.10.006

Zestcott, C. A., Stone, J., & Landau, M. J. (2017). The role of conscious attention in how weight serves as an embodiment of importance. *Personality and Social Psychology Bulletin, 43,* 1712–1723. http://dx.doi.org/10.1177/0146167217727505

Zhong, C. B., & Leonardelli, G. J. (2008). Cold and lonely: Does social exclusion literally feel cold? *Psychological Science, 19,* 838–842. http://dx.doi.org/10.1111/j.1467-9280.2008.02165.x

Zhong, C. B., & Liljenquist, K. (2006). Washing away your sins: Threatened morality and physical cleansing. *Science, 313,* 1451–1452. http://dx.doi.org/10.1126/science.1130726

Zwaan, R. A. (2014). Embodiment and language comprehension: Reframing the discussion. *Trends in Cognitive Sciences, 18*, 229–234. http://dx.doi.org/10.1016/j.tics.2014.02.008

Zwaan, R. A. (2016). Situation models, mental simulations, and abstract concepts in discourse comprehension. *Psychonomic Bulletin & Review, 23*, 1028–1034. http://dx.doi.org/10.3758/s13423-015-0864-x

Zwaan, R. A., Langston, M. C., & Graesser, A. C. (1995). The construction of situation models in narrative comprehension: An event-indexing model. *Psychological Science, 6*, 292–297. http://dx.doi.org/10.1111/j.1467-9280.1995.tb00513.x

Zwaan, R. A., & Madden, C. J. (2005). Embodied sentence comprehension. In D. Pecher & R. A. Zwaan (Eds.), *Grounding cognition: The role of perception and action in memory, language, and thinking* (pp. 224–245). Cambridge, England: Cambridge University Press. http://dx.doi.org/10.1017/CBO9780511499968.010

Zwaan, R. A., & Pecher, D. (2012). Revisiting mental simulation in language comprehension: Six replication attempts. *PLoS ONE, 7*(12), e51382. http://dx.doi.org/10.1371/journal.pone.0051382

Zwaan, R. A., Stanfield, R. A., & Yaxley, R. H. (2002). Language comprehenders mentally represent the shapes of objects. *Psychological Science, 13*, 168–171. http://dx.doi.org/10.1111/1467-9280.00430

Zwaan, R. A., & Taylor, L. J. (2006). Seeing, acting, understanding: Motor resonance in language comprehension. *Journal of Experimental Psychology: General, 135*, 1–11. http://dx.doi.org/10.1037/0096-3445.135.1.1

Index

About the Author

Rebecca Fincher-Kiefer, PhD, is a professor of psychology at Gettysburg College, where she teaches courses on human cognition, statistics and research methods, and an advanced laboratory course on embodied cognition. She received her doctorate in cognitive psychology from the University of Pittsburgh in 1988. Her research in inferential processing in text comprehension and the nature of the mental representations of text has been published in journals including the *Journal of Experimental Psychology: Learning, Memory, and Cognition*; *Memory & Cognition*; and *Discourse Processes*. She has also served in several administrative roles at Gettysburg College, including chair of the Department of Psychology for 6 years.